M000208189

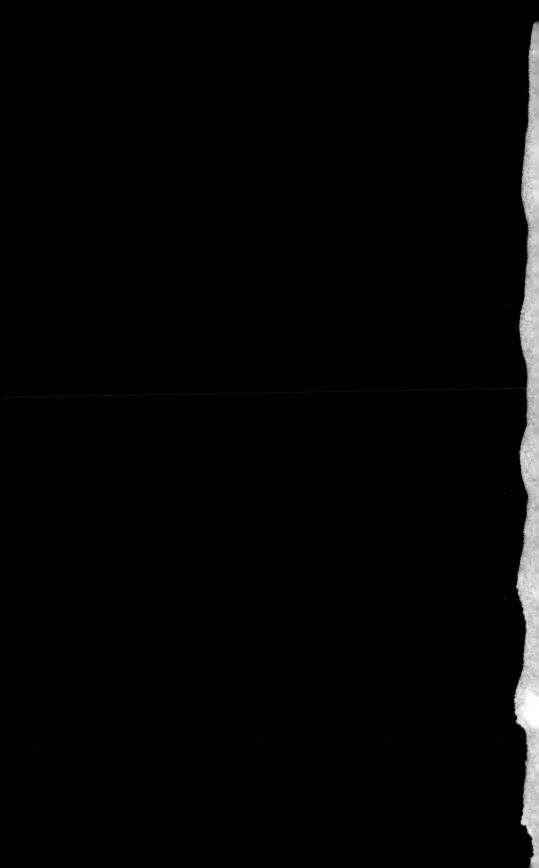

THE WOMEN OF SAN QUENTIN

Soul Murder of Transgender Women
in Male Prisons

Kristin Schreier Lyseggen

SFINX Publishing
Berkeley, California

SFINX Publishing

www.sfinxus.com

© **2015 by Kristin Schreier Lyseggen**

All rights reserved under International and Pan American copyright conventions. No part of this book may be reproduced or utilized in any form, by electronic, mechanical, or other means, without the prior written permission of the publisher, except for brief quotations embodied in literary articles or reviews.

The Women of San Quentin is a work of nonfiction. Some names, places, and other identifying information about people may have been changed to protect anonymity.

Cover and interior design by Kathrin Blatter and Andrew Johnson, www.un-studio.com San Francisco
Author photograph: Herb Schreier

Library of Congress Control Number: 2015906280

ISBN 978-0-9856244-2-2 (hardcover)
ISBN 978-0-9856244-3-9 (ebook)

Printed and Bound in California by Edition One Books
10 9 8 7 6 5 4 3 2 1

Between 1990 and 2005,
a new prison opened in the
United States every ten days

Bryan Stevenson, *Just Mercy*[1]

This book is dedicated
to people with gender identity
differences imprisoned
around the world, unable
to be who they are

To Marie, Mathea, Mikkel, and Jakob R., who give me hope;
to my parents, Bente and Stein; and to my love and
best friend, Herb

Contents

This book is for people like me, who grew up in a safe environment where issues of racism and poverty were not prominent. I want to share the lessons I learned from the people in this book who grew up never feeling safe, who were surrounded by others telling them that they should be "normal," and that their deepest sense of who they were was an error. As the number of transgender people "coming out" reaches levels we never before dreamed of, I hope this book will shed some light on the needs of people locked up twice in their lives.

I started this book before we learned that Private Bradley Manning was Chelsea Manning and before we knew about the popular Netflix TV show *Orange Is the New Black*. In real life, when most women with gender identity issues are jailed, they are put in male prisons with notorious predators. The only options for many of them in order to survive is to live isolated in cages, or become sex slaves for other inmates. For me to understand the reality of their lives, I had to gain trust from people I had never met and never expected to meet.

The project led me from the "war zone" in East Oakland, California, to the rundown, chaotic intensity of the Tenderloin district in San Francisco; I traveled from a boundary-breaking Transgender Health Conference in Bangkok to a clandestine LGBTQI advocacy conference in Nairobi, Kenya; from an event to raise funds for incarcerated transgender women in Oakland where one speaker was Angela Davis, formerly "most-wanted" by the FBI and now an African American professor at the University of California; to conservative Rome, Georgia, and Montgomery, Alabama; to a maximum security prison in the Central Valley of California.

Without exception, the stories I encountered during this project were diverse and different from one another in ways that were surprising and often disturbing. I was introduced to an almost-inconceivable struggle heaped upon the usual stories of people incarcerated in US prisons. In spite of the conditions of their lives, they taught me that regardless of what landed them behind bars, and the contradictory feelings one has about their crimes, there could still be the possibility of redemption.

The idea that we simply incarcerate people to keep the public safe is a gross over- simplification of more complex issues. Nothing is ever as black and white as the way we divide our society.

Kristin Schreier Lyseggen
Berkeley, California
May 2015

INTRODUCTION

When I moved from my native Norway to California in 2012 to be with the person I was to marry, I did not expect to write a book about people in prison. I had certainly worked with people who had been incarcerated: as a social worker at a crisis center for women with drug addiction and trauma, and as a journalist when I visited several prisons in Oslo. When I moved to Birmingham, England, in 2001 to study photography, I became engrossed in documenting the fringes of society, among them, transvestites and the glam of gay nightlife, and the three-story transgender-friendly nightclub, the Nightingale. My friendship with Michelle, documenting her life as both a man and a woman, led me to my working for the next several years with people whose body did not match their gender. When I returned to Norway in 2007, I interviewed and photographed people for my first book, *The Boy Who Was Not a Lesbian and Other True Stories,* published just as I moved to the United States.

My new life in Berkeley, California, seemed magnificent—an almost permanently blue sky, good wine, a mix of cultures and nationalities, and the company of a person who shared my interest in travel and transgender issues. But I was anxious about what to do next. My life had taken several surprising turns through the years. This was my third move to a new country (I briefly moved to Finland in 2008) where I had to start all over again. Experience had taught me I could do it, but I was a little older now and a little more jaded. All I knew was that I needed to find people who were not easily accepted in mainstream society.

When I read in a Bay Area newspaper about Grace, a transgender woman from Liberia who had spent considerable time in solitary confinement in a male immigration detention center in California, I was flabbergasted. I learned that imprisonment and time in solitary confinement, or "Administrative Segregation," was a common destiny for people with gender identity issues in the United States.[2] I knew then that my next project would be giving these people a voice. I would get to know a new country and a new culture through the back door.

To find people with gender identity issues who had experienced prison and wanted to share their stories, I asked my colleague Dr. Jamison Green,[3] whom I knew from my first book, for help. Through his contacts, in November 2012,

I was introduced to Janetta Louise Johnson, a 48-year-old African American transgender woman who had just been released from prison. She now worked as a coordinator for the Transgender, Gender Variant, and Intersex Justice Project (TGIJP), a nonprofit run by formerly incarcerated people that supports transgender people in prison. Janetta had been the only woman among a large population of men in the federal prison in Sheridan, Oregon, for three and a half years. Over time, she introduced me to other people who had been in prison and were now out, including Grace, whom I had read about in the newspaper. The US government officials had tried their best to send Grace back to her native Liberia, where she knew she could be killed for being who she was. She had been viciously attacked three times in San Francisco. It was also through Janetta that I met Tanesh, a married woman and grandmother of five living in the Nob Hill neighborhood of San Francisco.

After our first interview, in March 2013, Janetta helped me get in touch with incarcerated transgender women she was in contact with in prisons around the country. She sent out copies of my project proposal, inviting them to contribute their stories. Soon, handwritten letters started pouring into my mailbox from prisons in Illinois, Texas, California, and Georgia. The first one came from Jazzie, who defined herself as an African American transgender woman. She had been incarcerated for 17½ years and, at the time she wrote, was living at the California Correctional Institution in Tehachapi. During the period we wrote to each other, she spent a lot of time in solitary confinement.

Shiloh wrote me many letters from her cell in Salinas Valley State Prison in Soledad, California—some handwritten ones that I had difficulty understanding, and some that she got her cell mate, Kenneth, to write for her. She sent drawings and photographs of herself and her family from before her transition. I saw pictures of a handsome young man with black hair, a mustache, and a warm smile embracing family members. Shiloh told me she had tried to cut off her penis when she was 16. She had been incarcerated since 1981 and still claimed her innocence of a murder for which she was imprisoned for life without parole.

Usually, I rarely bother looking for mail, but now I found myself waiting for the postman. I was both eager and hesitant to read the emotionally charged letters.

Before long, Jennifer wrote from Kern Valley State Prison, where she was serving a 104-year sentence without parole because of the notorious three-strikes law. Convicted initially for attempted robbery, she had picked up her second and third strikes during riots in Folsom State Prison.

A few months later, I received a letter from Donna, who was at the maximum security prison in Marion, Illinois. I looked up her legal male name online and read news stories about her that made my heart race. Donna, a former member of the Aryan Republican Army (ARA)—an antigovernment, white supremacist hate group that had apparently committed more bank robberies than Jesse James (at least 22)—had at that time lived as Commander Pedro by day and Donna McClure by night. Donna was now serving a life sentence and was already taking hormones for her gender dysphoria.[4] I started feeling slightly anxious about giving my personal mail address to people with obviously violent pasts. At one point, I began looking under my car for possible bombs. Next I expected the Feds to knock on the door.

Daniella wrote to me over the months from various prisons in California's Central Valley as she was moved from one to another. Like many of the other women, she sent me a photograph of herself: a handsome, muscular guy in a blue prisoner's uniform. Her story was unusual. She had wanted to be in prison; being "out" in her community was hard, and she found it comforting to live behind prison walls where at least a few men treated her like a woman.

California is home to one of the largest correctional systems in the Western world;[5] it is therefore most likely also home to one of the largest populations of incarcerated people with gender identity issues. The state's inmates also spend the longest average time in solitary confinement compared to other prisoners in the US—thousands of them are held in "solitary" indefinitely on simple grounds: they have untreated mental illnesses; they are Muslims; they reported a rape by prison officials; they are gang members, sex offenders, gay, or have gender identity issues. Though several prisons claim to offer special housing and treatment for transgender people, this is rarely the case. Instead, they are often placed in solitary confinement as the only available way to "protect" them.

Once transgender people are in solitary, their situation can worsen. They are often forced to share their cell with a male inmate who is a sex offender or gang member. Many spend 22 to 24 hours a day in small, windowless cells and are only let out after business hours, when it is impossible to reach a lawyer. They are denied the education and socialization available to the general prison population. In addition, prison officials commonly block these prisoners' access to transition-related health care such as hormone therapy or gender reassignment surgery (GRS), even when these are prescribed as medically necessary by a doctor.[6]

Transgender people, in particular transgender women of color, are much more likely to be arrested and given prison time. While nearly one in six black men has been to prison,[7] nearly half of all transgender people of color have been incarcerated. Transgender women of color are 13 times more likely to be sexually abused while in prison by both other inmates and prison guards.[8] At meals, inmates often seat themselves by race, but since transgender people are usually not accepted in their own racial group, they may be forced for safety reasons to eat standing up. As their numbers increase in prisons, they face multiple challenges—sexual abuse, lack of medical and/or psychological treatment, being forced to share cells with men, time in solitary confinement, the enormous stress from months and years without hormone therapy. Often outcasts from their own families, they are ill prepared to re-enter society when their terms are up.

Health care professionals have begun to recognize that along with genetics and biology, early life abuse and bullying lend a strong hand in not only who we are mentally but our physical well-being and life expectancy as well. Between 40 and 50 percent of all homeless youth in America today identify with one or more of the letters in the LGBTQI acronym.[9] The National LGBTQI Task Force reported in 2014: "Transgender and gender non-conforming people face rampant discrimination in every area of life: education, employment, family life, public accommodations, housing, health, police and jails, and ID documents."[10]

As I began to form relationships with many of the people in this book—and several of them corresponded with me during the full two years of the project—I experienced a range of feelings: guilt when I was too busy to reply to all the letters, as well as some skepticism and awareness of my own naiveté. I had an almost bodily reaction to many stories I read or listened to. The fact that most of these women were forced to share their cell with a man made me nauseous. That so many struggled in vain to get the inexpensive hormones they needed in order to stay healthy and sane, the lack of which turned them into men with stubble beards, was heartbreaking. The fact that the judicial system insists on identifying them by the bodies they are born with and thus keeps them in male prisons while their authentic identity is female inspired the title of this book. San Quentin, California's oldest and most famous state prison, is where some of these women had previously been housed, although it has been an all-male prison since 1933. I live around the corner from San Quentin, as do some of the women in this book—I can almost see it from where I am writing, just across the Bay from Berkeley.

I came to understand that these women are moving toward becoming themselves, no matter the cost. But the trauma they experienced growing up will stay with them forever. If they didn't have trauma before they went to prison, they certainly will have it by now. These traumas are best thought of as soul murder. According to psychoanalyst Leonard Shengold[11] in his book *Soul Murder,* it is the crime of adults' willful abuse and neglect of children with such sufficient intensity and frequency as to be traumatic. He points out that the term "soul murder" was most famously defined first by the Norwegian playwright Henrik Ibsen in his play *John Gabriel Borkman,* and used by one of Sigmund Freud's subjects, Daniel Paul Schreber,[12] in his autobiography. Ibsen described it as the *destruction of the love of life in another human being.*

Should I—and could I—include all of these people's stories in my book? And how could I represent them fairly and honestly, particularly those women still in prison, who I had not met? I prefer the traditional approach to journalism and photography—sitting one-to-one with people, being able to see into their eyes, observe how they interact, or don't, with others and with me. Most important, I wanted these women to feel they could trust me. All of this was challenged by my limited interactions with them through old-fashioned snail mail. How could I truly communicate with people I could not see or call or email, much less reach on Facebook? I was glad that I could meet several of the women in person. I applied for permission to visit some of the incarcerated women. I did after a while get approved to visit a few, but was repeatedly turned down (or ignored) by other prisons. The women's handwritten accounts seemed endless, sometimes chaotic, just like their handwriting. Small pieces of information, weeks and sometimes months between letters, from nearly a dozen people—it was hard to follow their narratives and time lines. Many seemed lost, as if their sense of themselves was gone. As I read these stories, I remembered a statement in the book *Two-Spirited People*—that as many as 155 of the Native American tribes may have recognized three, even four or five genders. I kept thinking how much we lost by trying to erase those cultures that were perhaps wiser than our own.

Eventually, I decided to include excerpts from letters, lightly edited for spelling and grammar, in some of the chapters. This would give readers a peek into what I had experienced myself while reading them. By this time, I had interviewed and photographed Janetta, Tanesh, and Grace several times. Spending time in their worlds showed me a part of the Bay Area I had not seen before: the seedy neighborhood of the Tenderloin and then East Oakland, which felt like an odd mix of Bangkok, my old haunts in Birmingham, and Afghanistan without the soldiers. There were dirty, gritty, industrial factory buildings with bullet holes, young teens working the streets in broad daylight, their pimps nearby. East Oakland, with its high murder rate, seemed to be on fire. It was a stark reminder of what these already-vulnerable women had to face each day just going to work and returning home.

Toward the end of the project, opportunities arose to try to visit a few of the women in prison. In June 2014, an African American woman, Ashley Diamond, phoned me from inside a Georgia state prison for men and told me gruesome stories of gang rape and assaults by inmates and prison staff. She said she was afraid she would not live much longer. She sent me a "selfie" photo while making a video of herself that documents how, because the prison refused to provide the hormones prescribed for her, she was slowly becoming the man she had never been.[13] I flew to Georgia in October but was not allowed to visit her. However, her family and friends in the little town of Rome, Georgia, welcomed me warmly, and I was able to meet with her lawyers at the Southern Poverty Law Center in Montgomery, Alabama.

As I was wrapping up this book in early 2015, I was at last approved to visit Jennifer Gann in Kern Valley State Prison and Shiloh Quine in Mule Creek State Prison—both in California a few hours' drive from my home. Only a month earlier, Daniella was released from prison, and we met twice in person near her new place of work.

Many difficult challenges came up during this project. I felt a responsibility to accurately tell these people's stories, which otherwise might never be told, while being sensitive to those whose lives have been turned upside down by their actions and the families of those who had been harmed. I was also concerned whether telling their stories would compromise some of these women's safety, and I did not want these stories, once published, to in some way work in favor of the "antitransgender" movement (e.g., radical feminists, hate groups, and right-wing politicians). Because Donna had been part of the ARA, an organization that was classified as a domestic terrorist group by the FBI, I wanted to discuss her case with someone who knew her well. I was able to interview Dr. Mark S. Hamm, author of a book that is largely about Donna's life before and during her involvement with the ARA.

However, my main focus was to highlight the fact that these women have seen terrible hardship, and that the additional suffering they are forced to bear in prison goes beyond what society has prescribed in their prison sentences. Clearly, it was not my role to judge them for their crimes or whether they are innocent or guilty. The test of any society's humanness is to treat even hardcore criminals humanely, lest we lose something we all wish for in our lives. Some of the people in this book have been convicted of terrible crimes, but many have not. As will become clear, they are not asking us for forgiveness; they are asking for a minimum of decent medical care and for alleviation of the dangers to which they are exposed due to horrendous overcrowding in prisons, a situation declared inhumane by judges and by the United Nations.

This is not a book about criminal behavior, though it does not ignore the terrible aspects of the prison system; nor does it attempt to represent the gender variant population in general. Its purpose is to increase our awareness of a particularly vulnerable group of the population that is overrepresented in the US prison system. Most people with gender identity issues—and there are many more than anyone imagined—are not violent, but given the inequities of the society, too many of them end up in prison. My husband, a child psychiatrist working with children with gender variance, helped me navigate an ocean of research for this project. One statistic struck me: in Massachusetts and two other states, one in 200 households report that someone in their homes identifies as transgender or gender variant, and that number may be higher.[14]

In 2013 and 2014, the years when I researched and wrote this book, we witnessed the continuation of violence, murder, and hate crimes against people with gender identity issues, particularly transgender women of color. Several people with gender identity issues were murdered both in the US and worldwide: stories like that of the transgender woman whose body was found in a trash bin in Detroit, and the African American trans-identified woman who died while in the custody of the Berkeley police were commonplace.[15] More than 1,500 cases of killings of transgender and gender-nonconforming people, and people with gender variance, many of them teenagers, were reported between 2008 and 2014 worldwide.[16] Many such murders go unreported.

In Arizona and Florida, legal attempts were made to criminalize children with gender variance for their choice of public restrooms.[17] At the same time, several states passed laws protecting transgender people. Transgender issues received high and favorable visibility with news stories like Chelsea Manning's announcement of her female identity the day after her conviction for leaking US government classified documents, and the airing of the Netflix TV series *Orange Is the New Black*, with transgender actress Laverne Cox playing the transgender woman character Sophia Burset in June 2013.[18] (Sophia was housed in a female prison; this is not the case, unfortunately, for most imprisoned transgender women.)

While working on this project, my prejudices have been tested and my sense of humanity expanded. I have learned about a different kind of humanity from some of the most vulnerable people in the US. I have met wonderful human beings who are seen as criminals, whether fairly or not, and who get up each day and fight as best they can for freedom and protection and human rights for themselves and others. They fight to get rid of their internal demons and anger from years of abuse and to become better human beings. Many of them, I felt, wanted to share their stories not so much to get justice for themselves but to help others. They want other people to learn from their own mistakes—and from their captors' mistakes. As for the women serving life sentences, the last thing they can do for themselves is to live as the women they are (many "came out" during their time in prison) and to tell their truth, because everyone else has stopped caring.

Just as this book was reaching completion, a new Facebook friend from Norway, Lise, sent me a message: "Do you know Ubuntu? I have finally found what I have been looking for all these years." I looked up the word and found that Ubuntu is a South African Nguni Bantu term roughly translated as "human kindness," "humanity toward others," or more philosophically, "the belief in a universal bond of sharing that connects all humanity."

That is exactly what this book is about. Ubuntu. This book is about how we humans treat each other.

A GIRL FROM THE SOUTHERN WILD

On March 8, 2013, International Women's Day, I drove across the Bay Bridge from Berkeley to San Francisco and parked outside the Transgender, Gender Variant, and Intersex Justice Project's (TGIJP) office on Ninth Street—a trip that takes 15 minutes if you are lucky and 50 minutes during rush hour. When I rang the doorbell, I saw through a window Janetta Johnson waving at me before coming downstairs to let me in.

Janetta looked quite different from when I first met her a few months earlier. I would learn to expect this every time I met her. Today she wore huge heart-shaped silver earrings that accented her dark chocolate brown face and high cheekbones. Her large breasts were apparent under a black turtleneck; she had long, slim legs in jeans on a long, slim body. Her lips were edged with deep red, almost purple lip liner. Her hair was long and black, but other days it might be auburn, or brown with blond streaks; sometimes it was wavy and full, sometimes it was flattened. She spoke fast with a Southern accent.

In the TGIJP office, where Janetta worked as coordinator, we sat on one of those couches you disappear into, and I asked if I could take some images. "Sure, shoot away," Janetta said. After several photos I put aside the camera and placed my digital voice recorder on the glass table. I said I wanted to learn about her life and the lives of other incarcerated transgender women both inside and outside of prison. I wanted to know about their relationships with other prisoners and with prison officers, how they ended up there in the first place, and how they survived while they were locked up.

Janetta got up and poked her head into a large closet, fumbling, and retrieved a large brown envelope. "We are moving this office to East Oakland in two weeks' time," she explained. "I want you to take care of this for me. I tried writing a memoir while I was incarcerated. But now I want you to write my story." She handed me the envelope, which contained a thick pile of documents: handwritten letters, typewritten diaries, and legal mail. During our first meeting, Janetta had come across as businesslike, confident, and somewhat reserved. I had figured I was not going to get to know her quickly, but now she had just handed me her life in an envelope.

Sitting back down on the couch, Janetta began telling me about her childhood. I found later that she had written about it in one of her diaries:

> I grew up in Tampa, Florida in an area called Belmont Heights Project. I remember growing up in the sixties, seventies, and early eighties just being fascinated by the beautiful women with their beautiful dresses and shoes, hair and make-up. It felt like they had a style of their own, were strong and overcomers, and made life work. On one of the corner lots they served beer, wines, liquor, and other spirits. Across the street on the other corner was a fast food joint called Bexley's Chicken. Bexley was famous for their chicken sandwiches that were prepared on hamburger buns with mayonnaise. This mouth-watering chicken sandwich was dipped in a special sauce that had customers lined up out the door daily.

Growing up as an African American boy living in that neighborhood, Janetta experienced a tremendous amount of sexual abuse by African American men—close relatives and neighbors. By the time she was in first grade, she was regularly being raped by her older cousin. She started transitioning while still in Florida at age 17. By the time she went to prison at the age of 43, she had had breast implant surgery.

"While in prison, and being in a setting where everybody is divided by race, like the Bloods, Crips,[19] I was forced to be with the black men I had grown up with as a child," Janetta said and gazed at me intensely. It appeared that Janetta was ready to go deep with me; she seemed used to talking about her past. She began speaking faster, and I had to ask her to slow down.

Janetta was incarcerated in Sheridan Correctional Center, a medium security federal correctional institution in Oregon, from 2009 to 2012 for a nonviolent crime.[20] Her sentence was for more than five years, but she was let out early because of good behavior. Had she chosen to stay "protected" in solitary confinement by complaining to prison authorities about being sexually abused, the opportunities leading to early release would not have been available to her.

The purpose of what she called the SHU—the Special Housing Unit, also called solitary confinement—she said, was mainly punitive. This is where they put gang members; dangerous and violent men; pedophiles, who are at high risk for beatings and killings by other inmates; and people who have stabbed an officer. But it's also where transgender women are put "for their own protection." Solitary confinement cells generally measure 6 x 9 x 10 feet. Often the door is solid metal rather than bars, with a small window for receiving food and for communication with prison officials. Usually there is no television and no opportunity to socialize with other inmates. When Janetta was in the SHU, she explained, she could not go to the prison school, "chow hall," or gym or participate in any activities. She was handcuffed and shackled when she went to the visiting room or the shower. It was unquestionably punishment.

Being the only transgender person at Sheridan, it was better for her not to be too feminine. "The other inmates didn't want anyone else to know that there was someone in the

prison system with breasts. They didn't want to have to deal with the jokes and stuff like that. They didn't want the assumption made: 'Oh, this is what you guys do in prison,' you know."

"How did the inmates respond when you walked into Sheridan?" I asked. "They were pleased about it! But the thing is, while they were very happy and very excited, when it all boils down to it, they belong to gangs and they don't get to make their own decisions. If you are Blood or Crip and you mess around with a homosexual or transgender person, you represent the entire car, the whole entire gang. It's like you are the weak link inside the gang. Whatever you do reflects on the entire gang. These people, they say: 'Hey, you mess around with a faggot, you can go up to the SHU or you get beaten up.' These are the same people who ask to see my breasts, who say, 'Meet me behind the bleacher in the laundry room.'"

She was trapped with these men in close quarters with no outside support. Trying to connect with another race would create problems, she said. "They would say: 'Hey, you can't talk to her. We gonna beat you up, we're gonna do this and that to you.'"

Yet everyone inside the prison knew Janetta was a woman.

"It's not so much that the other inmates respected me, but they just knew that I never pretended to be anyone else. I was who I was. When they come into prison they are tough, and then all of a sudden they get their dicks sucked by a transgender or a homosexual. That is not okay. But I came in as a woman. First they weren't happy about me being in the compound, with a 38 double D and presenting myself as a woman. It took some time for them to accept that."

Like most other inmates, Janetta had to share a cell. The prison officials did not put her in a cell by herself because this would be asking for special privileges, and to have privileges was dangerous, even life threatening. Every time she got a new cell mate, she told me, "The man would say, 'I ain't want no room with a faggot, I don't like faggots, I hate faggots, I kill that motherfucker.'" But as soon as the door closed, he wanted to touch her, he wanted favors. If she didn't do what these men asked, she would end up in the SHU. "I was able to negotiate just giving people a hand job or a blow job just to make peace. I have had some guys pin me down to penetrate me, and I would beg: 'Please no, please no, I suck it for it, but don't put your penis... don't rape me....' They were gonna take me anyway, but I negotiated. Some of the guys were huge... and I was like: 'No, please no, I will give you a blow job!' I threatened to report them too, but the thing in prison is, you don't report anything to anyone. I would be punished by being put back in the SHU." The rapist might have been put in the SHU, too, for about two weeks to make it look good. But Janetta would have been there long-term, preventing her from going to school and completing the 500-hour drug treatment program, which allowed her to get out early. This meant that every move she made was a catch-22.

"At some point, I had to share a cell with this guy who was a Muslim for about eight months who used to wake me up every night fondling my breasts. I told an officer that he was waking me up every night, but the officer said, 'Wait a minute. Before you tell me this, I want to make sure that you know that if you tell me this (what I had already told him), the only place I can out you is in the SHU.' Because they were so worried about me wanting special privileges, but all I wanted was to be safe, and I didn't want to be touched."

Janetta in my studio in Berkeley, March 2013

If you are Blood or Crip and you mess around with a homosexual or transgender person, you represent the entire car. It's like you are the weak link inside the gang. Whatever you do reflects on the entire gang. These people, they say: "Hey, you mess around with a faggot, you can go up to the SHU or you get beaten up." These are the same people who ask to see my breasts, who say, "Meet me behind the bleacher in the laundry room."

— Janetta during an interview in San Francisco, March 2013

Later, I found this among the papers in that brown envelope:

> Another day I was chased into the SHU by a Bay Area gang
> and threatened with physical violence by six thugs, and
> being in the SHU for almost a week by myself reflecting on all
> that had transpired was more than I could handle. After the
> tenth day, I received a cellie by the name of Rick. A big black
> brotha, six foot four, 350 pounds, from Portland, Oregon. I was
> initially afraid and almost refused to accept a cellie, but then
> I remembered that refusal to accept a cellie could cause me
> disciplinary action, which could lead to loss of good time.
>
> The dude was not in the cell a good ten minutes before he
> stripped down to his boxer shorts and began masturbating
> and moaning like a big old lady. During that time, I was
> reading the only book I could find. It was Tom Clancy, my
> least favorite author. So I continued to read and not say a
> word. I tried to do my best and ignore him while he finished
> his business. I was not exactly sure where this was going.
> However, for some reason, I felt stuck and puzzled about how
> this thing is supposed to go. You have to be very careful about
> telling the officers about what goes on because they will put
> you on blast,[21] or if the word gets out that I am relying on the
> correctional officers to settle the situation, it could be a bad
> scene. With that said, neither of us said a word to one another
> for the next three days. However, during this silent treatment,
> I strategized on the best way to deal with this: what goes on in
> the SHU stays in the SHU.

Although Janetta did not report rape and sexual assault, she repeatedly filed complaints against the prison officials. They would refer to her as "the man with tits," and they refused to give her the medications prescribed by her primary care physician at Kaiser Permanente in San Francisco. She wrote in her diary: "I will build a huge wall of distrust for the mental health system, you calling me He, him, his, Mr. You might as well be saying fuck you to me because that's how it feels."

When Janetta had a chance to present her case in court, she did not show up because she was unshaven. Since she was not able to be herself, she felt she could not defend herself. She showed me a copy of the letter she sent to her lawyer from the SHU:

> **Hello attorney Dani.**
>
> **Just a few words to let you know that I am weathering the storm, just trying to figure out why. Do I have to always take myself to the school of hard knocks? I probably should have gone to school to learn all this stuff about the criminal justice system. Dani, I have grave concerns and unless I am on proper hormonal therapy, my six year sentence could be a death sentence. The reason I say this is, without my hormone dosage I am a person with a very sad, lonely, angry, sexually assaulted childhood trauma and abuse who wants to die. Two options: provide me with extensive acute trauma counseling or proper hormonal therapy in which I think I need both. I have so much fear right now, and just imagine if I cannot attend school, recovery programs, church, library, just locked in a cell with a full beard and mustache, I would lose my mind.**

The officers were sometimes abusive in other ways. One day while escorting Janetta to the showers, an officer handcuffed her so tightly that it cut off her circulation. "I screamed: 'Please! It hurts really bad!' But he just continued to shuffle me to the shower located in the annex. When I finished my shower, once again he used the same tactics, and I screamed and asked him to please check the cuffs, but he didn't. He just shuffled me back to my cell with my circulation cut off."

Participating in the prison's drug rehabilitation program helped Janetta gain perspective on her story. In therapy groups she got to see the similarities between other inmates' backgrounds and her own and how their childhood experiences had affected them. Many grew up with crackaddicted mothers and abusive parents. Abuse became part of their survival strategy, just as turning to prostitution had been part of her own. She also saw that the men she grew

Janetta embracing Miss Major at a fundraiser for TGI Justice Project, with Alicia Garza (left) and guest speaker Angela Davis (right). Oakland, California, April 21, 2013

up with were not so different from the inmates she was now living with. "They were the same men, the same sexual abuse as I was used to in prison, but the best thing was how I internalized all of this and my experience with the past. Before, I felt ugly, it was all my fault, but in prison I had the opportunity to really see who they are—that it is not all black men, but I realized that that culture in prison fit so well with the culture I grew up in.

"Fortunately, I did the best I could and stepped outside my culture and mixed with other cultures. A lot of my friends would say to you, 'Janetta is not black.' And also, for me being in there, I worked on trying to find my African pride. I wasn't proud of me as an African American person."

It was getting late. I gathered my gear and was about to go out the door when Janetta said, "If you write a project proposal, I can send it out on mail night next week to the people we write to in prisons." I told her I would be back with a bunch of them the next day, as the following week I would be a little busy because I was getting married. "A woman gotta do what a woman gotta do," she responded.

On the way out I turned and asked: "How many times were you sexually assaulted while in prison? "Seven times," she said.

When I got home, I sat on the porch with the documents Janetta had given me and read some of her writing:

> It was in the first or second grade when it all began. I can
> clearly remember my cousin who was much older getting
> on top of me humping and grinding. I thought that was OK
> because boys were supposed to hump on girls, however when
> penetration began I realized that this was when my whole
> world came crashing down. I knew that something tragic had
> happened. I remember being very sadly disappointed because
> my grandfather was in the twin bed right next to me. My
> grandfather was a severe chronic alcoholic, and was so drunk
> and passed out. He was a full blooded Cherokee Indian, and
> had to live with my aunt because his alcoholism caused him

to be homeless. My aunt was our babysitter, while my mother worked. In some aspects we were forced to sleep over quite a bit, especially on the weekends. During that time, I was my cousin's sex slave. I can remember falling asleep and waking up to him on top of me. He would be extremely heavy and was very strong. He hurt me so much that I would bleed. I tried to fight and scream, but then I lost my voice. I could only scream and cry silently. It was like hearing a whimper from an animal. I knew at that time, that I was ruined. This went on for years. Then there were other perpetrators throughout my childhood. My great uncle, my mom's boyfriends, and strangers.

I felt the rawness of Janetta's pain as I read on—the darkness of her suppression, the injustices done to her, the theft of her identity and self-worth. Abuse from childhood had followed her through life like a ghost. She was describing a modern form of slavery— how this society had failed her; about children who grew up in dirty houses with cockroaches, often with absent fathers, starving and crying; how tall, beautiful women like her were so readily picked up by police because of the way they looked. Being African American did not help.

Then I realized that during all those hours of my first interview with Janetta, I had not asked her about the crime that had put her in prison in the first place. I realized I was simply not so interested in that part of her story. This would be a recurring feeling throughout this project. I just wanted to know how these women had survived in the male prison system.

In April 2013, soon after I returned from a trip abroad, Janetta invited me to the TGIJP's new office in East Oakland, located on 47th Street around the corner from where I used to visit a friend. Janetta told me to call when I was outside the office. I knew this was an area of East Oakland where you don't dally once you get out of your car. My friend had said she could hear gun shots across the street at night.

East Oakland was always sunny, though dusty, and full of color with loud, gangster- banging music booming from car windows, chaotic intersections, and gas stations. But as I turned off Highway 880 onto East 12th Street, the city's usual pedestrian and car traffic yielded to empty streets lined with factories and tire stores. To get to work, Janetta had to take the BART train from downtown San Francisco to the Fruitvale Station, where Oscar Grant, a young black man, was killed by BART police in 2011.[22] Then she would take a bus to her office on 47th Street. Many people I know would never take BART to this area of town. They would take their car. But then, they would probably never go to East Oakland in the first place.

It was another Tuesday mail night at the office. Every Tuesday, Janetta put boxes filled with letters from incarcerated transgender women out on the tables and said, "Take your pick," to the many volunteers who turned up to help write letters back. "Where do you get all your strength from?" I asked Janetta when I managed to get her away from her work chair. We retreated to one of the empty rooms at the back of the office. It had bright blue walls. I photographed her as she told me more about herself.

"I started out as Jane. I was going through all this depression when I moved to San Francisco, and then I decided that I was going to do something really positive and good for myself. I was getting ready to go to the doctor and get paperwork to get my name legally changed, and I had been in a funk for a few days. I was really, really going through some stuff. This was in 1999, and I was on my way to get dressed for my name change, and then I thought about my auntie, whose name is Arnetta, who was the one who always took us to church just about every Sunday. Rain or shine, we were in church. And I was thinking about this spiritual piece that she gave us, and within this I had to separate my own God from her God and have my own personal relationship with God. Reflecting back, thinking about that time when I was asking and praying to my God to help me, guide me through my difficulties and situations, I felt that I got the strength to at least accept what was. I took 'etta' out of her name and put it on my name, and that represents this spiritual piece. My mother, who is a very, very strong woman, is called Louise, so I took hers as my middle name. And my last name is Johnson, after my first boyfriend. He is the only man I have ever loved, I think."

When Janetta still lived in Florida, she used to smoke crack and work the streets as a prostitute, and was once jailed for 45 days. When she got out, she tried to find a support network for transgender people to get off the street and off drugs. She went to all the treatment programs she could find and told them she was a transsexual woman. She asked to be housed with women, but they told her: If you want to come here you need to be a guy. You can wear makeup, but we will house you with men. She was exhausted and almost gave up.

Then someone told her about transgender people in San Francisco who had jobs and went to drug and treatment programs. Janetta got a phone number for someone called Miss Major, dialed the number, and said, "Hi, I'm Jane. I'm living in Florida and nothing is working for me here. If I move to San Francisco, do you guys have support groups? Do you think I can find a job?" Miss Major said, "If you move to San Francisco, I will help you."

Miss Major, the executive director of TGIJP, has been an activist and advocate in the transgender community for more than 40 years. She was part of the Stonewall Uprising in New York City in 1969 and an original member of the first transgender gospel choir. Janetta and Miss Major had a few more conversations, and two weeks later Janetta showed up at Miss Major's office. It was 1997. "I got on the Greyhound bus and moved here. And she has been my mama ever since."

Janetta also found comfort in San Francisco's City of Refuge United Church of Christ, where Bobby Jean Baker, also African American and transgender, was the reverend. "I love it there! That's where a lot of the transgender women go. And they have a gay community. They are very inclusive. It feels good to be part of a church. Growing up, one of my aunts took us to the church faithfully. I believe in God and I believe in a Higher Power. I don't necessarily believe in the same God and Jesus that my family believes in, but I believe there is this Divine that watches over us, gives us guidance, and gets us through things."

However, in San Francisco, Janetta had started selling drugs because of fears about not having enough money. She was arrested and then convicted of conspiracy to distribute crystal meth and sent to prison. She told me: "For me, it was not about being a drug dealer, but the fear that I had, listening to the media and seeing the state of the economy, folks losing homes, jobs, and businesses. Trauma and fear set in, and I was worried about being homeless. The department that I was working for in the Tenderloin Health Services laid off nine people and left four people to do the job that thirteen people were doing, including volunteers who had to stop doing volunteer work because they had to find a job."

When Janetta was let out of prison two years early in 2012, her transgender family was waiting to welcome her back. They had supported her throughout. She counted herself lucky. Now, she felt, it was time for her to help the people still in prison, those who had no one to come to visit, no one waiting for them when they were released.

When she returned to San Francisco, she learned there was a three-month waiting list to get mental health care. This was long enough for her to fall back into a state of dashed hopes and desperation. Janetta had repeatedly been told by both staff and inmates at the prison that she was not who she thought she was, that she was not a real woman but a man. After experiencing so much cruelty about her gender identity for so long, she again started to doubt herself. Four days after being released from prison, Janetta had a panic attack and ended up in a hospital emergency room.

Eventually she began going to therapy, then she started a transgender support group called Transcending. She told me this is what saved her. "I've been in and out of therapy since I moved to San Francisco. More in than out. I think that I'm okay being in therapy. I feel it's a good, safe place for me, based on all the trauma, abuse, and exploitation that has been heaped upon myself and my community. I'm also saddened that some of my sisters died on the streets of loneliness because they had no fair chance, especially transwomen that came out during the time I was transitioning, because we took a lot of really bad, traumatizing beatings, repeatedly, for just being trans, being in our gender expression. I must have been brutally beaten at least 23 times, shot at, stabbed, or knocked out, or had something thrown at me—eggs, bricks, bottles, sticks, and God knows what else. These were some very painful and hurtful situations. The emotional pains, scars, lumps, bumps, and bruises outweighed anything that happened to me physically. All the damage had been done a long time ago, throughout my adolescence, and then piling on top of that the physical and sexual abuse and misuse left me in a seemingly hopeless state of body. I had no idea what life could have been for me until I moved to San Francisco."

For the next six months, both Janetta and I were busy and met only occasionally. I focused on corresponding with the people in prison she had put me in touch with. Every so often she would send a text asking where I was or inviting me to stop by and meet some new people at her office. Sometimes she sent me the address of someone in prison who she thought would be good for the book. On November 21, I called Janetta and asked if I could take some more photos of her. She said, "Sure, come to the office, but I'm wearing a turban today." "Great," I replied.

A few hours later, Janetta sat posing in a chair in East Oakland, wearing her black turban and a different pair of large, heart-shaped, red earrings. I asked about her new friend David. "I met him a month ago. I was just hanging out in the Gangway [one of San Francisco's oldest gay bars]. He is 40 years old, pale skinned, true blue eyes, about 5 feet 8 inches tall. He's got really good personality."

Throughout this project, I rarely asked the people I communicated with about their surgeries. I had observed over the years that some people think they have a right to ask a transgender person about their genitals, a question they would never ask others. But I did feel I needed to ask this one time because I knew Janetta well enough and felt she would have a thought-provoking answer. "I am comfortable with being a lady with a penis," she answered. "I identify myself as a black woman, just a typical woman. I feel fine with being a woman with a penis."

Then I changed the subject. I asked about Janetta's relationship with her family. "I knew some of my uncles and aunties were ministers," she said, "but I do not know where they came from. I often wondered. I have a good relationship with my nieces and nephews. However, I feel they love me because they see my sister and the mutual love and respect that we have for each other, not to mention that my sister is a big advocate for me and will not allow anyone to disrespect me."

Janetta during our first interview in San Francisco on March 8, 2013, International Women's Day

Janetta's grandfather was 100 percent Cherokee, she told me. Her grandmother was black and Navajo. "My mother's father was basically white, but he had soft, curly hair. My grandmother was very light skinned, but she had complete African American hair." I could see the Native American characteristics in Janetta—her cheekbones, her almond-shaped eyes, and her mouth. A few of her grandparents' offspring were light skinned, some were dark, which made some people question if they were really full siblings. Her mother was given to her grandmother's sister when she was a baby. "Mum is still carrying that she was given away because she was the first black child. Actually, my grandma gave away two of her black children. She gave them to her sister. She kept the light-skinned children and got rid of the black children—that's how they felt all their lives. And they were questioned all the time if they were my grandfather's children. I think they are all his children. That's the way the genes work, you know."

During the second half of 2013, Janetta lost three friends. In June 2013, Jazzie Collins (age 54), a longtime trans activist in the Bay Area, passed away. One Monday morning in September, Melenie Mahinamalamalama Eleneke (age 53), Janetta's Hawaiian colleague at TGIJP, was found dead in her home in Daly City. Then, on New Year's Day 2014, the minister of Janetta's church, Bobby Jean Baker (age 49), was killed in a car accident in Oakland on her way home from a nighttime service. I sent Janetta an email with my condolences and asked her how she was doing after all that had happened. She wrote me back a few days later.

> **I experience the grief and loss of my trans sisters, who I hold in very high regard. It seems lots of us came with our own set of pain and trauma and behaviors that are based on the marginalization and disenfranchisement. And as a result of God, Recovery Discovery, organized religion, or we just got sick and tired of being sick and tired, we grabbed ahold of whatever it was that gave us the strength and courage to overcome, to pull ourselves up and begin to fight off some of those oppressions, and cultivate a life to be very proud of living and knowing. And I've worked with a lot of my sisters as a sister, as a friend, a colleague, a mentor, and I know that they**

passed with lots of self-love and respect, dignity, and care for
themselves and others. They did so much amazing work within
the community: social services, social justice advocating in the
San Francisco Bay Area, creating positive change for poor folks
to have better access. They have helped many folks—straight,
LGBT, Gender Variant, Queer and Questioning folks—to find
their path. As they got better, they helped others get better. Real.

In mid February 2014—just as CeCe McDonald, an African American
transgender woman who was wrongfully convicted was released from prison—
Janetta flew to Bangkok, Thailand. It was her first time abroad. Janetta, along
with trans activist Cecilia Chung, a senior strategist at Transgender Law
Center; my husband, Herb; and I were to present a symposium on incarcerated
people with gender identity issues, in particular, women in US male prisons,
at a World Professional Association for Transgender Health (WPATH)
conference. Five hundred health care professionals had signed up, and most of
them attended despite the political unrest in Bangkok.

Janetta arrived in Bangkok two days before Herb and I did. The morning after
we arrived, with only a couple of hours' sleep, Herb and I, with help from a
friend, Mikael, from Norway, rushed to put up a photography exhibition on the
conference hotel's patio. I had still not seen Janetta and was wondering if she
had arrived safely. She had not seen the photos I had taken of her blown up this
big before, and I wanted to observe her reaction. Herb and I went back to the
hotel room to change, and by the time we came downstairs, hundreds of people
were gathering around the exhibit and around the refreshment tables. It was
the conference's opening night.

Suddenly I saw Janetta walking towards me wearing a bright yellow blouse
and long skirt. She looked stunning. We had drinks and watched people
looking at the photographs. The music was infectious and I invited Janetta to
dance. "Are you kidding me?" she said. "I'm not dancing, I never dance." And
she sat down.

Our presentation the next day went well. Janetta fluently and gallantly talked
about her experiences in prison, about her childhood abuse, and what she

is working on at TGI Justice Project. I presented a slideshow, with music, of photos of people who would be in this book. The following morning, Janetta sat down with Herb and me at our breakfast table in the hotel's huge terrace restaurant and said, "I am going to ask some people for money. I will start with my surgeon in San Francisco. He is here."

"Why?" I asked.

"Because I do not have any money. The crowd-funding money has not yet come into my account, and my credit card does not work in this country."

It had been with the help of a crowd-funding website and support from the community that Janetta had collected enough funds to cover her expenses for this trip, including her hotel room and registration fee. Two other trans-identified people were supposed to be on our panel but did not have the money to attend. Of the six of us, the four who identified as transgender were the ones who could not afford the trip without assistance. I remembered what my friend Fresh! and other people I knew from the transgender community had told me, especially about people of color: they had no financial backup, not from their birth family, not from the state's health care systems. When they were broke, they were broke.

Janetta stood up and walked over to her surgeon. I saw them talking. He smiled, she looked more serious. Then she came back. "He said no. This is so embarrassing." I gazed at the ocean of wealthy, white, middle-aged professionals on the terrace, just a few people of color among them. When I got back to the room, I started crying. Janetta had no money, yet she had traveled across the world to represent the devastating reality of so much poverty in modern America.

The phone rang. It was Janetta. "Hey, girl, what's up? Are you coming to meet the Asian girls at the Lotus Room?" "Janetta, you are such an amazing woman," I said, "and I can't imagine what it must have felt like for you to go around begging." "Kris, don't cry!" Janetta said immediately. "I'm doing fine. See you downstairs in a few minutes!"

Later that day we had a cold drink on the patio near the water. We talked about the transgender women in Thailand, and then she said, "I think I'm asexual." I felt puzzled by her comment but didn't ask more. Then she added, "I do think that if I had not had a penis, things would have been much easier between me and the people in my previous relationships. It became too complicated for the people I was with at the time." She lit another cigarette and went quiet. A little later, I asked her to tell me more about her family.

"My dad lives in a Florida state prison. His name is Elijah. He received three consecutive 99-year sentences for which I think he will be discharged after doing over 20 years this year. Our relationship is a little spotty. I'm one of the middle children and the only one that he has very little contact with. I don't really have any special moments with him that stick out other than him taking us to bars and dope holes so he could score his dope. He was an intravenous drug user, and I never remember him doing anything other than popping up on occasion in Tampa to use me and my brother as props to transport drugs in large amounts while looking like a father taking his kids on summer vacation. Part of his goal as well was to make sure we knew our siblings on his side of the family, and to connect with our cousins who we visited in the summers in early adolescence. It was great to see them and aunties and uncles in our adolescence. I'd say from first grade to about sixth grade we went to see my grandmother—his mother—every summer for about three weeks. That was a joy. However, my father was never there. My brother and sisters have a cool relationship with him, and he makes an effort to stay in contact with them. I stopped reaching out to him because I felt like he wasn't reaching back, so I just let it go. I wish I could have had that father figure in my life. It will always be a small piece in my life that is empty and unfulfilled."

Her mother, she said, still lives in Tampa. "I was always impressed with my mother because she was a diva, especially when she applied herself. She wore wigs galore. I can remember her having at least 20 wigs in her collection. She also had lots of perfumes, lipsticks, high heels, and dresses. I can also remember painting her long, beautiful nails for her and clipping her toenails. I just could not wait for the day I could do the same thing for me."

Janetta grew up with a stepfather, James, who would come home drunk. "I used to have such intrusive memories of him calling my mom a whore and a bitch and she was no good. There's so many incidences. He physically attacked her, and sometimes she would throw the first blow because she knew he was going to hit her. He cut her, gave her black eyes, hit her in the head with objects, chased us out of the house with knives and guns, bats, anything he could get a hand on. He beat my brother once for something he did bad. He never hit me or my sister physically. I was sure he was killing our spirits. My friends and neighbors saw my mother and stepfather fight in the streets. My stepfather beat my mom down like a dog in the streets so many times, I'm sure it was close to 100 times. I've witnessed so much violence— emotional, physiological, and physical abuse—that I knew I was damaged goods. On top of all that, I was being sexually abused by my cousin, being fucked, I mean penetrated.

"My mother killed him [James] right in front of me and my brother's eyes. There was an ugly argument and a fight ensued out of it. James pulled out a rifle, and my mother overpowered him and took the rifle from him, accidentally killing him. I can remember my mother being arrested, and my brother and I were taken to our grandmother's house. My grandmother was really my mother's aunt and thus our great aunt. My mother was given to her as an infant by her older sister. She was our loving grandmother through and through. I can remember Grandma showing me and my brothers how to plait her hair. We would brush and comb and grease her scalp just about every weekend through my entire childhood.

"Today I have lots of love for my mother, and that is based on the fact that I have healed from so many stripes on my back, and on knowing her story in terms of being a single black mother with two children in the mid-'60s when black folks were so marginalized. There ain't no need to hold her hostage. She had her first child at 18 with no real education and not a lot of resources. It took a lot of work on my part and lots of therapy, recovery, and discovery to find my safe place in this world. She's learned to accept my transgenderism. A lot of it is that they didn't understand, and some of it is that they were buying into the fact that me being who I am is a sin against God. I know that a lot of the things I've taken myself through were based on what I felt as a child: lack of love, understanding, and compassion. But today I know what it means when parents say, 'I did the best I could with what I had.'"

The next time I saw her, Janetta shared that she had befriended some gay guys from her hotel with whom she explored Bangkok by night. She said, "We went to a cock fight last night," and then laughed. "Wow, did you win?" I asked. It took me a few seconds to realize she was talking about the red-light district.

She made a dismissive gesture. "But seriously. I'm very happy with my David. He is a very good man." She smiled and lit a cigarette. "My relationship with David is good. It's kind of shifted. It's like we're kissing cousins. I'm very fond of him, and he adores me. However, based on the fact that he spent so much time in prison, I suggested and encouraged him to go out and experiment and find his flavor. Not to mention: I don't want to be in a committed relationship. The relationship I'm committing to is taking good care of myself mentally, emotionally, and physically so I can do the work that I'm commissioned to do by my Higher Power." Later she said she had passed David on to a girlfriend of hers who suited him better. Janetta didn't want to be in a relationship.

On the last day of this five-day conference, Dr. Jamison Green, an international figure in the transgender community and the person who first put me in contact with Janetta, was sworn in as the new president of WPATH. Then the Amsterdam-based organizing committee for WPATH 2016, to be held in Amsterdam, came on stage to welcome us to the next conference. "With our 176 nationalities we are a very diverse city," they said, before playing a promotional film showing lots of smiling white people. I was glad to see Janetta approach the committee after the ceremony to ask if they could please include people like her and other people of color in their promotional material in the future, and to say that she was looking forward to visiting.

Janetta, from humid Florida, and myself, from cold Northern Europe, are the only two people sitting on the hotel patio in the blazing 95-degree sunshine in Thailand. I am observing Janetta's calmness in the sun. Her calmness is making me calm. Our faces are turned toward the sunshine, an occasional breeze from the urban Chao Phraya River easing the intensity of the heat just a little. "Any bit of sun," I say. Janetta, with her thick, long hair, her makeup, and her napkin in hand to dry up the tears of sweat, adds,

"I love the sun!" followed by a smile of gold teeth. Then she crawls into a large old wooden chair on the hotel patio, puts her legs up on its arms, and falls asleep.

I had listened with amazement to the stories of this once-wounded bird who was so determined to be free. She had lived in fear even before her freedom was taken away from her in prison. Being the only woman in a male prison was torture, but the isolation of solitary confinement was worse. Her self-doubt grew louder in solitary. Within those four claustrophobic walls, she could not escape awareness of what had been done to her. Now, being with her away from San Francisco and East Oakland, observing her engage with people from across the planet, I could see that Janetta was doing fine. Seeing her walking around Bangkok in her sandals, her bright pink and white dress, enjoying the atmosphere, the people, the food, I understood that she was less scared and she was taking care of herself.

I wondered if she felt free now—or, after all she had been through, if she could ever feel free. "Embrace and forgive," she would say to me. I knew Janetta had found peace and space within herself and gained strength by helping other abused women.

Laverne Cox, Miss Major, and Janetta Johnson at an event in San Francisco, 2014

Janetta in her office in East Oakland, November 2013

Janetta during a WPATH presentation planning dinner in Berkeley, December 2013

Janetta with her colleague Danielle Marilyn West (right) from TGI Justice Project speaking at a
demonstration against the killings and violence of transgender women of color after the murder of
Taja de Jesus, San Francisco, 2015

2

FAR FROM HOME

As soon as Grace and I set foot into Club 21, the bar at the corner of Turk and Taylor streets in San Francisco, we heard a spewing of expletives. It had been my idea to walk down Turk a few hundred yards from Grace's apartment building to this seedy, rundown bar, which I had passed a few times on my way to meet Grace at her place. I wanted to get to know this neighborhood, San Francisco's notorious Tenderloin, where Janetta used to live and Grace was still living.

The entrance was wide open, but Club 21 was everything but welcoming: broken windows with dark thick drapes, cracks taped over with cardboard, curtains of dusty fabric heavy with history. It looked like a place for those spoiling for a fight, a place not to venture into unless you were a regular.

As we made our way into the bar, we heard a male voice roar: "Get your fucking black ass out of here, you black bitch!" Since Grace was the only one with dark skin in the place, it was clear to whom he was referring. Never since coming to the States two years earlier had I witnessed direct racism like this. But Grace walked gracefully into the shower of hate and sat down at the bar, as far away from the screams as she could, though the bar was only a few feet long. This was nothing Grace couldn't handle.

I looked at the young, slim bartender wearing a black Misfits sweater, my heart palpitating as I asked him, "Could you please kick this man out?" The bartender looked much too gentle for this place and seemed puzzled by the incident. I could not read what Grace was feeling. Sadly, I was reminded of the fact that people in her situation often experience so much cruelty that they train themselves to hide their anxieties under fire.

The bartender followed my request and told the guy to get out. The man, probably in his 30s, with short, blond hair combed back flat, appeared from behind an ATM and walked out with no fuss. But once he was outside the bar, he started shouting again. I sat down next to Grace, ordered two Sierra Nevadas from the bar's white picnic cooler packed with ice, then got up and drew back the large curtains to get a better look at him. Only a broken window separated Grace and me from an all too easily imagined disaster. She continued to appear unmoved about the whole thing. The man raised his arms, pretending to hold a machine gun pointed at us. Then he thundered with a sneer: "I am going home to get my rifle, then I will come back and shoot you!"

We kept drinking. I could not fathom my own feelings, or Grace's. It was easier to continue ordering Sierra Nevadas from the cooler.

The bartender's name was Simon. He was from Sweden and had just started working in the bar. I asked him in Norwegian what the hell he was doing in this neighborhood. He smiled and replied in Swedish, "I like it here. But what are *you* doing in this neighborhood?" Afterward I wondered why I didn't call the police.

Grace and I first met in the beginning of 2013 at the Transgender, Gender Variant, and Intersex Justice Project (TGIJP) office in East Oakland. Janetta had introduced us. I already knew parts of Grace's story from a couple of newspaper clippings. I had read a news article about her that blew my mind: Grace, an immigrant from Liberia living in San Francisco, was arrested several times, ended up in solitary confinement, and was almost deported.[23]

Grace was 45 years old when we met. The long struggle through disrespect, violence, and political unrest in her homeland had exacted its toll. There were scars all over her 6-foot-3-inch body, some easily visible, and she was emotionally traumatized from violence, hate crimes, and from spending a long time in solitary confinement in an immigration detention center in California. By the time the US immigration center tried to deport her, Grace had attempted suicide. But long before Grace ended up in an immigration prison, she had experienced what she described as worse than the imprisonment and the physical attacks: the trauma of losing her African blood family when she told them the truth about who she was.

In Club 21, I had a tiny glimpse of what Grace and Janetta and many others in this book have experienced only too often: verbal assaults and degrading stares, racial and sexual slurs spit into their faces, the humiliation of not being taken seriously, physical attacks aimed at erasing their very being.

The part of Turk Street where Grace lived is one of the most visually bizarre streets in San Francisco: the sidewalks populated by toothless people begging for cash and cigarettes, elderly on heavy drugs wearing filthy clothes over fading tattoos. Turk runs through the Tenderloin, a neighborhood of halfway houses, shelters, single-room- occupancy hotels that rent rooms by the hour to serve the sex trade, rundown bars, and liquor stores. The first time I walked into this neighborhood alone, I felt both thrilled and nervous. It was like entering through a door to hell. No trees, no warm faces. Just horror. Fear. People's eyes screaming.

No one really knows how the Tenderloin got its name. Some say it is a reference to the neighborhood as the "soft underbelly" of the city. Some say the name is from the days when cops would receive "premium pay" for patrolling the city's seedy areas and could therefore afford great cuts of meat. Others say the term originated from the Tenderloin district in New York City, known for vice and corruption. The Tenderloin was San Francisco's first gay neighborhood before the Castro district took on that distinction. One of the country's first gay and transgender riots happened at Compton's Cafeteria on Turk and Taylor streets in 1966, three years before Stonewall in New York.[24]

Nothing could beat Club 21. It was frequented by so many interesting characters. Grace seemed accustomed to the diversity. "I've done it all," she would say. She spoke to anyone in the bar. Her exuberant body language got anyone talking. When we strolled through her neighborhood, she would speak to everyone she passed.

My being just 5 feet 2 inches, I felt safe with Grace. She would always walk me to the BART station after a night at the watering holes, sometimes holding my hand. She would tell me not to worry, even though I wasn't scared, saying that her big, pointed cowboy boots had metal tips, an excellent weapon if we ever needed one.

My first conversation with Grace was about Africa. "Grace, I have something that is really troubling me," I told her, knowing she was from Liberia. As a Norwegian, I felt somehow embarrassed that Norway had given the Nobel Peace Prize to the president of Liberia, Ellen Johnson Sirleaf, who publicly supported criminalization of the LGBT community.

Grace screamed in response: "Yeah! I have been thinking about this too, Kris. We have a lot of work to do!" So we made a date and decided to work together to write a petition chastising the Nobel Peace Prize Committee in Norway for their choice.

As a world map published by the International Lesbian, Gay, Bisexual, Trans and Intersex Association (ILGA) in 2013 shows, most countries in Africa have prison terms, and some have a death penalty, for any kind of LGBT identification.[25] Homophobia is widespread—with the help of Christian missionaries from the US. In some countries, like Sudan, Uganda, Somalia, and parts of Nigeria, the murder of gay and lesbian individuals is not prohibited by state legislation. In Uganda, even though the "Kill the Gays" bill passed in 2014 was later ruled invalid, it is even illegal for international organizations to "promote" LGBTQI rights in the country. Anyone who rents an apartment or gives a job to someone in the LGBTQI community can be imprisoned. However, there is much underreporting, and data on gender identity rights are sparse.

In March 2014, my husband and I presented our work at the first Pan Africa ILGA conference in Nairobi, Kenya, where there were lots of gay and trans activists from all over the African continent. It was clear that one of the challenges—and a way in—was to connect with religious leaders and build trust from there. A transgender woman, Leticia, from Kampala, Uganda, showed me images of herself after an attack and told me about her lesbian friend who was found at home, burned to death by boiling water that someone had thrown on her.

Grace and I met on May 17, a good day, since it was the national constitution day in Norway and also the International Day against Homophobia, Transphobia, and Biphobia. We spent all day at her one-bedroom apartment on the ninth floor. She had prepared some African dishes, and she waxed nostalgic as she showed me the photographs of herself with various colorful people on the nicely painted off-white walls and in photo albums. Grace was sweating. She told me she did not always feel well. She kept going to the doctor, who told her she needed to exercise more. "I had already lost my blood family," she said. "I naturally thought that if my blood family does not want anything to do with me, then no one will."

We wrote the petition, posted it online, and sent hard copies to the Nobel Committee in Norway and to Barack Obama at the White House. Grace told me later that she collected more than a thousand signatures during San Francisco's Trans March and Gay Pride weekend in late June.

We decided to create and post a YouTube video as well. Grace was wearing a bright yellow and green West African dress. She was confident and articulate. She said that life was very difficult for LGBT people in Liberia. They had admired Ellen Johnson Sirleaf for taking office and for speaking in favor of women, freedom, and liberation. Yet Sirleaf would do nothing for the LGBT community. Grace demanded on camera: "No leader of any nation deserves a Nobel Peace Price for criminalizing gay, lesbian, and transgender citizens. Please consider my petition and withdraw the Nobel Peace Prize from the Liberian president Ellen Johnson Sirleaf." We uploaded the video on YouTube.

In March 2012, journalists Tamasin Ford and Bonnie Allen from *The Guardian* (one of the UK's largest newspapers) had traveled to Liberia to do a joint interview with Tony Blair, a founder of the Africa Governance Initiative, and Johnson Sirleaf. The interview was videoed and also reported in *The Guardian*: "The Nobel peace prize winner and president of Liberia, Ellen Johnson Sirleaf, has defended a law that criminalizes homosexual acts, saying: 'We like ourselves just the way we are.... We've got certain traditional values in our society that we would like to preserve.'"[26] Grace and I could not stop watching the video on *The Guardian*'s website.

Grace was willing to let me photograph her. We set up photo lights and umbrellas. I took pictures with an old Rolleiflex medium format camera using 120 film. I had recently pretty much put aside my digital camera, seeking a way to capture a more intimate feel in the images of people I was photographing. Also I wanted to create a more serious, traditional style of portraiture, with black and white contrast, rather than press photo style. We covered her sunny windows in the living room with bright yellow and blue fabric backdrops. I noticed her eyes light up from the attention. She posed for several hours.

Grace was born in Liberia, West Africa, in 1968. She was one of many siblings, with responsibilities for her brothers and sisters. Early in her life, her parents divorced and Grace moved in with her father and stepmother. They had a large house on a big piece of land in a suburb of Monrovia, the capital, and lived well. Her father worked for Pan American World Airways, the largest US international carrier until the early 1990s, and took his family traveling around the world.

Grace knew early that she was a girl. She went to a boarding school in Ghana for two years before she came out to her close friends at age 16 as a gay boy. Grace had a steadfast clan of LGBT friends in the underground culture of Monrovia's back streets, and she would meet people in gay bars abroad in places like Paris, London, Amsterdam, and the United States. But she could tell no one about her gender identity issues. Transgender was unheard of wherever she went, and she figured it was too dangerous to reveal even to her closest friends. Grace said that at a young age in her home country she had seen people tortured and mistreated for their sexual orientation.

Despite the rampant prejudice in Liberia, Grace always spoke about her country with longing and love. Her great great grandfather had come from Virginia to settle in Liberia. "Liberia comes from the word 'liberty,'" she told me. "It is the oldest African republic, founded in 1847 by freed American slaves. The majority of Liberians were native Liberians who carried tribal names and spoke their native language. Monrovia, the capital, was named after the American president Monroe. Most Liberians today have American surnames like Johnson or Richards."

By the time Grace was growing up in Liberia, the country had long been plagued by conflicts between the native Liberians and the so-called America-Liberians. For decades, Americans had trained and equipped Liberia's armed forces and had supported Samuel Doe, who violently seized power in 1980 and became Liberia's first indigenous head of state. In the late 1980s, the Liberians grew tired of the corruption in Doe's government and his favoritism toward his native Kahn tribe, and the US began cutting off critical foreign aid to Liberia. The First

Liberian Civil War began in December 1989, when rebels and their leader, the America-Liberian Charles Taylor, entered Liberia from neighboring Ivory Coast to challenge Doe. Taylor had broken out of a prison in the United States, where he was awaiting extradition to Liberia on charges of embezzlement.

In 1990, the year Grace's family moved to the States, Taylor gained control and became one of the most brutal warlords in Africa. He resigned in 2003 as a result of growing international pressure and sought exile in Nigeria. After Taylor's resignation, Ellen Johnson Sirleaf returned to Liberia from the United States, where she had been for a decade. She won the 2005 presidential election and took office in 2006 as the first female head of an African state. Taylor was found guilty in 2012 of all eleven charges levied by the Special Court in Haag, including terror, murder, and rape, and sentenced to 50 years. His appeal in 2015 to serve his prison sentence in Rwanda instead of the UK was denied.

In 1986, Grace, then 18 years old, was sent to Texas to attend college, like many young America-Liberians. She showed me a yearbook picture from the Texas college of a pretty young man with short hair wearing a suit. "Look at me, Kris, can you believe this is me?" Grace laughed loud. She met other gay and lesbian people in the States and thrived living in an environment that was gay friendly compared to where she came from. It gave her hope. Every time she visited Liberia, however, she was reminded that she had to "walk and behave like a real man."

Grace had figured she must be bisexual. During her time in Texas, she had a college sweetheart whom she loved and whom became pregnant with a son. Grace showed me a photo on Facebook. "That's my youngest boy. We still talk. But he doesn't want to be my Facebook friend." Grace's relationship with her son's mother ended, and she moved on. "We were young and I was not ready to settle down. She was my best friend, but she was not ready for what I was about to become."

Grace's father died suddenly of a heart attack in 1988, and she went back to Liberia for the funeral. There she fell in love with another woman. They had gone to the same school when they were younger. "I was heartbroken about the loss of my father, and she was the only one I could confide in. We fell in love and went to Paris. From there we traveled to Geneva, where my second son was conceived." Grace and her new girlfriend got married in Liberia before moving to Minnesota with Grace's stepmother. "A lot of black women marry white American men and settle down there, and it was easier to get papers in the Midwest, where immigration was more relaxed," Grace said. "But like my previous love, my second wife was also not ready for my identity struggles."

Grace kept on trying to "behave" and live as "straight" as she could. She tried to live up to what was expected of her, now that she was responsible not only for her birth family but also for her new family. She absolutely loved them, but she struggled internally. Two years into her marriage and out of desperation, Grace found the courage to tell her wife and her stepmother that she was a woman. "My sons were never a mistake. My wife and I had lots of fun. I just could not live a double life anymore." Grace told me her stepmother and wife had gone into a rage and called Grace crazy, and then thrown her out. "They dishonored me. My relatives said I was doing a great sin against God." Grace packed two suitcases and fled to Los Angeles. She would not talk to her mother again for many years. "They are still not accepting me as a woman. I´m trying to reconcile with them, educate them about gender identity issues, but every time I try to reconnect, I end up getting very hurt. They use the male pronouns. They say 'he' and 'him.' It feels very humiliating."

In Los Angeles, Grace moved into a motel and started to sell sex on the Strip on Santa Monica Boulevard under the name "Africa." She was in constant pain from the separation from her family, but she knew she could never go back. "It all went downhill from there," Grace said. The stories she told me from this period were not clear, but it seemed so painful for her to talk about it that I did not push for more details.

Grace gave me permission to speak to her immigration lawyer, Cara Jobson, in San Francisco. I contacted Jobson in the spring of 2014. She told me that in 1994, Grace was convicted of a couple of theft crimes and sentenced to a prison term of three years and four months. "I do not have records of what prison she was in, but Grace tells me it was San Quentin. Some of the law enforcement records we have show that she was in 'Ad Seg' during at least part of her prison

Grace shows me scars from one of the three attacks in San Francisco. I took this photograph
during an interview at her home in the Tenderloin district in San Francisco.
May 17, 2013 (International Day Against Homophobia, Transphobia, and Biphobia)

In the detention center they tell us that transgender people cannot live in the general prison population because we will be attacked and cause disruption. So we live in a cage where we only get out one hour a day. Often this hour is after 5 p.m., when the lawyers have gone home, leaving no chance to call anyone. Some of us get very exhausted. Many give up and eventually agree to be deported and go back to Africa, Latin America, and elsewhere and live as the gender they were assigned at birth. They are in great danger in their home countries. I tried to kill myself twice because I knew there was no life for me in Liberia. I felt useless, worthless, and unwanted.

— Grace during an interview in 2013 about her time at an immigration detention center in San Diego term. Administrative Segregation in most prisons is essentially a form of solitary confinement."

Jobson continued: "In 1997, Grace was let out of prison but was soon picked up by Immigration and Custom Enforcement (ICE) and placed in deportation proceedings to remove her from the States because of her prison sentence. That year, an immigration judge granted Grace the right to stay in the US, based on a finding that she'd be persecuted in Liberia. The form of relief he gave her was relief under the Convention against Torture (CAT). Grace was free to stay. But the Immigration and Naturalization Service (INS) appealed, arguing that the regulations implementing the CAT treaty were not yet in effect and so the judge did not have authority to grant Grace relief. INS won the appeal, and Grace was sent back to the immigration detention center."

For the next several months Grace was in immigration custody in San Diego, which she described as far worse than being in the general US prison system. Recent reports on conditions in these prisons bear out how problematic these holding prisons can be. Grace told me, "In the detention center they tell us that transgender people cannot live in the general prison population because we will be attacked and cause disruption. So we live in a cage where we only get out one hour a day. Often this hour is after 5 p.m., when the lawyers have gone home, leaving no chance to call anyone. Some of us get very exhausted. Many give up and eventually agree to be deported and go back to Africa, Latin America, and elsewhere and live as the gender they were assigned at birth. They are in great danger in their home countries. I tried to kill myself twice because I knew there was no life for me in Liberia. I felt useless, worthless, and unwanted. I attempted suicide because they wanted to send me back to Liberia. I ripped the bedsheets and tried to hang myself, but a guard came just in time to save me."

"There are two common ways in which a transgender immigrant ends up in detention," Lauren Anderson writes in her paper "Punishing the Innocent."[27] One is when ICE arrests a transgender immigrant either crossing the border or living in the United States without proper immigration status. In the second, "transgender immigrants of any status can also be detained by ICE after completing a jail or prison sentence for a deportable crime." Anderson adds that "it is a common strategy to hold transgender inmates in solitary confinement. This creates major problems for transgender immigrants in the US."

The devastating psychological and physical effects of prolonged solitary confinement are well documented by social scientists, lawyers, and activists. Solitary, as is now well known, causes people immediate mental harm and very likely future psychological illness: nightmares, anxiety, chronic tiredness, nervous breakdowns, irrational anger, chronic depression, and suicidal ideation. It did not take long before Grace found herself struggling with many of these symptoms.

Grace was finally released in 2000 because ICE officials could not arrange for her removal to Liberia for lack of a valid travel document. "The US can't just fly people and leave them in another country," Jobson explained. "Due to sovereignty issues, ICE has to have a passport or some other document to show the receiving country that this is really one of their citizens. But then Grace was rearrested and sent back to San Diego in 2002 because they felt they were close to obtaining a valid travel document." This is when Jobson was contacted by a nonprofit called the Lawyers Committee for Civil Rights and started working with Grace.

By the time the Convention against Torture (CAT) was in place in the US, a new judge had denied Grace all forms of relief and ordered her removed from the country. Jobson and Grace appealed again, and the appeals were denied, but eventually the ICE no longer had a basis for detaining her, and she was released.

Grace went back to San Francisco, where she met Miss Major Griffin-Gracy and Sharon Grayson at the City of Refuge United Church of Christ. Grace told me, "They are transgender human rights activists who helped me find the courage to start my transition. Miss Major later started working at TGI Justice Project and they kept in touch with me." She said she felt great love for Miss Major. "Miss Major told me, 'Put your family and the past on the shelf for now, and focus on becoming the woman you are.' Miss Major supported me, bought me clothes and very large female shoes, and said to me, 'You may be big and tall, but you will become a beautiful woman.'"

A few weeks after the racist slurs attack, Grace and I went to Club 21 again. Swedish Simon put two shot glasses upside down next to our Sierra Nevadas (the bar sold only two kinds, a lager and an ale, both in bottles, no drafts). I asked him what they meant. "They're from Henry," he said and pointed to a man in his mid fifties sitting at the far end of the bar. "It means Henry has bought you two drinks."

We had another drink before we walked a hundred yards to Aunt Charlie's, one of the few remaining gay bars in the Tenderloin. The interior was incredibly pink: pink lamps, pink neon signs, pink everything. Or at least the lamps made it all look pink. The place did not have the feeling of a gay bar as we know it these days. It was secluded, no windows, frequently empty (except when the drag queens entertain twice a week). A gracious older man with white hair wearing a white wool sweater was serving behind the bar; Grace and I ordered white wine.

Grace opened up to me about the three attacks she experienced on the streets of San Francisco, which continue to haunt her. They occurred within just a few years of each other. One night in 2004, Grace was walking down Post Street on her way home after performing at DIVAS when a man in the street pointed a gun at her and, without warning, shot her in the head.

"I called 911, and the police and ambulance were there in four minutes. They saved my life, taking me to San Francisco General Hospital. The doctors said to me that they could not remove the bullet because it would kill me. It is still in my head. The police and a friend from the FBI office in San Diego investigated the case, but they could never find the man who tried to murder me. They could not even find any witnesses that wanted to come forward," she said. Grace tried to pull her life back together, but it was a continuous struggle. She could not find work. Having a bullet stuck in her head, as well as the attack itself, left her traumatized.

Two years later, in 2006, Cara Jobson and Grace went back to court before a third immigration judge. The judge finally granted Grace´s application for relief under the Torture Convention, finding that it was "more likely than not" that Grace would be tortured in Liberia. Only a few weeks after this good news from the immigration judge, Grace experienced yet another trauma. A woman walking toward her on Post Street screamed at her: "I know you are a man!" As she came closer, she threw battery acid all over Grace's face and chest.

"I knew who this woman was, but because I was on probation at the time, I could not just call the police. The police would quickly find out that I was on probation, and this attack, or 'fight' as they would most likely call it, would have been a violation on my probation so they would put me back in a prison. I knew that if I went to prison, I would also be sent back to Liberia." Grace suffered third-degree burns all over her body that left the keloid scars that commonly form on the skin of people of African descent after injury.

"My transgender sister Miss Patty, who lived in the same hotel as me, called 911 for an ambulance and came with me to the St. Francis Hospital's burn unit, where I stayed for three weeks," Grace said. "I told the SFPD that I did not know who poured the acid over me. I had to just go on living on the street, in a hotel room. I had to forgive this woman so I could move on with my life. I was so depressed and scared after that. It was so hurtful to me that this was the second black person in a matter of one year who had tried to kill me."

The following year, Grace experienced a third death-threatening attack. Late at night on November 21, 2007, seven men, probably in their 30s and seeming quite drunk, were laughing and shouting near Howard and Sixth streets. This intersection is usually busy and crowded, but at this time of night it was fearfully quiet. The men spotted Grace across the street: an African woman, taller and stronger than any of them, her dress sparkling, her makeup shimmering. The men started to shout to Grace, swearing and bullying her, calling her a whore, calling her a faggot in Spanish. Grace wanted nothing but to go home in one piece. One of them came up to her and asked for a light. She said she did not have one. The man slapped her buttocks, and she pushed him to the ground.[28] The others quickly joined in, and she panicked, fearing for her life. She fought back, knowing she stood no chance against seven of them. She pulled out a knife she carried for protection and stabbed one of them. Someone called the police. When the officers arrived on the scene, they found out that Grace was on probation. Fortunately, no one was killed. Grace was arrested and transported back to prison. This time, she was told, she would never see America again.

The day after her fortieth birthday, on April 7, 2008, Grace appeared in court, her 240 pounds trapped in an orange jumpsuit, handcuffed, short-haired, with no makeup, jewelry, or wig—without any of the necessities for her to dress as the woman she was.

When it was her turn to testify, she told the judge about her fear of being killed during the attack, and that the men had called her a whore and a faggot in Spanish. Although one witness said in court that Grace had walked away from the men and then returned to start another fight, the judge was sensitive to the trauma she had experienced after her previous attacks. Grace was not sentenced for the stabbing, but she still had to serve time for violating the law while on probation.

She was let out of prison in 2009 and eventually was given a place to live in the Tenderloin. The city of San Francisco covered most of her expenses. She also received therapy and plastic surgery and began planning to finish her reassignment surgery. "I thank everyone involved in my case," she said to me. "I am forever grateful for what the people and the city have done for me. Thanks to them, I am who I am today. I am a happy person now. I have contact with my family—well, on and off. They said they wanted to have me in their life again.

"I try to educate African families these days that this is something we are born with. Today's African culture and religion see it as a sin to be gay or transgender. Being gay in Liberia or any other African country is extremely stressful. You have to get married, be straight, and have children. But today my life is an open book."

When I was finishing up this chapter, I kept thinking of a question my husband, Herb, and I were asked during our trip to Kenya and South Africa in March 2014 to learn about and document LGBTQI advocacy and activism in Africa. During a short safari in Masai Mara, we spoke with a Kenyan barman named Elvis who worked at the safari lodge. His English was fluent, his skin dark brown. When he heard we were from America, he said, "Oh, may I ask you something? I met these friendly black American soldiers in Mombasa who would talk to each other casually, repeatedly saying, 'What's up, nigga?' What does 'nigga' mean?"

This innocent question highlighted the difference between what Africans and African Americans experience. Grace used to tell me that she did not connect so well with black people in America. She was proud of her skin and body, proud of being African. Although she had experienced brutality in enormous proportions, she did not carry the psychological burden that African Americans carried from generations of slavery, humiliation, and racism. Her struggles concerned the prejudice against her transition into womanhood. Although she experienced racism, she said, she could brush that off more easily.

Years after her attacks, Grace received a letter of approval for gender reassignment surgery, sponsored by the city of San Francisco. However, the "friendliest gay city of the world," widely known for its understanding, inclusion, respect, and tolerance for the LGBTQI community, had not been able to keep Grace safe from violence. There are still few jobs available for people like her. There are few if any shelters or separate housing for transgender or gender-nonconforming people. Instead, we hear of continuing abuse toward sexual minorities and trans- and queer-identified people, along with a dramatic rise in number of incarcerated people and the overrepresentation of LGBT adults and teens in American detention centers, jails, and prisons. Our society is unprepared for, or perhaps unwilling to accept, the increasing number of people who are coming out.

Grace often said to me, "I hope that I can go back to Liberia one day. It is my home." I too hope that she can go back. But with all that is already broken, the future looks grim for her country and for her return. Jobson told me in May 2014 that Grace's "immigration case has not yet been resolved. She has CAT and so the government cannot remove her to Liberia unless they decide to go back to court and try to convince the court that it would be safe for Grace in Liberia. ICE has not taken any action to try and remove her because they know they'd have to prove that she is now safe in Liberia, which I think would be hard to show, given the conditions there for LGBT people."

Even so, I can imagine Grace on a big stage in Monrovia much like the stage from which she spoke with incredible enthusiasm and strength during TransMarch in June 2013: "San Francisco, San Francisco! Let me hear you!

I love you. I love you. I love you. Do you want to know why? Because I am from Liberia, West Africa, and they told me I was a nobody, I was cursed, I should kill myself. I moved to San Francisco. Do you know why? Because of you, I am a lover today!" Grace's voice reached the entire Dolores Park, and people cheered. "I am the first transwoman from that country. And do you know something? Norway made a mistake to give the Nobel Peace Prize to the president of Liberia. She refuses to decriminalize gay and transgender and homosexual people. I have filed a petition to Norway, and I urge you to sign it today." She ended her three-minute speech with the words: "The struggle is not over yet. God Bless America."

Grace at home in the Tenderloin. May 17, 2013

Grace at home in the Tenderloin. June 2013

3

RUINS OF ROME

On a late October afternoon in 2014, I was sitting in Nick 'n Jim's BBQ in Birmingham, Alabama, waiting for my order of hot links, collards, and biscuits, and thinking about an announcement I had found on a Ku Klux Klan website: "Fall Fest with gathering of speakers, entertainment and cross burning organized by New Empire Knights of the Ku Klux Klan" in Adamsville. The idea briefly crossed my mind to drive to Adamsville, just 20 minutes away, to observe the KKK rally. But I was on my way to nearby Montgomery to meet with the lawyers who were working with Ashley Diamond, a transgender woman who had been sentenced to 12 years for probation violation in connection with a nonviolent crime she said she did not commit. The previous day, I had tried unsuccessfully to visit Ashley herself at Baldwin State Prison, a close security prison for men, in neighboring Georgia.

Montgomery is the city where so much began: 15-year old Claudette Colvin's, and later Rosa Parks', resisting bus segregation; Dexter Avenue Baptist Church, where Martin Luther King Jr. had been pastor; and the Alabama State Capitol Building, where he gave his famous "How Long, Not Long" speech after completing the historic march from Selma in 1965. Ku Klux Klan events in the 21st century were not news to any of the people I was meeting on my first trip to the Deep South, nor were black protests for basic human and civil rights. Such protests had started as soon as slavery ended in 1865, long before the Civil Rights Movement emerged. African Americans all over the United States continue to fight for these rights today. Ashley Diamond is one of them.

On November 14, 2013, I received the following letter from Ashley:

> **Dear Kris. I had been deciding whether or not to write you about your project and have made a decision finally. My name is Ashley Diamond. I am a transgender who is in prison. I have one hell of a story. I have appeared on Sally Jesse Raphael and Jerry Springer. I have filed a lawsuit in District Court, a story that can be found in *Rome News-Tribune*. Those same deputies are why I am here. Even more disturbing than the facts that brought me here is**

the huge mistreatment I have received in the Department of Corrections in Georgia. There is no way to explain the challenges I have fought and the fighting for my Gender Identity Disorder. I plan to file a lawsuit on the Department of Corrections in a few weeks to engulf a class action for the rights to care and counseling while in here. If you think you may want to use me in your project (which I give you kudos on) write me at the address below. Respectfully, Ashley

It took me a few months to reply to Ashley, since I was traveling in the early part of 2014, and had so many letters to respond to already. When I finally did write back, I didn't get a reply, and I left it at that. Then in June 2014, I received another letter from her. After studying the law for a couple of years and learning her juridical rights, she had filed the lawsuit against the Georgia Department of Corrections. It was so well written that it had sparked interest and found its way to the Southern Poverty Law Center (SPLC) in Montgomery, Alabama. The SPLC is one of the most controversial advocacy and lawyers groups in the country, with a reputation for taking on pro bono cases that no one else will.

She wrote: "At any rate, even if it takes my life to save others, I am willing to be that sacrifice. Life has been a wonderful mix of opportunities and disappointments as to be expected. But the turmoil of being in the wrong body has taken a huge toll. I am in the Bible Belt. Georgia is well known for more than the Confederacy, and fighting this in any other state couldn't possibly be as difficult as this has. I'd love to be a part of your project. There is so much to be done and it's only through education and projects such as yours which inform the world of our struggle for equality."

She also wrote a little about her early life: "It wasn't until my first suicide attempt as a young girl that any attention was paid to my 'situation'—it was only through my meeting a sympathetic endocrinologist, who started me on hormone therapy I so desperately needed to begin my transition. Living in a small town, no job, education, or self-worth, I was always targeted by police, jealous women, and bigots. While the world is raving over *Orange Is the New Black*, I am somewhat living it. I had a huge imagination as a child and an ultra-effeminate persona. That made me a target for bullies and teasing that would ultimately cut my chances for finishing school."

She quit school in eighth grade. Despite all her struggles, she knew early on that the world out there was a place she wanted to explore. Her fondest childhood memories, she said, were playing with her dolls and spending time with her best friend, Nicole. But she also experienced a lot of abuse. When people referred to her as anything but a girl, she responded, "I am a girl. I am a girl!" for which she would be spanked. "This was only the start of a life in torture. In prison I have been raped, urinated on, spit on, and beat up. It is too much to take."

A week or so later, someone called me from a Georgia phone number. I ignored it and let the caller leave a message, as I usually do with calls from unknown numbers. On the voicemail I heard a feminine, articulate, friendly voice. When the phone rang a few minutes later, I picked it up and the same voice said: "I am so pleased to speak with you, Kris. I finally got your letter and was so relieved to hear that you are still working on this book and that you will include me." In my most recent letter to Ashley, I had said that if we worked quickly we could see about including her story in the book.

"How did you find me?" I asked. She had seen my work while living in Atlanta, she explained. "I love your work and I respect what you do. You do what you love doing. It's such an honor talking to you."

"Where are you now exactly?" I asked. She said she was in Valdosta State Prison in Georgia, a close security prison for male adults located 20 miles from the Florida border.[29] "The men here are in for three counts of murder, some with multiple rape convictions. And here I am—a woman, a nonviolent offender. Why am I in here?" I could hear sounds from inside prison through the phone now—echoing sounds of shouting, loud and masculine.

"When you are living in the rural South," Ashley continued, "when you are an African American [child] and playing with all white children who had parents who were lawyers and doctors ... I was welcomed into their homes because they thought I was a girl, but as soon as they found out, I was banished. I was forbidden around their children. The kids would never go for it, and they would sneak out to see me, but it created a stigma, and everywhere I would go, I would be harassed. It took my family many years to adjust to it, but they finally did. And now, going from living as a woman for 20 years and then one day coming into a prison system which, even though I have a medical diagnosis, refuses to treat me. Even though the law requires them to do so, and their own policy requires that they treat me, they refuse to treat me."

It wasn't just being denied hormone treatment for her gender dysphoria diagnosis that worried Ashley, she said on the phone. "People should be very concerned about the inhumane treatment and the injustice that I am going through in here. I feel sorry for people who can watch this abuse and watch the sexual crimes being done to us. My friend Shannon was stabbed 20-odd times in here and was lying in a pool of blood while the officers did nothing. I was gang raped by six gang members [at Macon State Prison] and was unconscious for a long time, but no one cared."

"What do you have to do to stay alive in there? Do you have to be a sex slave?" I asked, sensing that I already knew the answer. "Yes I do, Kris." Her voice had been urgent and desperate. Now the line went quiet. Then I heard her cry. Silence again. Sniffles. When she began speaking again, she apologized for "losing her grip." "People hate me so much in here. I put myself in so much danger by fighting everyone and everything.

But I refuse to give up. If I had known what was waiting for me, I would certainly have chosen death before going to prison."

Ashley and I spoke for more than an hour. Occasionally I asked a question. Mostly I just let her talk. "I've solicited the gay community in Georgia to help me get a parole attorney. I'm a nonviolent offender. I was sentenced to 12 years for a violation on probation. I've lived as a girl since I was 15 years old. Now I am 36. How is it that I am so scrutinized and hated because of something that I could not help? My genetic makeup is not my fault." Ashley then said, "This is going to sound strange, Kris, but I need to underline this: I was never a promiscuous person. My first boyfriend and I were together for eight years. He was my high school sweetheart. I've only been with a limited number of men, and I always prided myself with that because I believe sex is important. It is a very intimate way to show your love with somebody, to consummate that love. But to have it become a mandated part of my everyday life, to have to service strangers, people who are predators...."

Then she changed the subject. "My mother was a military woman. She was gone most of my life. My father raised us, and my father was strictly Southern Baptist, just like his father, and we were going to church every Sunday. We were to do what we were told, and me playing with dolls was unheard of. I was possessed with the devil, is what they called it. All the stigma that does to a child! But my whole life I was never getting into any trouble, and then one brush with the law has turned my entire life upside down. I'll never be the same after this. I hope to be better, but there is a part of me that has been taken away. I'll never get that back, no matter what I do." Her voice was trembling now. Then she started crying again.

What led to her arrest is somewhat blurred. Ashley had fallen deeply in love with a man while in her 30s and living in Atlanta. "He was the only person who really saw me as me, but unfortunately he was a bad guy. I don't think he meant to be. He didn't even come from a bad family. He had money but he sold drugs. I was so in love with him and was not ashamed of who I was when I was with him, so I followed him everywhere and I would have done anything for him. I came to him one day, and he was asking me if I could take a saw to the pawnshop and pawn it and bring him the cash. So I take this saw to the pawnshop and I get the cash and I bring it back to him."

Two weeks after going to the pawnshop, she was arrested for burglary. "I'm thrown in the Floyd County Jail, which is in my hometown: Rome, Georgia. It's a Baptist land. I have breasts, so immediately I was scrutinized. I was spit on. I knew I didn't burglarize anything. I knew I didn't take anything, and I felt like I would be vindicated. Little did I know that when you are charged with a felony, you have to remain in jail until you go in front of a judge."

Ashley survived the abuse and bullying in jail until it was time to go to court. "I was under such duress and such pressure, but still I didn't give in because

I knew I was innocent. I went to this jury trial. They would not allow me to wear my female clothes even though it was my jury trial and, according to due process, I had that right. They took my wig off me. I proceeded to the jury trial, and there was a mistrial and they were not going to let me go. They wanted me to stay in jail for another six months until they had another trial. So the District Attorney came up to me and said, 'I tell you what. Since you've never been on probation, if you'll take this probation, we won't make you wait in jail for six more months. We'll go ahead and let you go.' And so I took the probation. I didn't think I would ever be in any more trouble."

Ashley's childhood friend Neal was doing well as an interior designer and had his own television show, she told me. "We've been best friends since we were 15. Once he started to get successful, he came back for me and said, 'Ashley, I'm getting you out of Rome, and you're coming to live with me in Gainesville [Georgia].' I went to live with him, and life started to get better. I didn't think I'd ever get in any more trouble." Neal gave her a job, and she started getting around with her music career. She was on the *Jerry Springer Show* and on a talk show hosted by Sally Jessy Raphael. "I was on the last episode of *Sally*, and she said, 'This girl is going places. She's going to be a star.' When she said I was going places, I had no idea that meant prison."

One weekend, Ashley came back to Rome in her brand new BMW to visit her family and friends. "I had breasts now, and I had wonderful clothes and jewelry. Some officers heard I was there, and they said they had a warrant out for me for theft by receiving stolen property. And so they broke into my mother's house. They attacked me. The neighbors saw it, and they were like, 'We saw what happened.' But the sheriff said to me, 'I'll tell you what. If you'll go somewhere around here and if you'll score some pot for us from somebody, we'll let you go.' After they had humiliated me, they let me go.

"I didn't return, and two weeks later I went to report to the probation officer, and they said they had a warrant out for my arrest for escape and theft, and that violated the probation right off the bat. First time, first time I ever violated. I didn't have any chance to even explain. The probation officer said, 'There's a warrant for your arrest. I'm not going to revoke you. I'm just telling you, Rome has to come and get you. If it was up to me, I wouldn't revoke you.

I'd keep you here, and we'd get to the bottom of it, but Rome has all custody of you in this case.' So eventually I was arrested and sent back to Floyd County Jail. I was called a bitch, and they would toss my bra around with the officers." She said the officers would come into her cell and bully her. "They would twist my arms. I was pushed into the wall. I would not get to eat. They would skip my food tray some days. It was really, really bad. And the officers that had arrested me were the joke of the town now because they let me go and said I escaped."

Ashley continued to fight. She went to a probation revocation hearing. She knew her rights, and she trusted that the truth would set her free. She couldn't accept going to prison now that she was just getting her life back together and getting ready for her gender transition. Grammy-winning record producer "Baby Face" Kenneth Edmonds, who had written and produced more than 25 number-one R&B hit songs, had sent her a letter. "She was head over heels about that letter," her friend Nicole told me later when we met in Rome. Ashley was trying to have a career as a singer, and she had petitioned several times for gender reassignment surgery to correct what she called "the problem."

"I created a bit of controversy," Ashley explained, "because everybody in the local jail was insinuating that the police had taken me behind the church and had sex with me. That's what made those guys, those officers, come for me even worse. They would come to my cell in the middle of the night, and they would throw my books around and my things down and do anything they could to make me get angry. As a matter of fact, on the way to the probation revocation hearing, they told me the best thing for me to do is to pack up my stuff and get out of Floyd County because if I continue to fight this, they're going to make my life a living hell."

At the second trial she fought. She fought alone. Her family members were present in court that day. They would later tell me how some of the law officials had shivered with disgust at the sight of Ashley and laughed at her for "pretending to be a woman." The judge said that Ashley's lifestyle was a problem. She decided to turn Ashley's 12 years of probation into prison time and added that by the time Ashley got out of prison, she hoped to have retired as a judge. "She showed no mercy, and every observation, every lawyer, even from the transcripts, they would give the overtones that it was all because of my gender identity."

While Ashley was in Floyd County Jail, she had asked the federal court to get her out of Rome. "They granted me that. They said that the conditions at Floyd County Jail were horrible. I requested to be immediately transferred to Georgia Department of Correction's custody. I thought that I would have an opportunity to better myself, to work on my case, to be in an environment where I wouldn't be harassed. But I was sent to the worst camp. That is when I was beaten and raped by six guys. I was forced to hide cellphones in my rectum. I was forced to hide marijuana in my rectum. I was forced to do the most horrible things you could ever imagine."

Ashley, with the help of some lawyers, later discovered that her transfer from Floyd County Jail was based on a fraudulent record, such that she was transferred to a close security prison—Macon State Prison—even though she had been assigned a medium security level and should have been placed in a medium-level nonviolent offenders unit. "They placed me in close security based on a disciplinary record that does not exist, and I have been on close security ever since," she said.

"After I had filed my own first lawsuit, I was raped by six inmates and had my bones broken and my teeth kicked out of my head and then was placed in a series of dangerous events. I started to do what I am legally entitled to do, and that's to request hormone therapy. I have to be able to reach out to somebody because there is no one in here that's going to help me. My mail has been tampered with. I don't get all the mail. But I got your letter today, and I was relieved that it was tonight. It was the work of God, the last letter you sent."

She said her hands were shaking now, that she was overly emotional. She kept apologizing and continued to tell me stories on the phone. She did not have a lawyer to represent her in the criminal case. She had no money, she said. She could not afford a good criminal lawyer. She explained: "No one dares taking on a case like this, representing a black transgender woman in Georgia. Lawyers here won't do it." She had filed her lawsuit against the Georgia

A photograph of Ashley taken inside prison in Georgia. July 2014

I can't fathom in my head how people can sleep at night. Even if I was a thief. Even if I did go out and steal something. Three years is enough to "rehabilitate" a person and put them back out there on an ankle monitor or house arrest. But because I have started this fight, you are going to drag me to the hole, you are not going to treat me, you are not going to protect me, and you are still not going to make sure I am safe.

— Ashley during a phone call in 2014

Department of Corrections for denying her hormone treatment pro se.[30] When the Southern Poverty Law Center in Montgomery learned about her lawsuit, they decided to represent her in the hormone case.

The background noise on the phone returned. The echoing and the male voices shouting were loud. Ashley apologized for the noise. Knowing that she was in that place alone made me wonder what she was made of. From all the terrible stories I had heard since the beginning of this project, however, I had learned that some of these women have an unusually high survival instinct. Their determination to fight for their basic human rights comes from a deeper place than their experience in prison. It began when they were young.

Ashley continued: "I have had to perform oral sex two or three times a night just to be able to go to chow the next day or to be able to go to the [prison] store and not have all of my things taken from me, to not be beat up or robbed. We transgender women are sex slaves to the gang members and to any and everybody who wants us. If we say no, if we go to the staff and complain, we're placed in solitary confinement. If you report a rape, nothing happens or you go to solitary confinement. I have spent a year and a half in solitary confinement just because I was raped. There was prior knowledge, and they knew. They knew that it had happened to me before, and they knew that it was a high risk that it was going to happen again. They didn't follow any of their own classification procedures as far as housing and where they put me, and they would put me in cells with rapists."

In solitary confinement, she explained, the temperature is often 100 degrees with no air conditioning and no one to talk to. Often Ashley would not get water or ice cubes. I asked her what kind of cell she lived in now. "I have a cell that is about eight-by-ten with bricks. There is no air conditioning. I sweat profusely. Coming off hormones and being in a place where there's not even a fan, it's like hell, literally. I have a door that is big—metal with no windows. You can't see out of the other side of it. But you know what? That's livable. What I can't live without is my hormones."

Ashley said she is housed with an inmate who is a gang member. She explained that there are all kinds of dangers, such as the gang members' use of smartphones. "They take pictures of me, and when I am being moved to another prison, they forward the images to others so they can continue to abuse me." She never mentioned her cell mate again in our conversations. I didn't ask. I knew it was dangerous for her to talk about other inmates.

"I just transferred dorms over here because I was in a dorm in a room where I was being sexually assaulted. Fortunately, [I have one doctor] who has been my only advocate and got me moved to this compound where I am now. But it's the same situation here. It's unending because it comes with the territory and the staff. I have written letters to the warden, to the ombudsman, to the Department of Corrections. I've done mass mailings. I've done everything to just get them to do what the guidelines say they should do."

I asked if she gets some kind of mental health care in prison. "Yes, we do. This is the extent of my mental health care: A counselor comes to speak with me with a notepad and says, 'How are you today? Do you feel like killing yourself today?'

"To know that I am transgendered and that I am in a place or in a room with someone who has two, three life sentences, who has been known to rape people.... My account [for making purchases in the prison store], because I filed a lawsuit, has been frozen, so I don't get to go to the store anymore. That's one of the ways that I'm being punished. I can't get things like other inmates can get because I have filed the lawsuit and it has brought attention to Georgia. They thought that I was just going to be just like any other person that they have destroyed, because I am not the first, nor will I be the last."

Ashley called again about a week later. In this second conversation she told me more about the rape, although details were still sparse and I didn't push for more. Six inmates had tied her up, beaten her, and brutally raped her. "They raped me. They stomped me. They kicked me. They spit on me. My arm was broken. My rib was broken. My tooth was chipped. I was literally beaten unconscious. They wrapped me up in a sheet, threw me on a bed.

"I had been approached by some gentlemen who were saying that they were my friends because they knew that I did law work. Little did I know that these guys had cell phone devices and were leaders in a gang, a high-up gang. I won't

On my way to see Ashley's mother, I saw that behind Rome's classical
main street façade lies more gloomy and poor neighborhoods

Ashley's sister Diana and their mother, Diane, with Ashley's two nephews.
Rome, Georgia, October 2014

say the gang name. Well, I'll say it to you. It's the Gangster Disciples. They're GD. And they run the whole prison. I check in. I was doing their law work, and things like that. They kept saying to me, 'You'll be all right, you'll be okay.' I'm thinking I'm making friends and I'm beginning to get accepted. Later on, they want sexual advances, and it started out gradually. And I'd be like, 'No, I don't want to do that because I have a boyfriend that I have been with for very many years.' So then it became, 'Well, you're going to do this. You are going to hide drugs. And you've got to hide phones.' Then I'd be like, 'Well, I don't know where I'm going to hide them.' And they're going: 'You are going to hide them in you.' It's called muleing. It is a prison term for taking things and shoving them inside your rectum."

She did what they told her to do. She didn't want to die. Ashley called her family and told them what was happening. They called the prison counselor to ask that Ashley be moved, so the prison officials had been alerted. "And they ignored it. They didn't care. They let me be raped. This is war, and unfortunately I feel like Anne Frank. I'm in the attic."

She explained that she had tried her best to find a criminal lawyer. "I cannot afford a lawyer, but I contacted someone with a very good reputation," she said. "Her name is Brandenburg. She's had a very high, high parole success rate. I wrote her a letter because her fees are so high. She believes she can get me out. Instead of her usual $15,000 fee, she told me to try and get $7,500. If I could raise it up, she would have me out in a few months." Suddenly Ashley said the prison officials were counting all the inmates and that she had to hurry and hang up.

After the second call, the phone calls from Ashley abruptly ended. I received a few rushed letters from her saying that she felt weak and scared. Nicole, her childhood friend, sent me an email in September saying that Ashley had been moved again, this time to Baldwin State Prison, another close security institution. Nicole was worried about Ashley. Letters from her had become few and far between.

I decided to travel to Georgia and Alabama to meet with Nicole and speak to Ashley's family, and to do an interview with Ashley's lawyers at the Southern

Poverty Law Center. I would also try to visit Ashley in Baldwin State Prison. I filled out the prison's special privilege visitors forms, though I knew the chances of seeing her were slim. Just before I left, I received a brief letter from Ashley stating that she had been transferred from Valdosta to Baldwin and that things were rough. She felt suicidal and sensed that her days were numbered.

On Thursday, October 23, I flew to Atlanta, where I rented a car and drove to the town of Rome. My plan was to spend a day or two in Rome meeting with Ashley's friends and family before visiting Baldwin State Prison and then driving to Montgomery.

I was anxious to get to meet Ashley. I also hoped to be able to photograph the prison from the outside, to observe the "atmosphere," read the other visitors' faces, experience just a tiny bit the prison staff's scare tactics if only to be a witness to a daunting and demoralizing prison policy. However, I was aware that with my appearance and my red Norwegian passport, I am hardly ever discriminated against unless it is because of my gender—not for my race, not for my culture, economic status, religion, sexual orientation, or gender identity. I have never been stopped at the airport, in the street, or when driving. Ashley, from the moment she was born, has had no such safety. This difference between us also means that I cannot go to the South— especially just for a weekend—and hope to find the whole truth. And feel the injustice in my body.

I had never been to the Deep South before (except for Atlanta). Family and friends warned me: "Be careful." "Tell people where you are staying." "Please don't do anything reckless." Yet I knew I was not in any danger. I kept thinking, *It is Ashley they should be worried about!*

Located in Floyd County an hour and a quarter northwest of Atlanta, in the foothills of the Appalachian Mountains, Rome has around 36,000 citizens—60 percent white and 20 percent black plus some Native Americans and Asians. Twenty percent of the population lives below the poverty line. Like the city it is named after, it is built on seven hills with three rivers running between them. It has a long history of commercial success in cotton.

I walked to Rome's "historical downtown" the next morning, passing the Carnegie Library building where the town's civil rights movement had started. Rome's city hall next door had a large statue out front of the mythical twins, Romulus and Remus, a replica of the one Mussolini gave to Rome, Italy, in 1929. According to the myth, when the twins were born, their grandfather's brother left them to die by the River Tiber. They were saved by a series of encounters: a she-wolf breastfed them, and a shepherd and his wife took them in. When they discovered, as adults, the truth of who they were, they killed the man who had left them to die. Later they founded a new city, Rome.

I thought of Ashley while I stood there. She was certainly a different kind of Roman, yet she too, once she realized who she was, knew she was meant to do something significant despite the hardships she faced. I thought again about how it would be to visit her in Baldwin State Prison. I was sure she would be pleased to see me the next day. But she has a stubble beard now. How humiliated she might feel to meet me while looking like a man—the man she has never been.

At 4:40 p.m. that afternoon, Ashley's longtime friend Nicole and her husband, Michael, met me outside the Rodeway Inn where I was staying. We hugged, and then they took me for a ride around town before parking on Broad Street.

Nicole is a young, beautiful woman, almost six feet tall, with long auburn tresses. She's a couple of years younger than Ashley. She told me repeatedly that Ashley is anything but a criminal, that she is shocked about Ashley's situation and does not know how to help her. As we got out of the car, Nicole stretched out her long arms and said, "This is where Ashley and I went out on the town. And this is the store, Koman's, where Ashley bought wigs. It's where she took Sally Jessy Raphael and the film crew when they came to town for the show. God, we had so much fun. I miss her so much. She is my other half. We are soul mates." She suggested we go to Curlee's Fish House & Oyster Bar where we could talk. She, Michael, and I shared plates of Boom Boom and Crack-a-Lacka Shrimp and each had a Shrimp Po-Boy.

"If you look around us right now," Nicole said, "how many churches do you see? We have at least seven in the town center." She continued, "We can't wait to get out of here. This place is so contradictory. Ashley was so brave to 'come out' in this town. As far as I know, no one who is gay in Rome is 'out' here. This town is extremely homophobic. You have them all preaching and praying on a Sunday, but I know what these people did out the night before."

The two grew up on the same street, and Nicole's mother sometimes babysat Ashley as a child. "We became best friends. We do not need to tell each other things; we know how one another feels. I was at the funeral for my great grandmother, and my family treated me really badly. I was all upset and begged Ashley to come and get me. She came. Little did I know that her father had passed away that same day. She would always be there for me, no matter what, even on the day her father died. He died of leukemia in 2000."

During our visit, Nicole handed me an article about Ashley printed in the *Rome News-Tribune*. To my surprise, the local newspaper had published at least three stories about Ashley since her incarceration, presenting her as a transgender woman and using the right pronoun. However, along with the articles, they kept publishing a horrible mug shot of Ashley looking like a man, which I imagined spreading like a disease on the Internet. Slowly yet too quickly, her female features and her femininity were being erased in prison.

The next day, I emailed the journalist and asked if we could meet for a coffee. I thought him brave to have written so many articles about Ashley in a town so full of bigotry, homophobia, and racism. He did eventually reply, but by then I was on my way to Montgomery. A few days later, after meeting with her lawyers, I emailed him again and included a photograph of what Ashley looked like before she entered prison. "May I ask you a big favor, to please use an image in the newspaper that is not a mug shot?" I wrote. "Ashley is not a man, but a woman, as you know, and the mugshot is simply inhumane. I will ask her friend to email you a decent image in case there is a next time that you will write about her. Her lawyer reminded me today, as well as her family, that the mug shot is depicting a criminal man. Ashley is neither of those two."

It is a 169-mile drive southeast from Rome, past Atlanta, to Baldwin State Prison. Baldwin only accepts visitors on Saturdays and Sundays, between 9 a.m. and 3 p.m. With no direct transportation available and no car of their own, it must be extremely hard for Ashley's family to travel all that way to see her, especially since, as Ashley had told me, they struggle financially.

I pulled into the prison parking lot, arriving half an hour early. Soon a woman in an official van pulled up behind me and said that I was not allowed on the premises until 9 a.m. She suggested I drive to a park nearby, which I did. On my return, I expected to see a line of people forming outside the prison building, but no one was around. It was freezing cold, so I put on my thick woolen sweater and walked up to the building. This place looked sad and forgotten. There was not a sound, not even a bird chirping. It reminded me of a concentration camp I had visited years earlier in Germany.

I was not allowed to bring anything into prison except car keys, my driver's license, and some quarters. Baldwin's visitor guide specifically states that women have to wear bras, panties, and slips. I brought a couple rolls of quarters so Ashley and I could buy some snacks and take pictures at the vending machines. I wanted to tell her that everything will be all right. But if they let me in to see her, I knew she would read my face and see that I was worried. The more I learned about the women in male prisons, the more I knew about the dangers they encounter.

Two women and a child lined up behind me outside the entrance. They carried small, transparent plastic purses filled with coins. I asked them if I had completed my visitor's form correctly. A huge sign outside the door glared in my face, stating the number of visitors arrested at the prison that month and warning visitors to be sure they weren't the next. *Oh God*, I thought, *I won't do anything wrong. I won't even take a picture of the building. They might be all too happy to find a way to arrest me.*

A slender young female officer invited me into the building. I gave her my driver's license. She looked at a computer screen for a long time. Then she said, "You are not on his list. He doesn't have anyone on the visitors list."

For a split second, I thought Ashley might get in more trouble if I said something. But of course she would want me to speak up. So I said, "Actually, it's not 'he.' Ashley is a woman, and she put me on the visitors list many months ago." "Aha, now I know who you are talking about," said the officer. "But she knows I'm coming to see her," I continued. My heart sank. I felt sad. Frustrated.

"No visitors on her list?" I carried on. "That is impossible. I have traveled all the way from California to see her. Can you please tell her that I am here?" "Sorry, ma'am, I am not allowed to do that." "Can I please call her just to say I'm here?" "Sorry, ma'am, you are not allowed to do that." "But I have to speak with her. How can I reach her?" "You have to contact her the way you normally contact her."

I was prepared for this, yet I felt so disappointed. "Aren't the inmate's visitor lists supposed to be transferred along with the prisoner when a prisoner is moved from one prison to the next?" I asked. "Yes, ma'am. But there are no visitors on his list." "Can you please tell her, at least please tell her … that I have been here to see her?" I looked at the young woman while placing my right hand on my heart, hoping to gently persuade her. She looked a little friendlier and said, "I'll see what I can do, ma'am."

I knew my failed visit would have one of three outcomes: the officer would pass my message on to Ashley and not think more of it; she would tell other officers, who would punish Ashley for "misbehaving"; or she would never tell Ashley I had been there. I walked back to the car. What else was there for me to do here? Should I wait and hope for a miracle? I drove outside the prison gates, and then called the prison on my cell. Another woman answered. "May I speak to an inmate, please?" "No, ma'am, inmates cannot receive calls at these premises. They have phones in their dormitories, and they can call you when they want to."

I felt annoyed with myself for not being able to get in, but mostly just disappointed on Ashley's behalf. If she had access to a phone, she would have called me on a regular basis. I drove back toward Rome for 47 miles, my thoughts churning, before I stopped to fill the tank and go to the toilet.

The next morning, Ashley's mother, Diane, called me at the Rodeway Inn. It was Sunday, and I asked if I could accompany her to church. She said yes, and

I drove over to pick her up. She came running out from a little white wooden house, got into the car with a big smile, and said, "Change of plans! I'll skip church and we'll go to Ashley's sister's house. I have already been to church once today, and that's when they sing, which is the fun part anyway. Take a turn here, it's not far. I am so pleased to meet you, Kris!"

Ashley's sister Diana opened the door when we got there, and then she opened her arms and hugged me. She sat me down on the sofa next to her and showed me a photo album. She talked about how frustrating this whole situation was. When I mentioned that I had not been able to see Ashley at the prison the day before, Diana told me, "They said the exact same thing to us: 'Ashley does not have anyone on the visitors list.'"

Diana said that even though she didn't understand what it meant to be transgender, she had accepted Ashley as a transgender woman and they loved her. Ashley's mother added, "God loves us all. You are no worse as a human being if you are a transgender, and you are no better. Transgenders have a right to be who they are. Amen."

Diana introduced me to her nephews: one of them about seven years old and the other an 18-year-old who Diana said was gay. I asked him if he was open about this in Rome, and he said, "Oh yes, absolutely." Diana said, "He has had a very difficult time. His mother, Ashley's other sister, Kelly, is addicted to drugs. Her two kids stay with me most of the time. We hang out here, and we somehow find a way. My nephew has very few friends. He has always been bullied and has struggled enormously in school because of his sexual orientation."

It was obviously important to Ashley's sister to talk about things the way they were. She was not interested in pretending things were okay when they weren't. Diana kept holding her arm on the left side of her stomach and now and then she would moan. She said she had been in pain for several years. She had had multiple abdominal surgeries, but the doctors didn't quite know what was wrong with her. She was only 30 years old. I asked if I could take some photos. She said yes but wanted to put her wig on first.

Shortly before Ashley's mother and I left, Diana said, "Kris, I want to add to this conversation, despite my mother being present, and say that our childhood has not been easy, especially not for my two oldest sisters, Ashley and Kelly. There was no food on the table during our childhood. Both our parents were alcoholics. They were always drunk. We were always hungry. We had nothing. But Ashley never got into trouble. Ashley is not a criminal. She always knew she was much better than that, and she knew what she wanted. She is much smarter than me, but she always supported me."

I drove Ashley's mother home. She posed for more photographs on the lawn and on the balcony of her little white house. She liked being photographed; she said she felt like a Hollywood star. She smoked a cigarette and said, "Ashley's father passed away in 2000. He was 13 years older than me. He was just old enough to experience the cotton. Imagine, 13 years difference and I missed it, just like that." She gave me a big hug and said she hoped that we would meet again.

I left Rome and headed for Birmingham and Montgomery. As soon as I crossed the Alabama state border, which was only 30 minutes away from Rome, I spotted some cotton fields. I had never seen cotton fields before. It was after harvest. Most of the cotton plants were chopped down, but there was cotton flying across my windshield and scattered along the highway, looking like snowflakes. All I could think of was cotton's role in the history of slavery in this country. (The United States is still the world's top exporter of cotton.)

I drove through Birmingham to get a quick feeling of the place, stopping there for lunch, while deciding not to take a chance at the Ku Klux Klan rally nearby. In Montgomery, 90 minutes away, I checked in at a hotel downtown and walked up to "Rosa Parks' bus stop" and what used to be the old slave markets. From 1808, when the US government banned the importation of slaves to the US, until 1860, the enslaved population in Alabama grew from less than 40,000 to more than 435,000.[31]

My appointment at the Southern Poverty Law Center (SPLC) was at 2 p.m. the next day.[32] I arrived three minutes early at the modern building on a hill on Washington Avenue. The security guard, well equipped with weapons and walkie-talkie, called someone: "Are you expecting a Kris Lyseggen?" I waited a few minutes in the reception area, after going through a security check point, before a young woman took me upstairs to a sunny office overlooking the church Martin Luther King Jr. pastored.

"The first thing we need to talk about is what happens to people like Ashley *before* they get to prison," said David Dinielli, one of Ashley's lawyers, as soon as we sat down. Dinielli is a friendly looking man with square glasses and short, black hair. A fellow attorney, Chinyere Ezie, was there with him, as was Kyleah Starling, the communications assistant with whom I had been corresponding. A fifth person was present by speakerphone, presumably to record the interview. I had not expected to be in a room with so many people. They had asked me to give them my questions earlier that week. They thanked me for my interest in Ashley's story.

"There are certain things we cannot discuss," Dinielli explained, "but in general, Ashley wants people to know about her case. She has decided that she doesn't want this to happen to other people. Even if it is going to put her in even greater danger, it is important to her to try and survive, not just for her, but for other inmates as well." Then he continued: the story of Ashley Diamond and the stories of many people like her begin with the circumstances that force interactions between law enforcement and transgender and gender non-conforming people. "In many states throughout the country and especially in the South, there is no protection for people like Ashley— not in the workplace, not in the public. Transgender people can therefore not act as full citizens and participate in the economy. I think that made life hard for Ashley."

"Ashley does not have much on her record, does she?" I asked.

"No," he answered. "In fact, she doesn't have much at all."

"It seems very important to her that she always did everything she could to stay away from the law," I continued.

"True," Dinielli said. "And even the things that landed her in jail are nonviolent. So I think the background is very important. Do we want to operate a society where we exclude certain kinds of people from participation? With Ashley, it is very clear that she was not violent during the time of her incarcerations. She has been in multiple prisons now and has been housed with extremely violent prisoners."

Dinielli had kind eyes, and I sensed his genuine concern for Ashley's safety. I said I had tried to get into Baldwin but was told that Ashley didn't have anyone on her visitors list. "Isn't the list supposed to be transferred when she moves to another prison?" I asked.

"Generally, yes," Dinielli replied. "It is a black box in many ways. Even [for us] sometimes, as her lawyers, there have been times we think that things she has tried to send us have not gotten to us, even though we have the absolute legal right as her lawyers. We also ran into roadblocks where people said we needed to have certain permissions.

"Individuals have a lot of power in those institutions. I'm sorry you didn't get to meet with her; she is a pretty spectacular person."

"Is she in danger now? Have you spoken with her recently?"

"We were visiting with her two and half weeks ago at Baldwin," Dinielli continued. "I hadn't seen her in some time. As always, I found her to be resolute, determined, and strong, but also describing situations and circumstances that are so plainly mean, it is hard to believe they exist in what ought to be a modern country."

Dinielli explained how they had first heard of Ashley. "We learned that she had filed a lawsuit on her own. One of my former colleagues decided we needed to go and investigate and see this person. At that time, the lawsuit she had filed addressed a number of issues. Here in the US there are very strict laws according to which inmates can bring lawsuits challenging essentially anything regarding their conditions. The law requires that inmates follow procedures and are not allowed to go to court until they have dotted every 'i' and crossed every 't.' This is why it is challenging sometimes to represent prisoners. Ashley sent in the right piece of paper at the right time. Only then does the law even permit her to walk into a courthouse in the first instance. That first lawsuit ended up being dismissed. During all this time, of course, she has been transferred between various prisons."

He continued: "We got in contact with her and asked whether she would be interested in bringing a lawsuit that was really challenging Georgia's refusal to provide appropriate medical care. Her case is compelling. The fact that she has been outright denied is something to me that shocks the conscience. There is no dispute at this point in what is appropriate treatment for people who are transgender, and we couldn't figure out why in the world this was being denied to her. But of course several other things are happening to her as well that are equally shocking. The stories she is telling us are harrowing, frightening, and put into question if the people who run these prisons have any sense of humanity at all."

"Ashley told me you are only representing her in the hormone case. Why not in the criminal case?"

"We are interested in helping her in any way we can. We are moving piece by piece. There have been cases that are exhausted, and as a tragic result of these laws, it isn't possible to present all the things that have happened to one particular person in a single lawsuit."

Dinielli then said that the number of transgender people in prison is extremely high compared to the number in the general population, the number of transgender women is even higher, and the number of black transwomen is the highest of any.

Chinyere Ezie chimed in: "Within the transgender community, they are frequently denied the life chances they need in order to survive. Transgender people drop out of school at alarming rates because of relentless harassment and bullying, and are repeatedly fired from jobs when employers learn that they are transgender. Because of this pervasive discrimination, black market activities become the only option for survival for some individuals. But even when that is not what people are doing to survive, it becomes the perception of law enforcement that all transgender people are sex workers and/or criminals."

"We were seeing in a lot of cases previously where the police were stalking transgender women on the street," Dinielli continued, "searching their bags, and when they found condoms, using that as evidence that they were sex workers. There are so many things wrong with that presumption that I don't even know where to start.

"Just recently they passed a statewide law in California that eliminates the ability to use condom possession as evidence," he said.

"What about Ashley's conviction? Doesn't she have a very long sentence for the kind of crime that she is accused of?" I asked.

"Frankly, I don't have a reason to believe that the length of time was out of the ordinary for the type of crime that underlies the conviction," Dinielli replied. "We haven't focused on that, to be honest, but I'm sure you are aware that throughout the United States in general we overcriminalize people, we overincarcerate people, and we keep them in for far longer than the rest of the modern world. What I am saying is: I don't know if the length of her incarceration is because of the fact that she is Ashley or the fact that the state of Georgia overcriminalizes people and keeps them in prison for too long."

"I echo that," said Ezie. "It is a system-wide problem. A lot of prisons are operated privately, and it is lucrative to keep people in jail. The people who own the prisons do a lot of criminal law lobbying for things like the three-strikes laws and private probation, which keep you in the system. It's more of a reflection of our incarceration in this country more than anything specific to people like Ashley."

"Are you aware of any cases where they are giving hormones to anyone in prison in Georgia?"

"Ashley told us there is someone in her prison," Dinielli said. "The GDC has a formal written policy stating that, 'We will help you where you left off, but we are not going to help you beyond that.' For Ashley that means she should be maintained on hormones, and we can't think of any legal justifications for their denial. The only thing they have said in response is: 'Well, we don't know why we should believe her.'

"This is yet one more circumstance in which, for some reason, there seem to be a 'trans exception' to every rule. If you end up in prison and you have diabetes, I don't think people question that you are telling the truth. It is absurd to think that if you just happen to be arrested you also happen to have your medical record on you. The GDC's first response was: 'Well, we will need to see your medical record, and see all the prescriptions.' But of course most transgender people don't have a medical record. In the United States you get medical care through your employer, and so if you have never been able to have a job, most likely you've never had insurance. If you haven't had a steady income, you can't waltz into your doctor's office and be treated the way other people get treated. Many transgender people are forced to get their treatments essentially on the black market. Ashley got her treatments through a variety of ways that changed over time. Her circumstances are currently hell."

He said that when Ashley was first brought into the prison system, they recognized her as someone with gender identity disorder, but their only advice was that she should learn some coping mechanisms while in prison. "That is not medical advice," Dinielli said. "That is the most outrageous, malicious, and destructive medical advice I have ever heard."

"Is she in danger because of this lawsuit now being filed?"

"It's really hard to know," Dinielli answered. "Certainly she has told us things that make us think some of the conduct by guards and official treatment may result from the fact that she is standing up for herself. We do know there have been instances where soon after she has received visits from lawyers, that she has been put in solitary confinement. It is suspicious when someone who had essentially no record of poor behavior in prison finds herself in solitary confinement days after receiving lawyer visits."

"What are you going to do from here regarding Ashley?" I asked as the interview drew to a close. They were getting ready to rush into another meeting.

"We are going to file a federal lawsuit against the Georgia Departments of Corrections on behalf of Ashley Diamond. As it is, with SPLC, we seek justice not just for one individual, but [also] for others in her situation. Both Chinyere and I are extremely hopeful that Ashley's case will not only help her but bring Georgia into align[ment], acknowledge what the law is, acknowledge what human decency requires, and to make sure this doesn't happen to other people. Interestingly, there has been some progress in terms of what transgender people need, for example, the law that recently passed in California to include transgender people in a bathroom policy, and people made every effort to sabotage it."

"Just to be a little bit more controversial," Chinyere added, "it is not just religious people in the South that need to do some soul-searching. A few years back, there was a lot of debate around a push to get federal employment discrimination protections for gays and lesbians to also include transpeople, and one of the leading advocates said, 'No, let's just go ahead and get the gay, lesbian, bisexuals, the low-hanging fruit, in first. People are confused by transgender persons, so they can wait for the next turn around.' So I think historically and in recent history the LGB community hasn't been the most embracing of the T. There is a lot of pushing we need to do, and a lot of public education. Again, I wouldn't say it is reserved for a particular demographic."

As I drove back to the Atlanta airport that afternoon, I reflected on what Ashley had described to me on the phone, how her body is drastically changing. Her body fat has been redistributed. Where she was once shapely with hips and buttocks, she is now thin as a rail. The color of her skin has changed. Her legs are as thin as pencils, her face has lost its fullness. Her voice has dropped. She has hot flashes, a lot of anxiety and sweats.

Ashley is being forced by prison officials to shave with barber clippers. It causes bruising. It abrades her skin. Her facial hair has begun to grow underneath her skin, which is creating bumps on her face. "It's like growing warts all over my entire body," she explained to me. These changes could be irreversible. Because she transitioned using hormones as a teenager, she never had to grow into a man. Until now. "It is a horrible thing to force someone who has lived her entire life as a woman to live as a man," she told me the last time we spoke. "That must be the cruelest and evilest thing that anyone can ever to do someone. I've lost everything, every single thing." I could not agree with her more. And now I knew that her lawyers agree with her too.

"I can't fathom in my head how people can sleep at night," Ashley told me. "Even if I was a thief. Even if I did go out and steal something. Three years is enough to 'rehabilitate' a person and put them back out there on an ankle monitor or house arrest. But because I have started this fight, you are going to drag me to the hole [solitary confinement], you are not going to treat me, you are not going to protect me, and you are still not going to make sure I am safe."

I have read many "opinions" about Ashley on Facebook posted by people in Rome, the little town where Ashley was born. They say that she deserves it, that she should have thought about all of this before she went to prison. The comments are degrading, blaming her for her misery, blaming her for the way she was born, blaming her for fighting back against the perpetrators. I'm sure some people think to themselves: *Why can't Ashley just pretend to be a man in there to keep herself safe?* But Ashley cannot pretend to be a man any more than I can.

Sometime after the gang rape, Ashley had gone to a counselor's office. The counselor asked her, "What is your problem?" Ashley had started crying and said, "This ain't right. Someone has to do something." The counselor said to her, "Well, nobody's going to do something because this is Georgia." Ashley responded, "Okay. Well, I'm going to do something." The counselor had laughed in her face, telling her, "What are you going to do? You're behind bars yourself. Do you think you're going to go up against the Georgia Department of Corrections and you're going to have any leeway?"

That did it for Ashley. She decided to do something herself. She read every legal resource she could get her hands on, and she studied. She handwrote her lawsuit.

On February 19, 2015, Southern Poverty Law Center filed Ashley's lawsuit. A couple of months later, on Saturday morning April 4, I walked downstairs to pick up the newspaper on our doorstep and saw an article about Ashley

Diamond's case in the middle of the front page of the *New York Times*: "Transgender Inmate's Hormone Treatment Lawsuit Gets Justice Dept. Backing." The Justice Department, perhaps for the first time in history, had discussed whether hormone treatment for transgender inmates is necessary medical care that states are required to provide. The Department now considers blanket policies denying new hormone treatments for transgender inmates as unconstitutional. Ashley's battle; however, is not over.

Ashley's lawyers at Southern Poverty Law Center, Chinyere Ezie and David Dinielli.
Montgomery, Alabama, October 2014

'Every Day I Struggle'

Transgender Inmate Cites Attacks and Abuse in Men's Prison

By DEBORAH SONTAG

ROME, Ga. — Before she fell on hard times and got into trouble with the law, Ashley Diamond had a wardrobe of wigs named after her favorite divas. "Darling, hand me Aretha" or Mariah or Madonna, she would say to her younger sister when they glammed up to go out on the town.

Ms. Diamond, 36, had lived openly and outspokenly as a transgender woman since adolescence, much of that time defying the norms in this conservative Southern city.

But on the day she arrived at a Georgia prison intake center in 2012, the deliberate defeminizing of Ms. Diamond began. Ordered to strip alongside male inmates, she froze but ultimately removed her long hair and the Hannah Montana pajamas in which she had been taken into custody, she said. She hugged her rounded breasts protectively.

Looking back, she said, it seemed an apt rite of initiation into what became three years of degrading and abusive treatment, starting with the state's denial of the hormones she says she had taken for 17 years. But on Friday, Ms. Diamond and, through her, all transgender inmates won the unexpected support of the Justice Department, which intervened on her behalf in the federal

lawsuit she filed against Georgia corrections officials in February.

"During intake, I kept saying: 'Hello? I'm trans? I'm a woman?'" Ms. Diamond recounted in a phone conversation from prison a few weeks ago. "But to them I was gay. I was what they called a 'sissy.' So finally I was like: 'O.K., I'm a sissy. Do you have a place where sissies can go and be O.K.?'"

They did not provide one, she said. A first-time inmate at 33 whose major offense was burglary, Ms. Diamond was sent to a series of high-security lockups

Before going to prison, Ashley Diamond lived as a woman.

for violent male prisoners. She has been raped at least seven times by inmates, her lawsuit asserts, with a detailed accounting of each. She has been mocked by prison officials as a "he-she thing" and thrown into solitary confinement for "pretending to be a woman." She has undergone drastic physical changes without hormones. And, in desperation, she has tried to castrate and to kill herself several times.

"My biggest concern is that she survives to get out of prison, which I worry about every day," said Stephen Sloan, a counselor who treated her at Baldwin State Prison and whose pleas that Ms. Diamond be restarted on hormones were ignored.

In her lawsuit, Ms. Diamond asks the court to direct prison officials to provide her hormone therapy, to allow her to express her female identity through "grooming, pronoun use and dress," and to provide her safer housing.

She also seeks broader changes in policy and practice. And the Justice Department, in its support, declared hormone therapy to be necessary medical care, saying Georgia, and other states, must treat "gender dysphoria" like any other health condition and provide "individual assessment and care."

Continued on Page A12

Obama Calls The Iran Dea 'Our Best B

By PETER BAKER

President Obama strongly fended last week's prelimi agreement with Iran as a " in a lifetime opportunity" to the spread of nuclear weapor a dangerous region while assuring critics that he w ran ultimately cheated.

As he sought in an interv with The New York Times to the tentative deal to skeptics cusing him of giving away much, Mr. Obama emphasize Israel that "we've got tl backs" in the face of Iranian l tility. And he suggested that could accept some sort of vot Congress if it did not block ability to carry out the agi ment.

"This is our best bet by fa make sure Iran doesn't get a clear weapon," Mr. Obama saic an interview with Thomas Friedman, an Op-Ed columr for The Times, published on S day. "What we will be doing ev as we enter into this deal is sei ing a very clear message to t Iranians and to the entire reg that if anybody messes with rael, America will be there."

In the interview, held Saturd Mr. Obama provided new deta

Continued on Page A8

Front page story, the *New York Times*, April 6, 2015

Ashley as a teenager. Undated photograph. Courtesy Nicole Carter

Ashley and her close friend Nicole Carter, undated. Photograph courtesy of Nicole Carter

5-/26/15

Dear Kris,
Thank you for the beautiful
book excerpt and photos. I can't
wait till its complete. They have
transferd me to get a (fuck hole)
another prison. Excuse my french.
The Eletric Chair is a tourist attraction.
I was pleasantly suprised, and
extremley gratful for the funds.
You and I devolped a close bond
and vision from the begining.
I thank you for all owing
me to subject in your
fabolous book. I'm loss for words
at my current situation. GDOC
rem ains the enemy, but its
my friends like you that help
me get through. Life begins at
the end of your comfort Zone."
Taking Glory and running..."
I promise, promise to be
in touch this week by Wens day
Much love
Ash —— aka Jem

Ashley's mother, Diane Diamond, outside her home. I later mailed this portrait to Diane,
who sent it to Ashely in prison. The prison guard forced Ashley to rip it into pieces.
Rome, Georgia, October 2014

Donna with her nanny in Saipan, July 1959

4

THE BRAVEST THING I EVER DID WAS TO WEAR A DRESS

As he was being prepared for medical treatment, under the watchful eye of [FBI special agent] Ed Woods, nurses undressed Langan to find that he had an enlarged knuckle on his left hand, two scars on his shoulders, a bullet fragment from a previous gun battle lodged in his chest—and no body hair. Langan had shaved his chest hair, his leg hair, his pubic hair. The only hair he had was on his head. It was dyed red and fell below his shoulders. His fingernails were two inches long and his toenails bore the remnants of pink polish. Langan told the doctors that, for several months, he had been taking black-market birth control pills. Defying all stereotypes of the modern Aryan warrior, Pete Langan was a preoperative transsexual, a poster boy for Nazi homoeroticism.

— The scene at the medical intake after the arrest of Donna Langan on January 18, 1996, in Columbus, Ohio, where she survived 47 gun shots by FBI agents[33]

Sometime in April 2013, I got an email from the federal maximum security prison in Marion, Illinois. The sender's name read Peter Kevin Langan, but in the email the writer introduced herself as Donna. She said she was interested in my project and would write to me again soon. I Googled her name, and the hair on my arms stood on end as I read news articles, including news reports in the *New York Times* and *Los Angeles Times*, describing Langan and her Aryan Republican Army gang as violent and dangerous bank robbers, "Mid-Western Bank Bandits," and white supremacists who had robbed more banks than Jesse James.

To my surprise, I also found a book called *In Bad Company* by Dr. Mark S. Hamm, which revealed Langan's and the ARA's possible involvement in the 1995 bombing of a federal office building in Oklahoma City that killed 168 people. I ordered a copy of the book online and quickly found that much of it was about Langan: her birth as a boy in Saipan, the kindness and care she received from nannies while growing up in Saigon, her family's involvement in the "American War" in Vietnam, and their relocation to suburban Wheaton, Maryland, after they had to evacuate. Hamm's book read like a crime novel.

Hamm, a former prison warden and now a professor of criminology at Indiana State University, replied to my request for an interview immediately. I found our phone conversation as intriguing as his book, raising many questions even as it provided new information and answers. It was, however, a little confusing to switch back and forth from my questioning Hamm about Donna—to Hamm answering me about "Pete." Hamm, at the time of our interview, was not aware that Donna was now living full-time as a woman in prison.

Donna had already told me that her father had worked for the CIA and been stationed in Vietnam during the war. Her mother worked at the US embassy, where she narrowly escaped a bomb attack on the building. As a young boy growing up in Saigon, Donna spoke, read, and wrote French, Vietnamese, and English fluently. During my hour-long interview with Hamm, he told me that Donna was incredibly smart and charming, that she could quote Shakespeare. As a child she had played with the children of South Vietnam's President Diem (soon to be assassinated, along with his brother, with CIA complicity; Hamm writes in his introduction that Donna said her father was involved in the assassination) and his wife, Madam Nhu, known to many as the Dragon Lady.[34] In his book, Hamm describes one of the first traumatic events Donna experienced as a child: standing on the roof of their apartment building in Saigon and witnessing a Buddhist monk protesting the war by immolating himself.

Hamm told me about Donna's initial involvement with the Aryan Republican Army. "He meets up with Guthrie, who is totally antigovernment and a very destructive person who had been in the Navy Seals but [was] booted out, knows how to build bombs, and hates the government. This is when Langan is transformed into a paramilitary criminal. And it is at this point that they [Langan and Guthrie] eventually form the ARA. Langan emerges as Commander Pedro Gomez, leader of the Army, and as this identity grows, the cross-dressing escalates. They go hand in hand. His crimes were directly related to the confusion he felt about his gender identity. And so as one problem increases, the other problem increases, to the point where, at one point, they begin to rob banks to fund the revolution to overthrow the government. Pete Langan then emerges as this unique character in the annals of American crime, in which he is by day Commander Pedro, dressed in camouflage and touting assault weapons and homemade bombs and robbing banks, and then at night he becomes Donna McClure, this cross-dresser in the Kansas City transgender community, complete with pearls, high heels, and makeup.

"The initial reaction when you say this to people is that they'll laugh," Hamm continued. "It's comic. Well, it was not funny at all to Pete. These were very serious roles. He wasn't playing. He was trying to work through them, and then some deep psychological issues were going on. Eventually, he threatened some bank tellers with a homemade bomb, and somebody was able to identify him. His name then became known to the FBI as the leader of the ARA, and that would eventually be the crime he would be arrested and sentenced to life in prison for."

I had read in Hamm's book that at the time of Donna's arrest, she was engaged to Cherie, who was already in the process of transitioning from female to male.

Hamm went on: "He is absolutely fascinating. I'm a former prison warden, and I've spent all my life around prisons and criminals, and I can tell you he is off the charts. He is a very unique person as far as criminals go. Langan has extraordinary charisma. Little guys, you know, it's always the little guys, the 'Hitlers' and the 'Mansons' of the world. They're always little guys who have this extraordinary charisma about them, and Pete's only, I don't know, five-five tall and 120 pounds or something. But he's been in prison most of his life, and he had to learn how to survive there, and he survived by sort of playing the role of the little guy. 'You know,' he told me, 'I made it clear. I'm not somebody to be fucked with.' He used to carry gasoline, and he'd throw it. He is potentially an extremely violent person. Now on the other hand, he was also a wonderful father, and a caring person. He babysat and puttered around the house like a homebody. He definitely has proven to be violent, [but] if you look in his record—his record is as long as your arm—he's never killed anyone. Let's put it that way," Hamm insisted.

He then said that Donna had never violently assaulted anyone other than what was necessary to survive in prison. "Now, he has kidnapped two people at gunpoint. He's robbed these banks. He has frightened bank tellers to such a degree that they went into hyperventilation and they had to be hospitalized, waving around guns and bombs. I don't say that Langan was directly responsible for the bombing in Oklahoma City, but I do believe he's on the periphery of a cell that was responsible, so he's got the capacity for violence. His father was an assassin, then part of the Phoenix Program in Vietnam.[35] There's a lot of explanations for how Peter Kevin McGregor Langan ended up the way he did. On his mother's side, there were some political criminals in her background as well, some staunch Irish nationalists."

Hamm told me he strongly believed that even the most hardcore criminal can change. He seemed genuinely surprised when I told him that Donna now wanted to go public about her wish to transition to being a woman and that this was one of the reasons she had contacted me.

After my conversation with Dr. Hamm, I was all the more intrigued by Donna's extraordinarily diverse life, which had taken such extreme turns, and amazed also that she had sought me out. I began receiving from her what turned out to be many letters. One letter included a poem she had written, "The Bravest Thing I Ever Did Was to Wear a Dress." She was upfront with me about her violent past from the beginning. She sent along statements denouncing her criminal acts and said she was tired of the sensationalism that had surrounded her life. She wrote that there must be a time when she could move on and let the past be past.

I sat thinking about how complicated this issue was. The victims of the crimes she and her cohort had committed, as well as their relatives and others who were left to grieve or had been scarred or hurt, might never be able to move on. I wondered too about what it would be saying to include her story in this book. I worried also about the scandalous aspects of her story, which could distract from the part that is relevant to this book: her gender identity and transition.

Important to my decision to include her is the fact that being more open about her identity as a woman and pushing for gender reassignment treatment puts her at greater, not less, risk. After all, there are likely people, in or out of prison, who would want her dead for being "deviant," as "Aryan brothers" are strictly against transgender or gay identities. Unlike most incarcerated people, she

THE BRAVEST THING I EVER DID

WAS TO WEAR A DRESS

I have a tale that I must confess

It is strange but true,nor more no less

I tell it freely and under no duress

If you thought you knew me,well you'd never even guess

The bravest thing I ever did,was to wear a dress

I had always wanted to do it,but it seemed such a wickedness

I fought the urge,till it I no longer could repress

It made me so crazy , I had to say yes

It felt so good, I felt sexy like a temptress

I do not want to argue or be querulous

But if I am wrong,then call me a villainess

I feel so pretty and witty,just like an heiress

It makes me confident and gives me finess

I'll nevermore settle for any thing less

So don't be scared,and get over the stress

Make a move,like the Queen in chess

Be brave and wear that dress

Listen to Your inner Goddess

And You She shall bless

Copy right June 28,2007 By Bella Donna Night Raven

Donna explained the photographs in a letter from a federal prison in Butner, North Carolina, on April 26, 2013: "Me at USP-Lee County, Virginia in 2004 during a family visit. As you can see, my hair was very long, it's even longer now…"

had been living in a one-person cell with access to a typewriter or computer and email. Yet since she was transferred to a medium security prison in North Carolina, because it was ostensibly more informed about gender reassignment treatment, her situation has worsened. Not long after her transfer, she wrote that she was not receiving good medical care for her gender dysphoria—and, in an ironic twist, was sharing a cell with a sex offender. After being a notorious inmate with a private cell, status, and privileges, Donna now has to face the humiliation and danger reported by other transgender women in prisons. Perhaps coming out as a woman is the only thing that can keep her alive— freeing the only part of her existence she has any meaningful control over.

Her letters force us to examine if, or under what conditions, we might be willing to compartmentalize a person's violent past, not to forgive but to allow that person to move on in his or her self-identification. If Donna's treatment were purely medical, this question would not even be raised. But when it comes to gender reassignment and thus changing her physical appearance, it stands out starkly.

Excerpts from Donna's Letters 2013–2015

Email from: Langan Peter Kevin
Send date: Saturday, April 27, 2013 7:51AM
To: Kristin Lyseggen
Subject: Hello 4/26/13 project info

Hello, Kristin, I received the info about your project but was in the hole and getting ready to transfer so it took me a moment to get to where I am now and settling in. I would be interested in participating in a documentary book and exhibition involving TGI Justice Project, as I think they have done a fine job and will continue to do so. I would not mind sharing a photo or two and some prose either. Snail mail works better for me, but I did mean to get an e-mail out to you before I wrote a letter. I'll get a snail mail off to you next week.

Take care and be well, Yours truly, Donna

April 26, 2013
To: Kris Lyseggen
From: Donna
US Penitentiary
Marion, IL 62959
Re: Photo project and related personal info

Dear Kris,

I hope it's ok to call you Kris. You may call me Donna. I hope this letter finds you well.

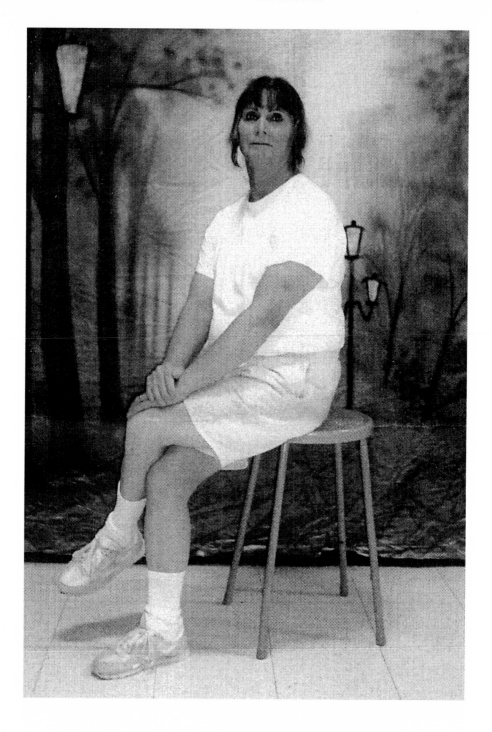

Donna in an undated photograph from the Federal Correctional Institution in
Butner, North Carolina, 2015. Photo courtesy Donna Langan

No doubt about it: I was a messed-up person. So I came to a point in my life when the cops were at my door and took me to jail. It was decision time. [I] chose to throw away my life for the cause and wanted to start the second American Revolution. I did pick up a gun and went on a multi-state/ nationwide crime spree.

— Donna in a letter from a maximum security prison in Illinois, 2013

As for myself, I am getting by ok as far as my circumstances allow.

I will try and type up the personal info about my past and my present as it relates to my gender dysphoria.

I am also involved in a struggle with my captors to be able to move my treatment forward. My captors are way behind as far as progressing my treatment. I need electrolysis or laser facial hair removal, and more in the way of real life experience (that would involve allowing the same items as female prisoners now receive).

I also wanted to ask you some technical questions. Can you and would you be able to "photoshop," retouch, or edit the photos sent to remove some things like darkening under the skin due to facial hair?

Also, can you return the photos and any finished editions that have been retouched?

Thanks. Yours truly, Donna

October 2013

Dear Kris,

My day-to-day survival in prison is due to my good/bad reputation. I am a good person to know and to have on your side and a bad person to cause trouble with. I follow the basic rules of prison survival, like no sex, no gambling, no drugs, no debt, mind my own business, assert and defend my rights, be a loyal friend and associate. Be on good terms with my own racial group, and be respectful of all other racial ethnic and religious groups. Stay busy at productive tasks. In prison terms, I am a convict as opposed to an inmate. As I have said, being a transgender has caused me problems in prison and could get me killed or raped one of these days. But I do assert my right to be left alone about it. And I am not flamboyantly effeminate. I am a 55-year-old woman and act accordingly.

October 14, 2013
To: Kris Lyseggen
From: Bella Donna Langan
US Penitentiary
Marion, IL 62959
Re: The how and why of I came to be a racist and extremist, and
how and why I changed and renounced those beliefs and practices.

I hope this letter finds you well. As for myself, I am getting by as best as I can. The reason for this letter and synopsis is I feel the need to restate my position on the subject of race, religion, bigotry, intolerance, and extremism as I believe and practice. The best way to do this is to relate to you my personal history and experiences.

I was born on the Pacific Island of Saipan which at that time was a U.N. Trust Territory administered by the US. I was born in 1958, and I think that era is significant and relevant to this synopsis. My father was of Irish ancestry, a former Major in the US Marines as well as a

former Member of the Canadian Air Force. He
joined WWII early to fight the Nazis and Hitler,
which he did as a gunner and radio operator in
1939. He was a US citizen and joined the Marines
after Pearl Harbor. My mother was of Scottish
ancestry and a Canadian citizen. She met my dad
while he was in Canada.

My dad was Catholic, my mom Protestant. This was
what was back then called a "mixed marriage."
All of us kids were supposed to be raised as
Catholics, but that did not take well on me. I was
the last of 6 kids: 3 born male, 3 born female.
My mom was 39 at the time of my birth. Things did
not go well for her, and she had to stay in the
hospital for a while after my birth. I was given
to an Island Native Woman (Chomoro). She was to
be my wet nurse and nanny. Somewhere along the
line it was discovered that she had TB, and I was
turned over to the care of my oldest sister.

The reason we lived in Saipan was that my dad was
then working for the CIA, and Saipan was a quiet,
backwater place to do whatever secret stuff he was
doing — mostly things related to Vietnam, Korea,
and China.

Our family briefly moved to the US, but by early
1960 we had moved to Saigon, South Vietnam. We had
a huge house and lots of Vietnamese servants. One
was assigned to raise me and to see to my needs.
My dad and the rest of the family went "Native,"
that is, we adopted much of the culture and customs
of our host country. We entertained the upper
echelon of the Vietnamese society. Some of those
same people would later be called war criminals.

As a child I really did not know that what was going on around me was a civil war. Nor did I make any distinction between White, Asian, French, Vietnamese, or English. Like a lot of children raised in multi-ethnic situations, I picked up the languages around me and spoke English, French, and Vietnamese very well. I could also read and write them by the time I was five.

Due to the ongoing civil war and strife, at times our home became an armed camp and rallying point for persons in the ex-pat community. It was not unusual to see pistols, rifles, and machine guns in my home. My mom was almost killed by a bomb that killed her boss at the American Embassy Annex, where she worked. The whole family almost got taken out by a bombing at a movie theater. We did not go that day, due to a last-minute problem.

Eventually, in August 1964 we moved to the USA, except Dad, who stayed in Saigon. It was culture shock for me. I started first grade that fall. I was put upon and called derogatory names like "gook" and "chink" by the other kids. I stopped speaking French and Vietnamese due in part to that. I also saw for the first time in my life black people. It was a new experience, but I did not view it in a negative fashion. And where I lived in Maryland, just outside of Washington, DC, there were not very many black people in my world. None lived on my street or even in my neighborhood, or went to school till one showed up in sixth grade (1969).

I had seen on TV the riots after Dr. King's assassination and was somewhat troubled by it.

It reminded me of Vietnam, and my oldest brother started carrying a gun to work, just in case. But things eventually went back to normal. George Wallace was also shot in Maryland about that same time.

Everything was in a state of change during this period. As a child I just kind of took it all in. At home we were not allowed to speak in a derogatory manner about other races or people. On our street we had, besides the usual WASPs, Irish, Jews, and Mexicans, but no blacks.

I had a lot of other things on my mind besides the status of race relations in the USA back then, not the least of which was my gender identity disorder. That scared the hell out of me.

Then my dad came home in 1967, and died suddenly a couple of months later. My whole world went into a tailspin and my gender identity problem got even worse.

My first negative experience with a black person happened when I was sent to a summer camp for disadvantaged kids between 5th and 6th grade. We bumped into each other, he pushed me, I pushed back, and we fought. It was a pretty even match and nobody got seriously hurt. I got a black eye, he got a bloody nose.

I started junior high school about 1970 or so, and race relations got a bit more complex. There were about a dozen black kids in my school. But they kept to themselves mostly. I started to use a lot of bad language, and the n-word came into my vocabulary. I used it mainly in reference to getting a cigarette filter wet while we shared a stolen smoke in the boys' room of the school.

As I got around more on my bicycle and on the bus, I saw more blacks but never gave them much thought. Even though I had a gender identity problem, I loved girls! And being around them and kissing them. In 7th grade I had an 8th-grader for a girlfriend, Carolyn W. She was Jewish and French-kissed. There was no interracial dating or mixing in my social circle. The Teen Club at school had a few dances for all of us kids, and I don't recall any mixed-race couples.

My next major exposure to black people was at work. At the age of 14, I got a job at a car wash. About half the people who worked there were black. I got along well with all of my co-workers because I was a good worker and did my job well without complaint. I also shared my pot, and/or bought pot from them. The drug world did a lot for race relations in my day. People who may never before [have] dealt with each other came together for drugs! I find that ironic, but it's the truth.

Due to my drug use and my gender identity issues, I came into serious conflict with the law. I was a chronic runaway and truant. I spent some time briefly in juvenile detention facilities, but never very long, and had no problems with blacks in them. That all was about to change, as I had a major conflict with the law and went on a crime spree when I was 15. I was arrested and shot after a robbery in Florida. I had been to a few jails under a fake name and lied about my age. [But now] I got sent to adult prison with a

20-year sentence. I can't even begin to describe the totality of my horrific experience, not in this brief synopsis. But let me try. I became the target of every rapist, pedophile, wannabe pimp, and creep in prison. As a young white boy, it was a given that I was going to get turned out. I was not, though. I did get raped by a white pedophile, and lots of blacks tried to get me, but I learned my lessons fast and well.

I found protection and a safe haven among white racists: people who hated blacks, Jews, and anything that was not white. I had to be willing to fight for myself and my race. But once I did prove myself, I was safe for the most part, or as safe as one can be in prison. At least they were not trying to sodomize me or pimp me out.

This was the early '70s and Florida had just integrated its prison system. It was open racial warfare and dog eat dog. I saw and was involved in several race riots. I had a choice: fight or be some black man's fuck boy! Or anyone else's, for that matter! People, black people, constantly got in my face and tried me, and then went on to someone else because I would fight and I had back-up. In those types of situations, you survive first and worry about ethics later. I had several close calls with people trying to rape me again and even a few more whites tried to do it to me, but they failed. My life was a nightmare and a living hell. But I survived and I came to be very bitter toward blacks and homosexuals. My gender problem never went away, but I had to hide it to survive. By the time I got out of prison, I was one bitter, twisted son-of-a-bitch.

When I got back home, I thought I had left all of that behind me. A lot had changed, and a lot had not. There were more mixed couples and interaction between the races, especially in the drug world. But folks still mostly divided along racial lines where I lived. I made up for lost time and worked hard all day and had fun at night. Eventually I grew bored with the party life and I got married and had a child. My son was born in a Catholic hospital, delivered by a Jewish doctor and a Chinese anesthesiologist. Along with my son came a pile of unpayable hospital bills. At best I was working poor, at worst I was downwardly mobile and scraping the edge of poverty. My financial problem got even worse when I became a custodial parent.

While the area I lived in was very liberal, I was moving in the other direction. With every layoff, set back, denied job, or other needed thing like housing, car loans, government benefits, I became more bitter and desperate. For me to blame others for my failings or for those failings of our society was wrong. I can see that in hindsight. But then I was in dire straits and desperate. So to blame the Jews and or minorities for my problems came pretty easy. Add to that mix an untreated severe gender identity disorder [GID] and it's a wonder I made it as far as I did.

One of the things people with GID sometimes do is to overcompensate to try and get rid of the problem. So I became super-macho, a mad dog, biker, militia maniac. I also became a religious zealot of the conservative Christian persuasion. I never got better, I got worse. I justified my crimes as plundering the Egyptians as in the

While hiding from the FBI between 1989 and 1996, Donna was secretly dressing as a woman and involved in the Kansas City transgender community.

A funny thing happened on the way to the revolution. I came to terms with my gender identity disorder, became active in the local transgender community (unknown to my racist buddies), and became involved romantically with another transgender. Before I could resolve this conflict in my life, I got busted, sent back to prison with a life-plus-35-year sentence and a very nasty reputation and a host of problems that could get me killed.

— Donna in a letter from a maximum security prison in Illinois, 2013 days of old. I also believed that the End Times were at hand.

No doubt about it: I was one messed-up person. So I came to a point in my life when the cops were at my door and took me to jail. It was decision time. [I] chose to throw away my life for the cause and wanted to start the second American Revolution. I did pick up a gun and went on a multi-state/ nationwide crime spree.

Please let me be very clear here: I was not out to hurt the common man. I never committed a "hate crime," fired a shot in anger, or shed one drop of blood. But I was one bad motor scooter hell on wheels, if you may. And I spouted a mix of racist, Nazi, religious, and otherwise offensive ideology and advocated a host of nasty things.

But a funny thing happened on the way to the revolution. I came to terms with my gender identity disorder, became active in the local transgender community (unknown to my racist buddies), and became involved romantically with another transgender. Before I could resolve this conflict in my life, I got busted, sent back to prison with a life-plus-35-year sentence and a very nasty reputation and a host of problems that could get me killed.

Now, what has happened to me since then is that I have tried to survive, that is number one. Number two is: I have resolved to deal with my transgender issues in a positive way and be active in the transgender community. I have been in prison since my arrest in January 1996. I do not have HIV, Hepatitis A, B, or C, any STD. I have not been raped on this trip, but I have had some close calls. And sexual predators are a constant problem, as is the possibility of being the victim of a hate crime (perpetrated by folks of any race) for being transgender, refusing to have sex (celibate since 1996), and most recently, for starting my gender transition. In March of 2012, I started on hormones and anti-androgens, and am seeking sexual reassignment surgery. Of course this has caused me a host of other problems. But I will deal with them.

I want you all to know that I have tried over the years to be a better person, mostly by letting go of my old attitude and ideals about race and religion. I do not judge people by their race or religion any more, nor do I advocate violence as a means to an end. I am not a perfect person. I still have preferences and biases, mostly against bad people and for good people. I live in a racial cauldron, not a melting pot, and I have to get along with my own people as well as others. I am a convict as opposed to an inmate. I respect all people who are of good will and deed.

I hope that you can forgive me of my past, have a little bit of faith in regards to my sincerity, and judge me by my current and future actions. Thank you for your time and consideration.

Yours truly, Bella Donna Langan (formerly known as Peter Langan)

P.S. There is a lot more for me to say and do about this subject. My synopsis is just that. My number one task and mission in life right now is to complete my gender transition. My life is a work in progress. My total self-improvement will be done as able and needed. I could use all of the help I can get along the way.

October 14, 2013

Dear Kristin,

Hi, I hope this letter finds you well. Thank you for the material you sent (part of your book). I liked it very much.

I also want you to know that it is very hard to convey my feelings and remorse for my past behavior and beliefs. They were bad and so was I. But there comes a time in everyone's life when they must leave the past behind. By living my life as I do now and trying to reach out to the transgender community, I hope I can do some good to make amends for my past. And quite frankly, I have had to make the changes in my life so that I can continue living. What I mean by that: I just could not go on living as a man and would have killed myself if I had not been able to make the change.

October 31, 2013
To: Kristin Lyseggen
From: Bella Donna Langan

Dear Kris,

Hi, I hope this letter finds you well. Things are rather tense and stressful for me right now due to a delay in having some of my gender dysphoria treatment issues dealt with on an official level.

I have asked for what is pretty much taken for granted in the free world for someone in transition: evaluation for reassignment surgery, and the surgery, "real life experience," that is, to be able to have the same items as born-female prisoners, and/or a transfer to a women's prison. I have also asked for an adjustment to my hormone regimen to add medroxyprogesterone (to enhance breast growth). And for electrolysis or laser hair removal of my facial hair.

I have spent half my life in prison and expect to spend the rest of my life there. It is hard to convey the reality of prison life to someone who has not done serious prison time. Almost like it is hard to tell people about being transgender who are not. But the effort must be made. Because for one thing, there are people in the transgender community who are willing to write us off. What I mean by that is: while many transgender people do have conflict or involvement with the law (in a bad way), some don't. I am not sure it is due to luck, circumstances, or character. All I know is that my being transgender put me at odds with society, and I ran afoul of the law. It's not an excuse for my bad behavior, but a big reason for it. Also, there are many innocent people in prison.

No matter the reason for being in prison, if you are transgender, it becomes a horrific nightmare, with no good outcome. You will most certainly be sexually assaulted. People will try to put you into sexual slavery. Or if you survive that, you may become a violent and dangerous person as a result of having to do so to survive. And you may fall victim to both results. It is a no-win situation.

March 25, 2014
To: Kristin Lyseggen
From: Bella Donna
Federal Correctional Institution
Butner, North Carolina

Dear Kristin,

Hi, I hope this letter finds you well. As for myself, I am a little bit worse for wear, due to my recent transfer, a process that took six weeks, two plane rides, and two bus trips. The whole time I was in transit I was in the hole. But I am happy to report I am [now] at my destination and not in the hole.

Please drop me a brief note (or a long one) letting me know you have my new address. And how your project with the new book is progressing. I also want to hear how things went at the symposium in Thailand.

Well, I have a ton of change of address letters to write, so I will keep this letter brief and close for now. Take care and be well.

Yours truly, Donna

April 10, 2014

Dear Kris,

Hi, I hope this letter finds you well. As for myself, I am not doing well.

Let me give you a bit of background info about what is going on now and recently. I was told around January 13, 2014, that I was being transferred, and the transfer was because the Bureau of Prisons (BOP) was going to advance my treatment for GID and my new location would be better able to assist in that process. I was told this by my case manager, the warden of Marion, and the chief psychologist. They told me that all of my issues regarding my "real life experience" had been resolved as well as other treatment issues like facial hair removal [and] speech therapy, but they would not address the reassignment surgery until I had one year of real life experience.

Well, when I got here, no one from psychology was aware of my situation, nor did they know nor were they made aware of any new treatment plan. I was forced to double cell, and my new roommate is a convicted sex offender whom the BOP feels is so dangerous they may civilly commit him at the end of his sentence.

I have received no "real life experience" items and a lot of runaround about it, but no specific answers. They have denied my repeated request for single-cell assignment and are delaying any response to my Administrative remedy. Today at lunch I spoke to the psychologist assigned to me here, Dr. Gray, and he did confirm that he had spoken to Dr. Patterson of Marion and confirmed much of what I had said treatment-wise.

Kris, we (transgender prisoners) are close to some important accomplishments and achievements in getting the treatment we have so long needed. But it will still take a lot more doing to get us to where we need to be. I am glad that I can be a positive part of this struggle. Maybe it will make amends for some of my less kindly deeds and actions.

Yours Truly, Donna

P.S. Perhaps it may be easier for us to keep in touch via email. I have tried to email you a few times but I never get any reply. It works ok for me and my son, whom you know lives in Thailand. Anyhow, ciao for now. Donna

---

July 2, 2014

Dear Kris,

I am really having trouble getting my transition on track. So many promises were made that were not followed thru on and so little progress has been made that I am pretty upset.

After six months of time, trouble, and travel, all I have to show for my efforts are 5 pairs of women's panties, some new bras, and some "maybes" on a very small quantity of female-oriented items (woman's watch, tennis shoes, and some Emery boards to file my nails). I am getting the classic runaround on everything else, and even the new stuff is not a sure thing.

I am in a very bad place and way mentally. I have a lot of discouraging thoughts and troubling ideals. I am scared and depressed and feel very alone.

It seems like I will have to fight tooth and nail for every little thing, and that I will no doubt have to go to court to get any further or substantial changes made. I get so sick of the lies and sexual harassment — and this is from staff.

I am forced to share a cell with men. So far I have had two sex offenders, one homophobe, and a gang member. It's hard to tell that I was sent here to advance my treatment when it looks like I am going backward at times.

I hope that your book project is going well.

My friend, I am weary of struggling and hope that I am up to the task. I know it is more than just my life and transition at stake, and that is what keeps me from giving in to hopelessness and self-destruction. But I am as close to the edge as I have ever been, and even a few words of encouragement would do a lot to lift my spirits.

On a more personal note, my son is or has moved to Shanghai, China, for a better job. It is my daughter's birthday on the 5th of July, and I miss her. My sister is coming to see me at the end of August, which is another reason for me to hang on a bit longer.

Thanks for your interest, time, and trouble. Take care and be well.

Yours truly, Donna

November 3, 2014
Federal Correctional Institution,
Butner, North Carolina

Dear Kristin,

I hope this letter finds you well.

I have a part-time job as a suicide watch companion. This involves me sitting outside a suicide watch cell on a 4-hour shift. I am available to talk to the person on suicide watch, and/or I just watch to make sure they are not actively trying to hurt themselves. It pays ok and has some social value in that it helps people. I don't make much money, but every little bit helps at this stage. I start another job next week that involves some light cleaning and clerical work. I briefly had a job caring for an older prisoner in a wheelchair, but he became verbally abusive and combative. It happens so often I feel like I am being set up. We don't have a toilet in our cell, so we have to share a common bathroom with 30 other prisoners. So we have to walk past a bunch of men who are barely dressed to use the toilet, whose seat is constantly urinated on. And with so many people sharing the toilet, there can be a line of people waiting. The weather here is milder than a lot of places that I have been, but we still get cold and snow.

I express and present myself as a woman and have people address me with correct names and pronouns, even staff. I'll try and get some more pictures taken.

Take care and be well, yours truly,

Donna

5

THE BATTLE FOR SHILOH

One of Shiloh Quine's fondest wishes, she told me in her letters, was to be photographed, since the only photos she had of herself were taken back in the days when she looked like a man. She has been incarcerated for almost 35 of her 55 years, with no visitors during the last 15 of those years.

Two years into our letter correspondence, on a Sunday morning in December 2014, I drove to Mule Creek State Prison to visit Shiloh. It was a strange feeling, knowing I would be the first person to visit her in so many years. It would also be my first time inside an American prison. Mule Creek, just outside the town of Ione in Amador County, is a farming and tourist area two hours' drive east of the Bay Area. Shiloh and Kenny, her cellmate, had both been transferred there recently. They had written that Mule Creek seemed safer compared to the abuse and hostility they had experienced in other prisons.

Despite my dishearteningly unsuccessful attempt to see Ashley Diamond in a Georgia prison two months earlier, I felt optimistic. A prison guard had explained on the phone that I did not need an appointment since I was already approved to visit Shiloh. Still, as is the way with the prison system, the compound could be on lockdown. And Shiloh did not know I was coming.

"Bring nothing but quarters for the food and photo vending machines and a picture ID," the visitor's instructions read. "Take off the alarm on your key ring, bring only one key." "No blue denim, blue chambray, or orange tops with orange bottoms; no forest green bottoms with tan tops; no camouflage unless identification shows active or reserve military personnel; no skirts, dresses, or shorts that expose more than two inches above the knee; no wigs, hairpieces, extensions, or other headpieces except for medical reasons and with prior approval; no hats or gloves, except with prior approval or in inclement weather; no shower shoes."[36] I felt disappointed about having to leave my own camera (and voice recorder) behind.

I had followed the visitor's guide carefully, making sure that I was wearing a bra with no metal, that the bra wouldn't show under my blouse, and that I was dressed in ordinary, nonprovocative clothing. I had read about women who, after driving for hundreds of miles and waiting for hours lined up outside the prison, were refused visitation because part of a bra was showing.

Herb, who had come with me but did not have visitor approval, was told to drive off the prison property immediately after dropping me off, so we said good-bye, aware we would not be able to communicate for the next several hours.

He waited on the other side of the road that ran by the prison, parked next to a fenced-in cow pasture.

To my surprise, there was no line of visitors waiting to get into Mule Creek. I walked into the visitor processing building, where a female officer greeted me and said, "How can I help you today?"

I thought I had prepared well for the visit, but I had forgotten Shiloh's inmate number in the car. The officer grumpily reprimanded me: it was important to bring the number if I wanted to see someone. Otherwise, she said, she had to search through thousands of names. But then she asked: "What is his name?" "Ehhh... it's a woman actually," I said and felt a shiver tousle my whole upper body. She answered: "Ma'am, for your information, this is a male prison. Everyone in here is male."

I found it difficult to use Shiloh's legal, male name, but though I felt intimidated, I managed to reply: "I know this is a male prison. Please search for Rodney Quine. But for your information, she is a woman." I went on to ask if she could kindly search for Kenneth Kent, Shiloh's best friend and cellmate, too, and if it would be okay for me to see him that day as well. To my surprise she said, "Yes, ma'am, you can come out and walk back in here again and call for Kent later." She found Shiloh's inmate number and handed me a piece of paper with a passport photo of a woman with thick, long black hair, to take with me to another building. I passed through a walk-through scanner and then several gates, waiting for each one to open and hearing it clang shut behind me. I found the "A" compound. The visitation room was filled with people. Half of them were wearing light blue shirts and loose, dark blue pants stamped with "Mule Creek State Prison" in large yellow letters. Things felt strangely calm, except for the thumping of my heart inside my chest.

06/06/2015 13:54

Shiloh and her cellmate Kenneth Kent wanted a photograph of the two of them together. This required both Herb and I to visit so that they could be in the visiting room at the same time. However, since Mule Creek State Prison did not allow us to photograph them together, we morphed them in Photoshop.

Shiloh and me at Mule Creek State Prison. Ione, California, December 2014

A prison guard told me to take a seat at table 10 and pointed to a hard, blue plastic chair at a low, round table, where I waited for Shiloh. Doors opened and closed, people came and went, prisoners embracing their wives and kids, but no Shiloh. I saw no photo vending machine but spotted a tall, white inmate holding a small digital camera. There were a few photo backdrops that looked as out of place as the backgrounds in photos other incarcerated women had sent me: a jungle scene with tropical birds, fake Christmas ornaments, and a big American flag.

In all the pictures Shiloh had sent me of herself with her family, she looked like a handsome young man. When Shiloh finally walked into the visitation room 30 minutes later, I saw a tall, beautiful woman. She smiled and we embraced for what seemed like a long time. I had not expected her to look so well. We sat down, leaning toward one another for privacy.

In her letters, Shiloh had explained how she got incarcerated. In 1980, when she was 20 years old, she had told the police that the gun used to murder someone was hers, even though it wasn't. She was serving a life sentence without the possibility of parole for a murder she said she did not commit. At the time of her arrest, Shiloh could not read or write.

As we sat there close together, she repeated that she had no hope of ever being released. Her case had been reopened in 1989, nine years after her arrest, because of a scandal involving the district attorney's office in Los Angeles. The killer, a previous lover of hers before she was married, had given false testimony during their trials for a deal with two jailhouse informants. She told me about a similar case, that of career criminal Leslie Vernon White, reported on *60 Minutes* in 1990. White said he had lied to give prosecutors the testimonies they "needed" in up to 40 cases.[37]

When no relief was offered to Shiloh in 1989, she had forced herself to let that hope go. Instead, she said, she was going to fight for gender reassignment surgery to become a whole person. Shiloh was finally prescribed female hormones in 2009. In the fall of 2014, the Transgender Law Center in San Francisco, in conjunction with pro bono co-counsel from the law firm of Morgan, Lewis, & Bockius, had filed a lawsuit on Shiloh's behalf against Governor Jerry Brown and the State of California, demanding that she be approved for surgery. That seemed to be going well, she said. She told me there were at least 10 other transgender women at Mule Creek.

"How come you are allowed to wear makeup?" I asked. "Oh, these are tattoos. I did it myself," she said and smiled. Lines in beautiful shades of dark blue and turquoise provided eye liner and defined "plucked" eyebrows.

When I asked her what she wanted to eat from the vending machines, she said she would eat anything; compared to prison food, it all seemed good to her. We looked at the limited selection: cans of surgery soda, chicken or ground beef sandwiches, and sausages in a two-pack with a bun. We watched other people warming their purchases in the microwaves placed near the vending machines. She said she didn't know what the various sodas were, as she had not seen any in 15 years. We purchased two cans of tomato juice, a twin sausage pack, and a chicken sandwich. She asked if I could help her warm the sausages, since she had never used a microwave before.

Shiloh was born in Los Angeles. I knew from her letters that her father had served 15 years at San Quentin before he met Shiloh's mother in Northern California. Her mother had two daughters from a previous marriage. The new family relocated to Arizona. Shiloh's father was physically and emotionally abusive throughout her childhood. When she was 16, she felt she could no longer live in a male body and attempted amputation of her own penis.

One of the photographs Shiloh had sent me was of herself and her mother taken just before her mother died. Shiloh had managed to transfer to a prison in Arizona, where her mother still lived, and they were able to say a final good-bye.

It had always puzzled me that Shiloh and most of the other incarcerated people who wrote to me would send treasured personal items they had managed to keep safe for many years—original photographs of and with their loved ones— and trust that I would scan them and send them back. What amazed me was how they had managed to keep these vulnerable pieces of paper in such a good condition for all those years as they were moved through a jungle of prisons in multiple states, confined to solitary cells, in a system that wants its inmates deprived of anything offering hope for redemption.

After we finished lunch, Shiloh gently asked if it was okay with me for us to be photographed together, and if she could put her arm around my shoulder while the pictures were taken. We exchanged knowing smiles as we chose the American flag as our backdrop. The "in-house photographer" was friendly and let us look through the images and choose the ones we liked. Then he printed out four of them with a little Canon SELPHY printer. Shiloh smiled shyly as she looked at them. I noticed that she felt good about what she saw while not quite believing that the woman in the picture was her. We decided she would pick two images to take back into her cell and show Kenny, and I'd take two home to scan, making extra copies for her. Time went fast, and I made up my mind to put off meeting Kenny so as not to break the flow of our conversation.

Shiloh and Kenny had asked me in multiple letters if my husband could come with me next time, as then they might be able to get a photo taken of the two of them together. They had relied on each other for many years. If Shiloh got her surgery, she might be entitled to transfer to a female prison and they would likely never see each other again. They were already preparing for a final separation. I promised Shiloh to make that photo-op happen.

Shiloh and I stepped outside the visitation room into a small concrete yard where we had to keep walking in circles while talking. She said she felt better since her transfer to Mule Creek, but her journey as a whole had been painful, and she had experienced unbelievable amounts of abuse while incarcerated. She appreciated the greenery that surrounded Mule Creek and loved looking at the bits of green lawn squeezed between compounds inside the prison. I told her I was particularly moved by her description of the trees she could see from her cell window at Soledad.

She responded that Soledad was the prison where her two daughters were conceived on a conjugal visit with her second wife, Adrienne, in one of the private family rooms. They had reconnected and married after Shiloh's divorce from her first wife, four years after she was sentenced for life. "And now both my daughters are working as prison guards," Shiloh said.

I recalled what she had written to me a few months earlier, soon after being transferred back to Soledad, where she had first been incarcerated in 1981: "I remember 35 years ago: the trees were real little as I was twenty and starting my prison sentence. After returning 30 some years later, they are so so tall and I am so so much older staring out my cell window."

On April 3, 2015, Herb read me a headline from his computer screen: "California to Pay for Inmate's Gender Confirmation Surgery, Judge Rules." A federal judge in Sacramento had ordered California's Department of Corrections to provide a transgender inmate in Mule Creek with sex reassignment surgery, saying refusal to do so violated the inmate's constitutional rights. This was not Shiloh but one of her fellow inmates, Michelle-Lael Norsworthy. Norsworthy's lawsuit was filed by the same lawyers who filed Shiloh's. Newspapers around the country and abroad reported the story. This was the second such judgment in US history, and the first in California.

Excerpts from Shiloh's Letters 2013–2015

March 26, 2013

Dear Kristin Lyseggen,

Hi, I am Shiloh, a transgender. I've been in prison 34 years. I've been on hormones for 4 years now. I'm 53 years old. My cellie is Kent. He's been in prison for 17 years and he's 41 years old.

On 3/26/13, I mailed TGI (Justice Project) some information and pictures to fax to you, and I'd like to participate with your project. I did sign a release form and Mr. Kent would too.

I am an individual who would love to share whatever subject matter. I was in a documentary on 9/8/06 for National Geographic "Eric Strauss" at Corcoran prison. He did filming. I've never seen it. It was about violence in the 1980s prison gangs. I wasn't or have never been in a gang. I was a girl even then, just not transitioned yet.

Sincerely, Shiloh Quine

May 27, 2013 Memorial Day

Dear Kris,

This is not a gender-friendly prison. We appealed
when we got put in the hole and should have kept
our privileges. The appeal was granted in Corcoran.
Once here, Salinas Valley staff, without even
hearing, didn't honor the appeal. This is a mean
place. I have nothing coming, even have problems in
regards to hormone injections at times.

California Dep. of Corrections has wanted to kill
me for years.

Salinas Valley here took my cell status,
restricted me partially, meaning I can live only
with my race, "white," with a compatible celly.
Now if Kent gets transferred, I can get anyone. I
can't live in this place with just anyone.

Well, better go.

Sincerely, Shiloh

June 18, 2013

Dear Kris,

I was wanting to see if you are all right. I know
you had had some medical issues to which I'm kind
of very concerned. I pray you are, and wish you
the best in your life.

I'm here. Still with Mr. Ken Kent, still seeking understanding about how we can have so so much love, but can't seem to find our way to that special place within a relationship. This is his 1st. Poor guy!!! All and all, I'm all right here, making the best of it all. Looking at TV. I'm still hoping for a guitar to play soon.

Well, better let you go, in hopes you're all right and all.

Sincerely, Shiloh

July 26, 2013

by Rodney "Shiloh" Quine, life story

Salinas Valley State Prison CDCR

I was born in 1959 in Los Angeles County and moved to Northern California in 1964 with my parents and three sisters. At a very early age, though very confused, I realized that I was different than other boys, just to later on realize all along I had been searching to complete my true identity.

At 5 years old I had desires to play with girls' toys, clothes, and dressing feminine. I was raised around horses and farm animals. However, in my 8th-grade middle school in 1972, they had a contest called Weird Day. I dressed up as a woman in a dress with long hair and won the contest. Ironically enough, genders and gays were unheard of. On prom night a girl, Adrienne, whom I grew up riding horses with, had picked me up before I went

inside to the prom dance and before my travel to
Arizona with my mother at midnight. In those days
it was very homophobic, and yet I was pulled to
the prom over the boy I desired and had a dilemma
with. I had my first sexual encounters with the
above girl. I felt as a bisexual more than a
heterosexual, and I felt insecurities of fear,
guilt, worry, shame reinforcing my true identity
as a female.

I struggled constantly due to society and family
and community peer pressure. I started high school
in 1973 in Parker, Arizona, and as you could
imagine, I had experienced more encounters with
boys and girls in the closet. In 1977, I came back
to Visalia, California, where I met Terri and was
convinced after a suicide attempt that it was just
a stage I was going through: a desire for men and
wishing to be a woman. My relationship manifested,
and in 1978 I was married. January 14, 1980, I
was incarcerated. I had no intent nor did I shoot
the person that got killed. I had been in the car
when it happened. I was a dumb, ignorant kid that
never learned to read or write. My codependent and
lover (before I was married), Jerry, had come from
Visalia, California, to Arizona where my parents
lived, then to L.A. with Terri and I, where he
later killed a man. He falsely testified at trial
in 1981 for a deal with two jailhouse informants.
In 1989, per a 60 Minutes TV show investigation
on the subject labeled "Jail House Informant
Scandal," an informant showed how he and others
would cut deals with the D.A.'s office to get
out of jail for testimony and false conviction.
Two hundred fifty cases reopened. I went back to
court in 1989. There was a deal given to these two

witnesses by the D.A., and this dirty little secret of a deal was only known to the D.A. and them. They had testified they had received nothing for their testimony at trial.

My attorney and the jury and I were not made aware of the deals that could have made a difference in the jurors' minds to believe them or not. They perjured themselves. My father-in-law had given Terri and me a .22 pistol that Jerry later used. I couldn't tell the investigators that my father-in-law gave me the gun to take to Arizona with other items that he was going to collect insurance for by saying it has been stolen. So it looked as if I had taken it once [it was] tracked back to him. The gun was hidden, and I was not even sure it was used to kill anyone because I had been in the car and didn't see the killing, even though Jerry had told Terri and me he had killed the man on the way back to Arizona. I cut a deal to get Terri cut loose from jail by telling the cops where the gun was and made a statement after I realized that Jerry didn't tell the truth when we talked him into turning himself [in] and clearing us of what he may have done. I felt the truth would have set us free. I should have kept my mouth shut. The false testimony, i.e., evidence, was what convicted me of the actual killing.

The appeals courts didn't care. I have no money and I am poor. I am so, so sorry that someone lost their life and for their family's loss and grief and my responsibility in this matter. Terri was with me for the three years after I got locked up, and on conjugal family visits I would dress up in her clothes as a woman as I had done on the streets with her when we first got married. In 1984 we got divorced and she re-married. In 1986 I married Adrienne, had two girls, and still felt as [if] I was the woman, especially wishing I was the one giving birth. Subsequently, I never had the opportunity to take hormones for long in society. I am blessed with the love of these people to love me with the comprehensive that I felt as a woman but looked like a pretty man. I guess I must be attracted to both genders.

My struggles while in prison, and the greatest suffering in inhumane conditions from my first ride on the grey goose bus shackled to another inmate in 1981 going to the prison-industrial complex for my journey, and encounters that followed.

No, Kris, we really do not obtain counseling/ therapy other than what we can obtain, pills/ psychiatric medications. I'm good on this. I'm enclosing a few pages of material I wrote/put all together for girls here. However, we have nothing going here at these so-called "transgender friendly" facility prison yards. I'm still with Kent. Worked our issues out. I'm blessed to be loved. As a woman in a man's prison, it gets intense due to being loved, hated by so many. Kent never would hurt me. Staff at Corcoran prison would take me from a compatible celly housing (2009-10-11) and put me in with inmates who have raped and killed women. Abuses of officials' power and hate for us girls. I filed legal complaints for better employee training and standards for equal treatment and changes. It is getting better.

I wish I could see you "visit." I'm not getting out soon, that I know of. I hope I have established what you need. The artwork is of the pure unicorns and of an evil leopard jumping at them. This is how I feel here always. Look out. I'm so happy you have Herb, and it sounds like a very nice place to be. That is so so special [that] you do not wish to hurt the fish. I'm like this with bugs or any life. Thank you for the TGI picture and Grace, the beautiful advocate/activist and caring person. I have now few family members. Can I call one day? What do you feel in regards to all I've shared, and what will become of all of this? Is my story worthy to share with the world? Did you get the drawing?

So in 2008, I had transferred to a prison closer to my mother in Arizona to see her one last time and was lucky to do so. Well, in the new prison I had met some transgender girls that shared information that we were allowed hormone treatments from 1997 within prison, but officials would not acknowledge or provide. So in 2009, at last, I was able to obtain hormones after getting them off and on through the black market. It is a myth that exists in our cultural beliefs that trans people wake up and decide that we want to change our gender and identity and that this is not a real need but a luxury on our part. This is wrong.

Society's viewpoint is expressed by moral beliefs that incarcerated individuals do not have a right, and reject that prisons provide treatment for GID inmates. At Corcoran Prison in December of 2011, I was attacked as a woman and have had numerous incidents. I'm happy to hear your back isn't hurting too bad. Yes, I'm safe and have lots of love in my world. I and Kent are together 24 hours a day inside a cell or out of it. I work out a lot, and all gets [to be] too much from time to time. We seem to keep it all together. Sorry about my writing at times. I move fast. I miss my typewriter. I miss my guitar, not allowed here. Officials hating on me, so I got sent here. No grass too. Oh well. I take power from it all.

Let me put Kenny — my typewriter — back on paper. He can be oh so sweet. If he was just not part kick-ass, he would be perfect. Hee! Hee! Most guys hate me or hit on me when others are not looking. I've had cops [and] staff tell me: "If I was in prison, I'll be your cellie." "Hey, you gay, bro?" My presence causes drama for numerous reasons: some are sickos, women killers, have been abusive to women in the past. Some desire but are not secure and can't stand on their own two feet, or they are drug users or gang members or jealous homeboys making statements to each other: "If you go down that path, then you'll be gay."

I have breasts but am not considered as a woman or male. Magazines showing breasts are not allowed in prison. I shower in a dayroom full of men. A lot of trans are whores for the money. As a beautiful woman, you can only imagine the issues that go with all of this for me. I live in fear of losing Kenny to "transfer." I can't live with him or without him. He's an amazing man. I used to fight a lot due to the fact that this is the mentality of inmates I'm around. I've been blessed with my skills and training — fear is all these people respect, which is really not the solution. The new

SNYs [safety needs yards] are more violent now because anyone can come here easily, and it's all just a circle-and-twist game for staff.

I want to thank you for sharing a little part of your world and self my way.

I have lots of memories, good ones/bad. I was in so much pain from traumas. I was very sensitive, and I'm a very intense kinda person.

I am thankful for [what] you're doing and as aforementioned possibly for you becoming a part of my life. Hugs and best wishes.

Sincerely: Shiloh Quine

P.S. We've been cellies 1½ years now. I almost moved. But he is sweet and good to me. He loves me, his first true love. I love him too. In 1965 at elementary school, [when I was] around 6 years old, the principal was going to spank me for wearing lipstick and stated [that] boys don't wear lipstick. I threw an ashtray at the wall and ran before he could spank me, and I ran home to the barn to see Boots, my horse, and hold him.

Could you please place my name/address at the end in case someone needs someone who may be able to understand them? You know I have no reason at all to [have lied] about my case in 1980. I'll never ever get out. I realize this to be a fact. It just eats at me. I never killed no one but am considered a killer. My part within this, I guess I'm as responsible. You would think a D.A. — now a judge — would have enough to get it right. He is not dumb, I'm sure he knows I didn't do the actual murder. But yet he lives with this knowledge, and that is where it began and ends.

R. Shiloh Quine C34058
Kenneth Kent K95444
CDCR
September 11, 2013

Dear Kris,

It was nice to get your 8-28-13 card. I hope this finds you and Herb well [and] in the best of health.

Ken and I went out to the facility yard, which is all dirt and rock because this is another form of only a few prisons, as this one [is] designed to make you pay for fighting against the evil. But we make it a positive — we hit the punching bag in the yard. Good workout. I got so sore. My whole body hurts. Also, we get to enjoy the joy of just being together sharing all these very special times dear to us both.

I'll let Ken write. My hand is as old as I. Besides, he misses me. I have not yelled at him in a while. Hee! Hee! Just playing.

Hi Kristin, this is Kenny. I hope this finds you and Herb well. We are kickin' back trying to make the best of every day. This prison labels itself "transgender friendly," but in all actuality there's nothing friendly about it. It's just the opposite. "Transgender friendly" is a sarcastic lie. Well, anyways, I just thought I'd share a couple thoughts with you. Take care. Kenny

I'll write soon, and thanks for all you and Herb do to help us all out.

Sincerely: Shiloh Quine

September 16, 2013

Dear Kris,

I'm enclosing 5 pictures dear to me so you'll see me before hormones and my family.

Hormones have changed me so much to match my inner gender I.D. Shiloh is dyslexic.

In 1985 while in prison, I married Adrienne. We had 2 children, even though she knew from 1973, being the first girl I was with ever, that I was identifying as a woman back then at 13 years old. I used to dress up as far back as I can remember and not understand why my body didn't match how I felt inside. As I grew up I understood I was a woman trapped inside a man's body.

Have a nice day — Shiloh

P.S. Please mail pictures back when possible

Peer Whispers in Your Ears
By Shiloh Quine
CDCR No. C34038
January 1, 2014

Mental walls in your halls, transgender dreams no more seems, walking tall, within forsaken laws, wanted so long hormone therapy, it's not wrong, winner now if [at] all, waited oh so so long, beating on walls, lost in mental halls, we are strong.

Poor boy wishes day and night if he could only hold her oh so tight, with all his heart and might, he only wishes his population wouldn't take it too bad or to fight, peer pressure it's a sin, she's still my delight, if only I could make it all right, she's loving and nice, can't you see her, I see her in your eyes, you're not right.

Trapped within, it's no sin, her beauty will win again and again, this world is cold, but gender women are so bold, let it be told, we must surely all know, she's from the skies above, they gave her inner love day and night, she can make it all right, she is pure delight, it's all right, wanna-be haters should be her CONGRATULATORS.

Corrections in the name of the laws, mental all for money, trapped and that's all, fight gender beauty, they're lost, you know discriminators ain't right, but yet you still cry in pain in this life, wounded within, who really made this the bigger sin, hold on tight to yourself at night, cry with all your might, love is the winner here tonight, your darkness isn't right, so come to the light, your desires you cannot hide from this woman who had to fight, for hormones and freedom, womanhood all of her life.

June 1, 2014

Dear Kris

Hope all is well? I and Ken almost got stabbed 5/17/14 in the hole, ad/seg safety concerns.

Going to a more hard place, (Kern Valley) Delano, the place I wrote about in an article for TGI Justice Project.

August 8, 2014
Vacaville, CA

Dear Kris,

Hope all is good.

From "The Journey Within" by Shiloh Quine.

Our challenges of extreme hate from staff and inmates became very dangerous till we became the top target of attacks from these gangs that work with staff to provide cell phones, etc. When guys accept you, they start to get harassed for being too close to you. No one wants to accept you as a cell mate.

So, Ken and I are in AD/SEG-hole. Now we need to say goodbye in hopes we will one day be together again. I was almost killed, given too much medication of the wrong kind. I vomited for 3 days till I slipped, fell, and hit my head. The cop said I was making myself vomit. On the 5th day, I fell out, then taken into a room, not E.R. room, and given an I.V. Almost well, getting X-ray of back of my head, tied to a board. Started choking on my vomit till I was rolled over.

So, I asked to go back to my 104 cell. I get there, and in 103, 105 are the guys that almost stabbed Ken and I. I talked to one of the girls off the yard. 10 LGBTQ inmates (one stabbed) and 10 gang inmates got into riot in the yard a week after Ken and I went to the hole.

I'm sick still. Ken got transferred from crisis bed. To achieve safety I cut myself, went back to crisis bed. Next day transferred to a crisis bed at San Luis Obispo, again given wrong medication. Sick again. Then I was transferred here to Vacaville CMF [crisis management facility] crisis bed.

I hope you're ok and all is well.

Shiloh

BY: R SHILOH QUINE
#C34038

WELCOME TO YOUR HOME
YOUR JOURNEY HAS BEGAN

CDCR

`SHILOH`

MY BIRTH NAME IS RODNEY QUINE, I GO BY SHILOH. IM A 54 YEAR OLD TRANSGENDER. DIAGNOSED BY PROFESSIONALS TO HAVE A PSYCHOLOGICAL CONDITION LABELED GENDER IDENTITY DISORDER (G.I.D.). ACCORDINGLY, I HAVE BEEN INCARCERATED FOR 34 LONG YEARS, UNDER THE CDCR INSTITUTIONAL CARE WITHIN CALIFORNIA. AS A PRE-OP INMATE, IM SEEKING SEX-REASSIGNMENT SEX-CHANGE SURGERY THAT IS APPROPRIATE FOR A PATIENT THAT IS ASSIGNED THE WRONG GENDER AT BIRTH. AS A CHILD I HAD EXPERIENCED LITTLE AMOUNTS OF HORMONES. HAD ATTEMPTED AMPUTATION OF MY PENIS AND CASTERATION DUE TO MY EMOTIONAL TURMOIL THAT HAS INTENSIFIED. PRISON ONLY PROVIDES HORMONE THERAPY, IM SEEKING ALL THREE ELEMENTS OF TREATMENT REFERRED TO AS "TRIADIC THERAPY" (1) HORMONES (2) REAL LIFE LIVING EXPERIENCE, I.E. AS A PATIENT LIVING FULL-TIME WITHIN THE NEW DESIRED GENDER (3) SURGERY FOR FULL TRANSITION FOR THE GENDER INDENTITY TO MATCH FOR A SERIOUS MEDICAL NEED. CONSTANTLY, WE FACE THE DEPRIVATION OF DISCOURAGING MEDICAL CARE DUE TO A "BLANKET POLICY" OF STRUGGLES OF ABUSES AND INHUMANE OPPRESSIONS THAT MANIFEST, WITHIN THE FORMS OF HATE FROM STAFF/INMATES THAT OPENLY EXIST WITHIN PRONOUNS CALLING MR. NOT SHE, OR OUR NAME OR INMATE. GIGGLES FROM ANTI-TRANS VERBAL AND WE PERSONALLY CONSTANTLY FACE MORE THAN THE ORDINARY DAY TO DAY LIFE IN PRISON. FROM STRIP SEARCHES TO SHOWERING AROUND NUMEROUS MEN THAT ARE NOT EVEN ALLOWED TO LOOK AT BREAST IN MAGAZINES DUE TO A LAWSUIT DUE TO HARASSMENT TO FEMALE STAFF, ON THIER BEHALF FILED IN COURT. THE GOVERNMENTS OBLIGATION IS TO HAVE A COMPREH-

SUPERIOR COURT OF THE STATE OF CALIFORNIA COUNTY OF LOS ANGELES

IN RE RODNEY QUINE,)
)
      Petitioner,)   CASE NO: A196140
)
on Habeas Corpus.)
)
)

DECLARATION BY TERRI BECK

I, Terri Beck, declare under penalty of perjury the following:

I was in the Torrance Court in 1981 in order to give testimony in Rodney Quine's trial in case number A196140. However, out fear, I did not testify. Rodney Quine was my husband.

The testimony that I would have given is the following:

On the day of the shooting, Sunday, February 17, 1980, Rodney Quine and Jerry Devin Naylor came to Rodney's Aunt Nina's house to pick me up. They said that we were going back Arizona where we had come the previous day. On the drive back to Parker, Arizona, Naylor told me that he had killed a man. Naylor's testimony at Rodney's trial that Rodney told Naylor and me that he killed the man is not true. Rodney told me that he did not know that Naylor had killed the man, although he had been in the car with Naylor and the man. Naylor had decided to tell the police that he shot the man. He was also going to tell the police that Rodney had nothing to do with the shooting. However, when he did talk to the police, he changed his story. I could not believe that he had told the police that Rodney killed the man because he was so remorseful after shooting the man. On the drive back to Arizona, Naylor kept saying, "Why did I do it? Why did I do it?"

Based upon what I know, there is no doubt in my mine that Jerry Naylor and not Rodney Quine killed Shahid Ali Baig.

                                         Terri Beck
                                       TERRI BECK

Executed on February 19 1993 at Visalia, California.

I LOOK NOTHING LIKE THAT NOW!, I WAS ON 60 MINUTES WITH DAN RATHER IN OR ABOUT 2005, IN REGARDS TO MY CHARGE OF MURDER, WHICH I STILL CONTEND THAT I AM INNOCENT OF THE MURDER! STILL TRYING TO BRING SOME TRUTH OUT OF IT. MY FAMILY, MY SISTERS STILL LOVE ME. NOT SURE HOW THEY ARE HANDLING THIS GENDER WITH ME NOW?.I MAY SEND THEM A COPY OF ALL THIS INFORMATION. THEY ALREADY KNOW I'M A TRANS. DON'T WANT TO WORRY OR CAUSE THEM PAIN BEYOND LIFE. THIS FOR A LOT OF REASONS. MY FAMILY KNOWS MY HEART, AND THAT I'M A CARING PERSON.

Today, the CDC will remove from the general population any prisoner who poses a severe danger to safety, security, or an on-going investigation.[134] Nearly every CDC prison has an administrative segregation unit in which to house prisoners who have been removed from the general population and are awaiting a decision as to whether they will be returned to the prison's general

The new (SNY) "Sensitive Needs Yards" = (PC) Protective Custody, but they're not. (SNY) mixes higher inmates of a higher security risk criteria from assaults that occurs from them, with us, gangs or said to be ex-gang also, it's so overcrowded and groups of inmates have so much drama. One can easily obtain (SNY) placement, once here away from violent (G.P.) general population groups, it starts up again. It's so overcrowded things happen from violent from harassment over the course, daily harassment faced by genders from inmates or staff, now CDCR   there own lack of policy for placing trans, is felt on many levels it takes on many forms.

If you have ongoing proceedings, or need to file in Federal Court in order to preserve your rights to federal review, you must continue to pursue these actions on your own.

Shiloh (middle) with her sisters and her mother. Soledad Prison 1985.
Photo courtesy Shiloh Quine

04-12-205

Dear Kris,

Hope All is good For you BOTH?. Ken AND I ARE Fine. Hope you got $30.00 BACK RETURN on packAge And AGAin THANKS.

well, michelle NORSWORTHy WHom HAS SAme ATTORNey SAme JuDGe got APPROveD FoR SuRGeRy. My CASE IS RIGHT 'iN BACK oF HERS I Hope I Get SAme Decision MAYBe AS HeR. ITS All OTHeR NewS T.V.

I HAve ANoTHER ARTiCLe ENClOSeD FoR you.

I miss you AND I Hope youR OK. LACY IS A TRANSGeNDeR wHo got KilleD By celly I WROTe ABOuT.

Shiloh was able to transfer to a far-away Arizona prison so she could see her mother one last time before she passed away. Arizona, November 2006. Photo courtesy Shiloh Quine

6

A GIRL NAMED HARVEY

I met with Tanesh Watson Nutall for the second time at the end of 2013. She had invited me to her small apartment in the Nob Hill section of San Francisco. I walked up to the third floor of a bright white apartment building and quietly stepped into an even brighter living room full of people. Tanesh was sitting on a sofa bed holding a baby girl. "This is Mamonte," she said proudly. A girl about eight years old with braids in rainbow colors came up to me to say hello, and a man named Gary reached out his hand to greet me. Pierre, Tanesh's husband, welcomed me warmly to their home. Then the two men gathered the kids and a Miniature Pinscher and went out for a walk.

Tanesh was wearing buttoned-up red silk pajamas and thick knitted socks with flip-flops. Pierre's name tattooed on her chest above her heart was not visible today as it had been the first time we met. The pictures I took of them that day in East Oakland are among my favorites. They had been in a hurry but kindly posed for me anyway. She looked stunning in stark makeup and high heels, ripped blue jeans, and a glossy, flowery jacket. She sat calmly and patiently, looking directly into the camera, answering my questions about her prison time while I shot away. Tanesh was glowing, and I felt I could capture that glow. I exhibited these photographs, along with those of Grace and Janetta, at the World Professional Association for Transgender Health (WPATH) conference in Bangkok, in February 2014.

Prison hadn't been such a horrible experience for her, Tanesh told me at that time. She didn't have to live through the sort of trauma that many of her trans-sisters had experienced. "Do you want to know why I went to prison?" she asked. "I was convicted of a burglary. That was my very first offense." At the age of 23, Tanesh, along with her older brother Jimmy and another person, had burglarized her grandmother's friend's house. She still feels terrible about it. "I robbed her of all her jewelry. Later our friend got very scared when questioned by police and told on us. The police came to Grandma Mack's house and arrested me. We were crack addicts, but still, what a terrible thing to do to an elderly lady, your grandmother's best friend.

"I stayed in prison for 18 months and then did one and half years on probation. It was an old army estate turned into a state prison. I was in a single-person cell but not in a special unit for people like me." The whole experience made her promise herself to never go back to prison.

Today, in Tanesh's sunny San Francisco apartment, I asked about her upbringing. She was her parents' sixth child; they named her Harvey. She knew she was different from other boys. She figured out that she must be gay at a very young age, maybe five or six. As she grew older she found women beautiful but was never attracted to them physically.

Shortly after Tanesh was born, in Rahway, New Jersey, in 1965, her mother and father divorced. She was taken to live with her great grandmother, Grandma Mack. Being raised by Grandma Mack, Tanesh felt like an only child, though she was not lonely. She had her own room, in stark contrast to her siblings. Her four brothers lived with their mother in the projects and had to share rooms. As she grew up, it became a routine to visit her mother and siblings every Sunday, although she had little contact with her father and his family.

"My mother's name is Cynthia, my father is called Marion. I always knew who my parents were, but because I was with Grandma Mack, I was Grandma Mack's baby. I was spoiled as a child, but I believe wholeheartedly today that my great grandmother always knew that Harvey was a girl." Tanesh would come home from church on Sundays, take off the little tie and boy clothes Grandma Mack had made for her, then run to her great grandmother's room and dress up in her clothing. "I would come marching down the stairs like I was one of those choir ladies at the church, and I would sing the songs. We had a piano downstairs, and I'd play the piano. Grandma Mack would let me do all of that."

One Sunday after church, Tanesh's grandmother suddenly paid a visit. When she saw Tanesh dressed up in one of Mack's robes, she said, "Mama, why do you let that boy dress like that?" Grandma Mack replied, "Leave Harvey alone. He ain't bothering nobody."

When Tanesh was 12, her relatives decided that she needed more structure and discipline than the elderly Grandma Mack could give, so she and her brother Kevin were moved to the home of her Aunt Margot in Scotch Plains. "Aunt Margot was not a warm and loving person. She kept telling us: either you get a job when you graduate or you go to the service. We were not going to do nothing and stay in her house—or she would send us to our mother in California."

In fact, the threat of joining her mother, who had remarried and moved to Los Angeles, sounded good to Tanesh. Margot was religious and believed that homosexuals go to hell when they die. Tanesh rebelled by bringing all sorts of people to Aunt Margot's house at night, and she started dressing up in feminine clothing. The more Tanesh felt comfortable with herself, the more uncomfortable Margot became.

Tanesh stayed in Scotch Plains through junior high and high school. When she finished high school, she told me, "Aunt Margot gave me 40 dollars and said: happy graduation. That was it." Instead of going to the graduation party, Tanesh wandered the dark streets alone, thinking about what to do with her life. She wanted to go to Los Angeles, but Aunt Margot had not offered to buy her a ticket. To have a roof over her head she knew of only two options: join the service or get a job. (There was never any talk about higher education.) Yet both options meant she could not continue to become who she really was. She had recently come out to her friends, but she didn't want to get a job for a few dollars a day where she would be ridiculed. Aunt Margot had always said "join the service" as if it were a challenge, so Tanesh decided to apply to the military just to show her aunt that she could.

Tanesh went to the recruiting station in Westfield, New Jersey, signed up for the National Guard, and passed all the tests. When she showed Aunt Margot the test results, her aunt responded: "I don't believe it. Are you really going?!" Tanesh was sure Margot figured that the military would straighten her out; she would start to act like a "real" man and have a good career.

Tanesh went into the service at Fort Jackson, South Carolina, in 1984. The attitude about people identifying as gay, lesbian, or transgender was strictly "don't ask, don't tell," and Tanesh quickly became homesick.[38] "I found that people started migrating to me, and I to them—meaning finding other gay people and coming out to them. But I missed my brother and my friends with whom I could be myself. I also have very bad feet and could not wear those combat boots." After only ten weeks, she approached the military officials.

They took X-rays of her feet and offered her two options: surgery or a medical discharge. Tanesh chose to be discharged and returned to Aunt Margot's.

"While I was living at home again, Aunt Margot's comment for the next six months went like this: 'I knew you wouldn't be able to go through with it! I knew you wouldn't make it!' That's when my drug addiction actually started, though I was already smoking weed and drinking to drown my sorrows."

After six months of belittling from Aunt Margot, Tanesh left, this time for good. She was 18. Her big brother Jimmy had recently come out as gay, and they decided to hook up and test fate together. They surfed a bit from motel to motel, doing drugs, stealing, living from one day to the next. Her brain responded well to the drugs; they made her feelings go away, and it was easier to escape than to deal with conflicts regarding her gender identity.

Eventually, Jimmy and Tanesh got an apartment together in Somerset, New Jersey, through social security housing. By this time, Tanesh was certain she did not want to look like a boy anymore. She wanted to be a woman and dress like a woman. Jimmy, who was three years older, knew who he was, and his confidence helped Tanesh to transition. Soon she no longer wanted to pretend or to use parties as opportunities to dress up as a female. She began telling herself: *This is who I am every day, and nobody can say anything because I'm paying my own bills.* Her memory of this period is blurry, Tanesh told me. She started calling herself "T," though by the late '80s she changed it to Tanesh, a name Jimmy chose for her. It was also around this time that she went to prison for the burglary. And she and Jimmy got themselves tested for HIV. Jimmy tested positive.

On Halloween in 1990, when Tanesh had been out of prison for almost three years, she and Jimmy dressed up and went trick-or-treating together. It was cold and raining heavily, and Jimmy got pneumonia. He was taken to the hospital, returning home the day before Thanksgiving. A few weeks later, Tanesh came home from work on her lunch break. Jimmy's bedroom door was open, and he was lying across the bed. "This was typical of Jimmy. He used to love to take a hot shower and lie across the bed naked to air dry, so I didn't think about it at first." When Tanesh came back downstairs, however, Jimmy

Tanesh during our first meeting in East Oakland, California, December 2013

I always knew who my parents were, but because I was with Grandma Mack, I was Grandma Mack's baby. I was spoiled as a child, but I believe wholeheartedly today that my great grandmother always knew that Harvey was a girl.

— Tanesh during an interview in Nob Hill, San Francisco, 2014 was still lying across the bed. She came into the room and saw that his eyes were rolled back in his head. The manager of the store downstairs called an ambulance. Jimmy was rushed to the hospital. He passed away that night.

Tanesh was devastated. She was in a daze through the funeral. She could not eat. She got high constantly. Sometime after the funeral she called her mother in California: "Mommy, I don't know what to do. I can't stay in this house anymore."

"Well, why don't you come on out to California?" her mother replied.

Tanesh and a guy she was seeing at the time took a Greyhound bus west, and Tanesh moved in with her mother in Compton, south of downtown Los Angeles. Compton was infamous in the 1980s for the hip-hop groups and rappers that blossomed in its neighborhoods. Later it became known for the violent gangs, such as the Bloods, Crips, and Sureños, that still figure prominently in prisons across the US. Less than six months later, Grandma Mack died. Tanesh was heartbroken. The two people she loved most, Grandma Mack and Jimmy, who had always been there for her, were now gone.

When Tanesh moved to Compton, her mother had asked her not to dress as a woman while she lived with her because her husband didn't know about Tanesh's female identity. "My mother was worried and had asked me: 'Please, baby, can you try and wear some boy clothes?'" Being sensitive to other people's feelings, she wanted to respect her mother's house and not make her new stepdad feel uncomfortable, so she agreed. But before long, Tanesh was bringing home girl's clothing. Guilt set in—guilt about not being the boy she was supposed to be, about not being good enough for her mother. Until this point, Tanesh had considered her drug use recreational, but now it became an addiction. She also started to appreciate how much the men she met liked the way she looked when she dressed up. They would give her drugs, sometimes for free, just to sit and look at her. Tanesh was naive, and she loved the attention. Her low self-esteem got a boost with every man she seduced and every toke of crack she took.

She said, "Then one day some of those same guys went to me and said, 'We don't want to look no more. We want to touch and taste now.'" She started giving them sex for drugs. She started selling sex in the back of cars, in parking lots. In a short time, she became a serious crackhead and a prostitute. Her mother kicked her out.

Her mother talked one of her brothers into housing her. She started hooking up with people in downtown LA. Her only friends were dope dealers. She found a "husband" who turned out to be abusive. But she was proud of being pretty on the strip, collecting more money than the other girls. Tanesh was the new face, and she was trustworthy. She didn't try to rob her clients. She was too scared to do that. "For me, it started out as a modern fairy tale, a Cinderella-type thing." She told herself it was easier to stand on a street corner and have a guy pick her up than to work a nine-to-five job. "There's nothing, literally nothing but the grace of God that I do not have HIV today," Tanesh said.

Because she was so pretty, the drug dealers regarded her as a money maker. "I worked down in the garment district area, Seventh Street, very industrial. We had this certain little section down there, and everybody knew where to find us. Every now and then you'd have a 'real' female, but mostly it was us trans women."

"It was all about the drugs. The black trans community I was involved in were all intocrack. I ended up getting close with a couple of them, we would watch each others' backs. The Latina girls, they'd come out there and they'd be beautiful, really beautiful—shoes, clothes, nails, hair, all that—because for them it was more about the money. They would get the money and pump it right back up into their bodies, get breast implants, et cetera, but us black girls were all about drugs."

She was also drinking heavily and did a lot of "boosting," meaning stealing things from a store and selling them. She and her friends started writing false checks. She was caught and went to jail several times. She was also in jail for prostitution. She would sell sex, get arrested, then spend time in the county jail in downtown LA, where she would hook up with other people she knew from the streets. "Honestly, I didn't have that many bad experiences in jail, either. But there was this one time, after being arrested and thrown into jail again, that I spotted a tall, muscular guy whom I tried to seduce." Tanesh had learned

Tanesh with her two granddaughters Denise and Mamonte and
husband, Pierre, at their home in Nob Hill, San Francisco 2014

the importance of finding a "jail husband" who could protect her. Instead, a jealous transgender woman dragged her by the hair into the bathroom and then grabbed her arms, lifted her body high up toward the ceiling, and dropped her headfirst to the ground. "That was my most painful and frightening experience," she said.

In between being on the street and spending a few weeks at a time in jail, Tanesh was in and out of drug and alcohol treatment programs. She would sign up for a program, get a few dollars together and a place to live, but she could not stay away from crack. For years, the only thing that mattered to her was getting high. With her fraudulent checks, stealing, prostitution, and drugs—and with the three-strikes law, which sent scores of nonviolent offenders like Tanesh to prison—she was pushing her luck.

In 2006, Tanesh signed up for yet another drug treatment program, her 63rd. And there she met Pierre, a tall, muscular guy with kind eyes. They started talking and would sit together during sessions. "Pierre is a heterosexual man, and I know he knew what I was. He knew I was different. But he fell in love with me, my spirit. He is such a gentleman. He has always been a gentleman. It was always me who started the arguments, it was me who did all the crazy shit."

Tanesh and Pierre didn't stay long with the treatment program. They felt they were ready to give up crack now that they had each other, but this resolve lasted only a few days. Drugs became a big part of their lives yet again. This time they were in it together. They were fighting. They were in love. They were desperate, living in shelters from Long Beach to downtown Los Angeles. Tanesh continued to sell sex. Crack made her extremely paranoid. She would often look at Pierre and think that he was going to kill her.

Pierre's only daughter was pregnant with her first child when Pierre and Tanesh first met, and the baby's birth became a turning point for Tanesh. She quickly developed a closeness with him, a kind of love she had never before experienced. She had always wanted a family of her own. In fact, that had been her biggest wish when she was little. She and Pierre were making a lot of money from boosting, and their drug addiction exploded—which meant they were not able to see their grandson as much as they wanted. They were torn. Pierre looked at her one day and said: "You know what, Tanesh? I want to go to San Francisco." Tanesh was scared to leave Los Angeles. She had just developed a relationship with her mother for the first time in her life. But Pierre convinced Tanesh that they needed a place to make a fresh start. They packed up and left LA.

Tanesh interrupted her narrative to tell me: "I am very much into my mom's life now, and she's very much into mine. I have a card up there that I'll never take down," she said pointing to the television. "It was my first birthday card from my mother since I got off drugs, and she addressed it to her daughter, and so now me and my mother have this wonderful relationship, and she looks at me as being her daughter."

When Tanesh and Pierre got to San Francisco, they quickly fell in with the same kind of people they had known in LA, and they were back on drugs. But not long after, they met a woman named Lydia who worked at the liberal GLIDE Memorial Church, known for its many social service programs. "Lydia started talking to us about addiction. She started making us believe that we could actually stop, you know? She really took an interest in us." Lydia also helped them with money management. Even though she was not supposed to keep cash for anyone, Lydia made an exception, locking up whatever money Pierre and Tanesh saved by staying off drugs.

It was around this time that Tanesh met Janetta. "There was a nonprofit down in the Tenderloin where she worked, and we ran into Janetta. We were so new to the city, and she knew I was transgender. She stopped us and invited us for a coffee at Starbucks. It was the first time in my life that I had ever been to a Starbucks. This was also the first time I had met a transgender person who was not on drugs. I felt there was no competition, the way I was used to feel with other transwomen. And I felt I could trust her."

A month went by, then another. All of a sudden, they had saved money for six months. Then they said to each other: Let's see if we can manage it ourselves. They met with Lydia, got their money, and walked home through the Tenderloin. "We had all this money burning in our pockets. We were very nervous. Pierre looks at me, I'm looking at him—I will never forget this—I got so scared, and he saw my fear. And then he said, "Baby, let's go to the movies." They managed to stay on their feet, and they were able to find a decent place to live: the one-bedroom on Nob Hill where we were sitting. "He has been clean for two years now, and I have been off drugs for four years in March this year."

The topic turned to religion. She told me she used to hate God because Aunt Margot told her she would die and go to hell for being gay. And Tanesh had hated being gay. However, she said, "There is this thing called speaking in tongues, when the Holy Spirit falls upon you. That is what I believe in, and that is something I held onto."

After Tanesh and I had talked for an hour, Pierre and the others returned from their walk. They agreed to having pictures taken. Eight-year-old Denise helped me bring in a tripod from my car for the photo shoot and wanted to know things about photography. This time also, the images turned out well. Denise is in the foreground staring impassively into the camera, just like her grandmother.

A year went by before I saw Tanesh and Pierre again. On November 24, 2014, I drove to the same apartment building on California Street. They had moved to a nicer, slightly bigger unit on the first floor. Pierre gave me a bear hug and asked if it would bother me if he smoked in the bedroom. "Pierre's daughter has another child on the way," Tanesh said and chuckled. "It will be our fifth grandchild!" The photograph I had taken of them the first time we met, in East Oakland, was framed and on display in the living room. Below the image were the words in large handwriting: "A love that will never die."

There was no smoke in the living room like the previous time I had visited because Tanesh had finally given up cigarettes. She was planning for her future now. She was on a waiting list for gender reassignment surgery and was following the guidelines to prepare, included quitting nicotine.

"I don't know if I ever told you," Tanesh said, "but I'm not an anal sex kind of person. And Pierre is heterosexual. So I would like to make love to my husband in that natural way, as a woman." In November 2012, the city of San Francisco had announced that, under its new health care plan, it would offer free reassignment surgery to all its transgender residents without insurance plans.[39] Tanesh commented that what San Francisco was doing was wonderful but also potentially dangerous. She knew transgender women living in shelters who would have no one to take care of them after the surgery and would have to go back out on the strip to sell sex before they had healed properly.

Tanesh asked me when this book would be published. She wanted to tell her church, the City of Refuge in Oakland, about it. I suggested we do a talk together when the book is out. "I would like that very much," she responded.

Tanesh had not told her grandkids her full story yet, she said next. They just know Nana has a very deep voice and that she has to shave every morning. Tanesh was pondering how to tell them about Harvey. She wanted to show them a photograph of Harvey as a little boy so they would know the full story of how she became Nana and learn to accept people with gender identity issues.

Just a few hours after my interview with Tanesh, I heard that the Grand Jury in St. Louis decided not to indict Darren Wilson, the white police officer who killed the unarmed black teenager Michael Brown in Ferguson, Missouri. Protests began that night all over the Bay Area. People blocked highways, and students at UC Berkeley protested for a fourth night. Forty or more police officers with gas masks and shotguns stood guard at the highway one block from where Herb and I live. Military armored vehicles were speeding around in the neighborhood, helicopters with searchlights buzzed uncomfortably loudly over our heads. I had never in my life seen anything like it. We went out in the streets and were humiliated by police carrying guns and sticks and shields. They shouted at us as if we were criminals, even though we were walking peacefully with our dog in our own neighborhood.

I was thinking about Tanesh, also Janetta and Grace, imagining they would want to take part in the protests, though it might not be safe for them. I thought of how much punishment they had already received from policemen, from prison officials, from society just for how they look. Janetta had told me she is afraid of closing up the TGIJP office (which had recently moved back to San Francisco, to the St. James Infirmary on Mission Street) at the end of the workday, worrying that the police might pass by and think she was a sex worker or burglar.

A few months later, my husband and I took a working vacation at a cottage in Clearlake, California. It was raining—big, heavy raindrops sweeping down the lake that turned to mist over the roughed-up water. I was reading the fourth part of journalist Nicholas Kristof's op-ed series in the *New York Times*, "When Whites Just Don't Get It," where he writes: "Because of the catastrophic experiment in mass incarceration, black men in their 20s without a high school diploma are more likely to be incarcerated today than employed, according to a study from the National Bureau of Economic Research. Nearly 70 percent of middle-aged black men who never graduated from high school have been imprisoned."[40] It occurred to me that, ironically, Tanesh and people like her would be included in Kristof's category "black men" because there is so little data on inmates with gender identity differences. The correctional institutions most likely never count their transgender inmates.

I was reminded of a similar trend I'd read concerning incarceration for drug offenses. Between 1980 and 2011, the number of Americans in prison for drug offenses skyrocketed from 41,000 to 500,000.[41] In 1986, the year Tanesh was sent to a state prison, drug offenders spent an average of 22 months in prison. By 2004, that average had increased to 62 months. If Tanesh were arrested and convicted today, she would serve a much longer sentence. Her chances of starting her own family would be vastly reduced.

When Tanesh told me, the first time we met, that her prison experience was not horrible, I wondered whether her story would fit in this book. I also wondered why I thought this. Was it because I am so drawn to the extraordinary that ordinary was not enough and I had suddenly found her story ordinary? The second time we met, I no longer had that doubt. Hers was a story of trying to survive on the street all those years and, against all odds, eventually getting her life together.

During my November 2014 visit, Tanesh told me: "I had to go through drug addiction, through jail, and through prostitution. I had to go through homelessness, all being a cycle because of what I am—an African American transgender woman." Then I thought, *Her story is an homage to the human spirit and a reminder of the many stories of violence against people of color, particularly people with gender variance.* Her story stands against all that we would have surmised about her had we met her on the streets of New Jersey, Los Angeles, or San Francisco 15 or 30 years earlier. Her time on those sweaty, dark streets, without education or a glimpse of something bright ahead of her, had been her prison time. Having a family and a life she could share with another human being was all she had ever wanted. Her incredible drive to become who she was and to have a home, and her great grandmother's acceptance of her had helped her come through the haze of addiction and out the other side, whole.

Grandparents Tanesh and Pierre with Denise and Mamonte at home, with friend Greg (right).
Nob Hill, San Francisco 2014

7

THREE STRIKES
AND YOU'RE OUT

We have abolished parole in many states. We have invented slogans like "Three Strikes and You're Out" to communicate our toughness. We've given up on rehabilitation, education, and services for the imprisoned because providing assistance to the incarcerated is apparently too kind.

— Bryan Stevenson, *Just Mercy*[42]

On Friday, February 20, 2015, I headed south on Interstate 5, husband and dog in tow, toward Kern Valley State Prison, outside of Delano, to visit Jennifer Gann. Herb and I drove through California's 450-mile-long Central Valley, where most of the nation's vegetables, berries, and nuts are grown—a valley of increasing drought and where many of the state's prisons are located. After four hours or so, we pulled into what looked to me like an odd little town a few miles north of Bakersfield. But Delano has an important history. In the 1960s and early '70s, it was a major center for the early farm workers' push for a union, headed by Cesar Chavez. Chavez's ultimate goal was "to overthrow a system in this nation which treats farm workers as if they were not important human beings."[43]

The first time Jennifer wrote to me, two years earlier, she was 43 years old and had been in prison for almost 23 of those years, serving a 104-year-to-life sentence in a maximum security prison without the possibility of parole. After many failed attempts to get permission to visit her, in February 2015 I finally received visitors approval from Kern Valley State Prison, enclosed with a letter from Jennifer saying she was excited about my upcoming visit.

I tried but found it impossible to make an appointment online or by phone, as the prison's website directs. So the day before leaving for Delano, I emailed Jennifer's mother for help.

Jennifer had told me her mother had always supported her, and she and Jennifer's sister were the only people who had visited her in now almost 25 years. They came twice a year, on Jennifer's birthday and during Christmas. She gave me her mother's email address, and we emailed each other a couple of times. Her mother wrote that she supported her son in every way possible, but she wanted to continue referring "to her son as Johnny." She was not comfortable talking about Jennifer's gender identity. My first thought was, *Not even her own mother, as much as she loved and supported her, could accept and value Jennifer for who she was.* Jennifer's mother wrote back:

> Good morning, Kris. I have never been able to make an online appointment either. Same problem. So I just go there to visit without an appointment. Just show up around 10 to 10:30. Once appointments are done, they start taking the non-appointment visitors by 11. You fill out a visiting form and wait until they call you. I have always managed to get in, usually by 12 at the latest. Just call the day before on the 800 number to make sure they are not on lockdown and visiting is scheduled. Thank you so much for all the kindness you have shown to my son.

She said Jennifer loves the vending machine food, which they don't get inside the prison, and reminded me to bring quarters. "It is really disgusting the way our prison system [is] run," she continued. I felt emboldened then to email back and ask for more details regarding Jennifer's case. She responded:

> As for the reason for maximum security, I still don't really understand our prison system. He's not ever murdered anybody, but he has been a threat at times when he was younger and hot-headed, as he has been in altercations, but I think mostly just to protect himself and not back down and show other inmates that he can protect himself. Early on, he got involved in the AB at Folsom, and his behavior earned him second and third strikes, thanks to the ridiculous three-strikes law. He was transferred to Pelican Bay and was in the SHU for 7 years, and in order to break gang ties, he asked for protection and got transferred out. Unfortunately, being in solitary a lot, and I'm sure with his hormone imbalance the severe depression he suffered at times, and he tried to kill himself a couple of times. So many of the guards at these prisons spend their time harassing and instigating aggressive behavior from the inmates, it's definitely not a place of

> rehabilitation in maximum security. I'm sure when you visit
> John he can fill you in on the last 20+ years better than I can.
> It breaks my heart what the prison system has done to my
> child over 24 years, but his strength and courage never cease
> to amaze me. I love him very much.

She asked me to give her "son a hug when I saw him."

The "AB" Jennifer's mother referred to is the Aryan Brotherhood, a violent
prison gang that is present in every prison across the country. Jennifer had
told me that when she was in Folsom Prison, she had to join her "own race" as
a means of survival during the days when gangs grouped by ethnicity, color,
religion, race, and belief were deliberately thrown together within the prison
walls. I imagined gladiators waiting to fight to the death in the Colosseum in
ancient Rome.

Jennifer was born in 1969 in Riverside, California. She grew up with an
abusive stepfather and struggled at school mainly because of behavioral
problems. She felt different. She knew she was not a boy, but she did not know
she had what doctors in prison would later call gender dysphoria. Nor did she
know yet that she had bipolar disorder. In her teens she started on birth control
pills and identified as gender nonconforming. She worked the streets selling
sex and doing drugs in Los Angeles and Santa Barbara. Shortly thereafter,
she was convicted of attempted robbery and sent to prison for 16 months, an
experience that launched her on a downward spiral she could not stop. She
was determined to change when she was let out, but shortly afterward, in
1991, she was involved in another robbery and was arrested and sentenced
again. During that prison term, she got involved with the skinheads and white
supremacists and ended up participating in one of the many riots for which
Folsom State Prison is famous. That earned her a second and then third strike
just as the harsh three-strikes law was introduced in California.

The infamous three-strikes law is a mandatory life sentence no matter how
small the criminal offense, giving the judges little way for leniency. It is
responsible for an extraordinary number of life-without-parole sentences even
for individuals convicted of nonviolent crimes as minor as shoplifting. Today,

more than half the inmates sentenced under the law are serving sentences for nonviolent crimes in California.[44]

In her letters Jennifer came across as a feisty, political, and radical woman who was never going to stop her activism until "justice was served." By justice she didn't mean that she shouldn't be in prison and do her rightful time. She meant that she had already paid for her mistakes, that 25 years was enough, that the three-strikes law allowed her no second chance and no opportunity to live free as the woman she is. By justice she also meant reversing the cruel and unusual punishment meted out to her and other LGBTQI prisoners in male prisons and the prison system's refusal to let her be in a female prison.

Jennifer had spent many years at two of California's most notorious maximum security facilities. Folsom State, opened in 1880, is California's second-oldest prison after San Quentin and was the state's first maximum security prison. Pelican Bay, where Jennifer spent seven years in solitary confinement, is considered one of the toughest "super-maximum" prisons in the country. A report from the Center for Constitutional Rights states that "more than 500 of Pelican Bay's SHU prisoners have been held in solitary confinement in the SHU for over 10 years. Over 78 prisoners have languished in solitary for more than 20 years. Prisoners are detained inside windowless cells, are not allowed to call home, and are served substandard or rotten food."[45] Now I was on my way to see Jennifer, not at Folsom or Pelican Bay, but at another maximum security prison, Kern Valley.

On Saturday morning the sky was gray, appropriate to my mission, as Herb and I looked for a breakfast place. We headed for a Mexican restaurant in Delano's town center, but when we spotted an old white Toyota in the parking lot, its trunk wide open and a rifle in plain view with no one nearby, we decided to eat elsewhere. Except for that experience, we enjoyed being in a town where most of the population was Latino, and we were treated with incredible friendliness.

Since Herb did not have permission to visit Jennifer, I left him and the dog at the hotel after breakfast and drove on my own toward the prison. I could see acres of prison buildings in the distance across fallow fields. I passed a big blue sign along the highway that read: "State Prison: Do Not Pick Up Hitch-Hikers" before I saw the sign for Kern Valley State Prison. There were guard towers on every other building overlooking the long road paralleling the prison walls for what seemed like miles ahead. I showed my ID to the guard at the checkpoint and drove toward the tall, white factory-style buildings.

After parking the car, I approached the crowd of people waiting in the "no appointment" line in the parking lot. I couldn't seem to get the dress code right, no matter how much I had prepared. A friendly young woman suggested I take off my scarf (the extra sweater I'd wrapped around my neck against the dampness and cold) and warned me that the metal buttons on my jacket might set off the scanner. And I could only wear one ring (I had two). I ran back to the car a few times to take off various garments, in the end wearing a black blouse under a black T-shirt, black jeans, and black boots. (No orange, no army green, no blue shirts, no blue jeans....) I asked several women if they also had trouble making appointments. "Yes," they confirmed. "It is impossible, both online and by phone. We always just turn up around 10:30."

When the tall, brusk, slow-moving correctional officer came to talk to us and distribute forms, I asked him if my outfit was okay. He said he couldn't say; I might have "too many layers on." I should get it checked out in a building across the parking lot—the opposite direction from where the other visitors were heading to get processed. "Well, I just really want to get in now," I said and hurried after them. It was already 11:30, and we hadn't even gotten into the main building. One woman had already been turned away, with tears in her eyes, because she was wearing flip-flops.

I was one of two or three white people in the group. The rest, mostly women and children, were Hispanic, plus a few young African American women who had come from Oakland. As we entered the building, several women were told that the men they had come to see—husbands, sons, brothers—were on lockdown. With no surprise in their faces, just sadness, they calmly turned and left.

Finally I was called up and went through the scanner. My wedding ring set off the alarm. After that, I passed through a series of wired gates and started looking for Facility C. The grounds were barren, sterile—no trees, no grass.

Once in the visiting room, I was directed to sit down at table 15, next to a man and woman—the only other white people present. I felt I was imposing on the couple's privacy, so I turned my chair away from them. All around me were women, nicely dressed with makeup and bright lipstick, sitting with men in blue prison uniforms who had tattoos on their necks, faces, and arms. The men were not handcuffed and were free to move around. I tried to imagine coming here every other weekend to visit my love. I couldn't.

Finally, after 45 minutes, Jennifer came out and we hugged. She was shorter and more feminine than I had imagined. She was also a lot calmer. "Are you okay?" I asked.

"Thank you for coming, Kris," she said and smiled shyly. "I am okay now that you are here. I thought it was my mother when they called me up. I was in the yard. We haven't been outside for two weeks because of the fog. The weather is not good here. We are not let out when the weather is bad."

We walked to the vending machines and bought Cherry Cokes and quesadillas with jalapeño that we warmed in the microwave. Then we sat down next to each other. Jennifer would every so often look up at the clock on the wall behind me. "We only have till 2:30 p.m.," she said.

"When did your mother last come?" I asked. "She was here for my birthday in October. She tries to come twice a year, and she usually brings my baby sister along. My sister is in a violent relationship. As much as I am trying to be there for her, it's hard from here. My mother is caring for my old and sick grandmother."

She talked about her life prison sentence. "I have done bad things and I regret them all. But I have paid for that now, and I have changed. Still, there is no way for me to get out. There is no second chance for me. I had to defend myself when I got my second and third strikes in prison." While at Folsom, Jennifer had hit someone in the head with a metal bar and was charged with possession of a weapon. Then she beat up another man and was charged with battery. "I have never murdered anyone. The way that the prison system was built was to get us into fights with one another, gangs against gangs, race against race, and I was under a lot of pressure and the violence escalated."

12/25/2012

Jennifer and her mother, Peggy, on a visit at Kern Valley State Prison,
California, December 2012. Photo courtesy Jennifer Gann

Jennifer and me during a visit in Kern Valley State Prison, California. February 2015

Jennifer celebrating her two-year-old sister's birthday.
Undated photo. Photo courtesy Jennifer Gann

Leaving Kern Valley State Prison, Delano, California, February 2015

The three-strikes law was first introduced in Washington state in 1993. A year later California followed, due to a well-financed lobbying effort by the strong, fast-growing California Correctional Peace Officers Association. The union has become one of the most powerful political forces in California, contributing millions of dollars to support "three strikes" and other laws that lengthen sentences and increase parole sanctions, increase salaries for the officers, and build new prisons. The three-strikes law soon spread to almost half of the states in the country. As with most laws concerning criminal behavior, this one fell disproportionately on the backs of black men.

The law has never been shown to reduce crime rates anywhere in the United States.[46]

In 2012, Californians voted in a referendum for a revision to the law (Proposition 36) that gave nonviolent three-strikers the possibility of a new trial. The proposition passed with an overwhelmingly majority vote in every county. In California, some 2,000 people have been released after the three-strikes law revision was enacted (between November 2012 and December 2014) and very few have gone back to committing crimes.[47]

"So what happened with your re-trial and Proposition 36?" I asked. I knew that a public defender in Sacramento had tried to get Jennifer's case reopened. "The case went nowhere," she said. "The judge took one quick look and said no. I wish I had had a chance to show I could do some good in society and not have the taxpayers spend millions of dollars on me in here. It's useless. And it is cruel."

Jennifer told me she was now sharing a cell with a 50-year-old black man who is Muslim and bisexual, and they have a good friendship. "I am doing okay for the time being, and I am for the most part safe. But every time we get transferred, every time we get a new cell mate, it is dangerous for us. Sometimes we need to be placed in Ad Seg [Administrative Segregation Unit], which is horrible. Ad Seg, or 'the hole,' is a terrible place to be. They say that Ad Seg is a safe place for us transgender women. But we have to share cells with sex offenders and gang members, and we cannot participate in programs." During a prison transfer from the California Institution for Men in Chino to

Kern Valley, which should not have taken more than 30 days, Jennifer spent seven months in "the hole" due to lack of bed space.

I looked at her painted arms. She pointed at one tattoo that read: "Riot Grrrl." Then she explained another. "'HB' stands for Huntington Beach, where I grew up."

"What do you believe is the solution to all of this?" I asked. "Clearly you do not believe in building more prisons, so what can be done for transgender prisoners?" "I think a separate facility within the prison, not to be mandatory but where women like me could go and be safe from all the male predators. We could end up like Carmen, who was killed here last year by her cellmate."

"How do you feel about your mother not accepting that you are a woman?" "It is hard. My mother has asked me not to sign my letters with 'Jennifer.' She is a Republican and very religious, and she just doesn't believe that this is natural. But my mom loves me unconditionally. She just doesn't want to call me anything other than 'baby' or 'Johnny.'"

It was getting close to 1:45 p.m. and we wanted to do a photo shoot. A sign said no more than one "retake" was allowed per prisoner, but the inmate house photographer, a friendly elderly man in a prison uniform and with a tiny digital camera, patiently gave us all the time we needed. Jennifer looked vulnerable and said her hair was a mess. I suggested she let it down. We took one photo after another and were finally pleased with fourof them, which the "photographer" went off to print for us.

On our way back to the vending machines for dessert, we passed another woman in a prison uniform sitting with her parents at a table. Jennifer explained that she was also transgender. Jennifer snuck up on her and gave her a big hug. "She is my friend, my homebody." We bought ice cream. Then I remembered and gave her an extra long warm hug. "This one is from your mother."

At 2:30, everyone in the visiting room stood up. Long hugs and some wet kisses were exchanged. Jennifer and I hugged a few times, and then I left. I walked back to the processing office, passing several other huge, white buildings before I was let out. I was thinking, *What kind of life can you really create for yourself in prison, knowing that you have no alternative?* Passing the yellow "Exit" sign as I drove out of the parking lot was particularly poignant, knowing that Jennifer would most likely never see it.

Excerpts from Jennifer's Letters 2013–2015

Kern Valley State Prison
April 7, 2013
Re: New Photography Project

Dear Kristin,

I'm writing in response to your flier requesting transgender prisoners' participation in your new project.

I'm a 43-year-old transwoman prisoner activist, blogger, and Siddha yoga student. I would be happy to meet you and participate fully in your project if possible.

I look forward to your reply.

Thank you!

Sincerely, Jennifer

Kern Valley State Prison, CA
April 25, 2013

Dear Kris,

Once you're approved, you may come visit me in person. Enclosed is my complete release form. I will try to have my mom email you my most recent photos from our visit last X-mas Day.

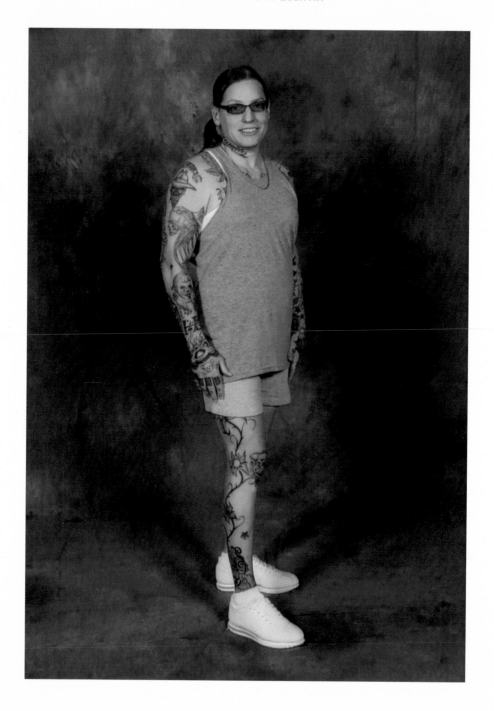

Jennifer during a photo shoot organized for prisoners by the administration
at Kern Valley State Prison, Delano, California 2014

I do now qualify to be represented under Proposition 36, the new Three Strikes Reform Act, but it's hard to obtain justice in this country for trans people like me. If only I had some community support, like CeCe McDonald had, I could maybe organize a campaign for my release. I've served 23 years in prison for petty offenses, never raped or murdered anyone! Sometimes I just want to die rather than live in this hell any longer!

— Jennifer in a letter from Kern Valley State Prison, April 26, 2013

In fact, you can email her yourself. Thank you, my sister, for all of your efforts on behalf of transgender people, particularly those of us in prison struggling for equality and liberation. I would love to know more about you personally, your motivations, preferences, etc.

Until next time, be fabulous and smile!

Sincerely yours, with great love and respect.

Jenni xoxo

Kern Valley State Prison, CA
April 26, 2013

Dear Kris,

Hello again! I thought maybe you could use a head start on your research for the book, so here's some questions and answers (I have written) that may or may not be useful.

Q: Where did I grow up and what was my childhood like?

A: I was born in 1969 in Riverside, California, and moved to Huntington Beach in 1979, both of which are just outside of Los Angeles. I grew up with two sisters, older and younger, my mom, and an abusive heroin addict stepfather. A typical white American working-class family, I guess. I did exhibit some psychological issues early on from my gender identity disorder, and had some behavioral problems in school.

Q: Did you have a lot of friends or social interactions?

A: Most of my friends were girls, who I seemed more compatible with personality-wise. I grew up with stoners, punk rockers, and skinheads, mostly, did a lot of drinking and drugs, and went to punk rock shows in L.A. in the '80s. I used to hang out in Hollywood or Long Beach. Most memorably, I've met Mike Ness of Social Distortion, Mike Reach of T.S.O.L., and Gwen Stefani of No Doubt. I also got on stage with D.R.I. Good times!

Q: How did I end up in prison?

A: Hanging out with boys, I always got into trouble. We got into fights, gang activity, and more serious crimes. Being unable to fit in, I was always trying to prove myself and overcompensating for my gender insecurities. I even took the rap for crimes I didn't commit, such as my original robbery convictions. If not for my drug-induced mental incompetency and psychological disorders, I would not have pleaded guilty and would not have a life sentence under the three-strikes law.

Q: Will you ever get out on parole?

A: Not unless I can raise some money and get a good lawyer. I do now qualify to be represented under Proposition 36, the new Three Strikes Reform Act, but it's hard to obtain justice in this country for trans people like me. If only I had some community support, like CeCe McDonald had, I could maybe organize a campaign for my release. I've served 23 years in prison for petty offenses, never raped or murdered anyone!

Sometimes I just want to die rather than live in this hell any longer!

Q: On a lighter note, what's my favorite color?

A: Pink and lavender because they're so feminine!

Q: Favorite food?

A: Mexican or Italian. I like salty and spicy foods and lots of cheese! Yummy!

Q: Favorite place?

A: The beach, enjoying the sunshine and ocean breeze. As for traveling, Europe, India, and Thailand (in that order).

Q: Other interests, likes and dislikes?

A: I love being femme, fetish fashion, leather and latex, tattoo art, and social justice activism. I dislike hatred, racism, and homophobia/transphobia. I want to abolish prisons and patriarchy and rebuild an Amazon culture! Long live the Amazons!

Sincerely, Jennifer

PS: I'm in dire need of some writing paper. If possible, could you send some?

May 14, 2013

Dear Kris,

Hello again!

Unfortunately, I'm sad to report that I received a notice of visitor disapproval dated May 6 which does not give any legitimate reason for disapproval.

Generally, nothing pleases me more than being a woman and feeling like a woman, especially when others accept and acknowledge me for who I am. I am a very femme woman, a girly girl at heart, but with a rough edge. I enjoy wearing makeup and women's clothing, styling my hair, and other forms of feminine gender expressions. However, I have a lot of tattoos, a violent criminal/gang member background, and kind of a tomboyish gangsta bitch persona (I'm kind of tired of having to live up to this image).

As for being a woman in a male prison, it is for the most part an absurd, nightmarish experience. Every day is a struggle against constant sexism, adversity, and opposition. Even for heterosexual gender-conforming men, prison is not easy or pleasant. For LGBTQ prisoners it is a hundred times worse!!! We (I'm not alone) are among the most vulnerable inmates facing discrimination and threats of violence on a daily basis from both inmates and guards. Transphobic hatred is not at all rational; it is ugly and vicious like a dangerous predatory monster! It is so heinous and scary to witness! Every day, I see a hateful look, a threatening demeanor glance, hear a taunting or sarcastic comment, face sexual harassment, discrimination, and disrespectful conduct. In spite of this, I am defiant and determined to shine like a light in the darkness. Like Rihanna sings, "We're beautiful like diamonds in the sky… shine bright like a diamond!"

June 3, 2013

Dear Kris,

Much of the time, I feel like I'm unfairly being ignored or intentionally insulted when prison staff address me as "mister" or throw other male pronouns in my face. It's hard for me to just roll with the punches and bite my tongue, as I'm very proud of who I am. I often want to directly confront these instances of gender and sex stereotyping.

My current cell mate professes love for me. He's very supportive and understanding, but also very sexually attracted to me. He's told me how much I've educated him and opened his eyes to the trans liberation struggle. It's very hard for us trans prisoners to find a compatible cell mate, but it's mandatory for us to live with a man according to regulations. Essentially, we are forced to "choose" a sexual partner under threat of disciplinary action, whether we want sex or not. This is just the way things are for women in a men's prison, we are coerced into unwanted sexual relationships. It's institutional rape! When we're lucky, we're able to find a man that we like, one who treats us like a queen and genuinely cares, who meets our needs and provides for our security on the yard.

This is ideal and not always a real possibility.

Some of the guards are nice and some are not. Some are professional and some are not. Some are accommodating and respectful, but some are openly homophobic and outright criminal in their conduct. Some are intimidating, threatening, and hateful towards us. Hopefully, I will get a visit from my mom this month. She has been my only true friend, my only visitor over the years. Although she's a conservative Christian and registered Republican who disagrees with the LGBTQ lifestyle and political agenda, she is still accepting and supportive of me individually. I will be always her "son" and she calls me "Johnny." She won't recognize the reality of me being a girl. I would really prefer if she was able to see me as her "daughter" and for my sister to see me as her "sister." However, we haven't reached that point… yet. It would make me soooo happy!!!

Well Kris, this is all for now. Write back soon!!! Thank you!

With much love and respect, Jenni xoxo

P.S. I share all of my literature and LGBTQ info/ resources with the other girls.

October 8, 2013

Dear Kris,

Hey girl! How are you? I hope that all is well. Thank you for the photos and enclosures on the

DOMA/Prop 8 victories! Yay! People have "marriage equality," but I think that just pink-washes U.S. imperialism and patriarchy. Gays serving in the military and getting marriage benefits is not "liberation" in my opinion… It also co-opts the queer liberation struggle by giving a false sense that we have "won" the struggle and now it's over. That's the furthest thing from the truth! I have experienced violence firsthand here at Kern Valley State Prison. When we are being beaten, raped, and killed on a regular basis in this society, "marriage equality" and military service doesn't really matter….

LGBTQ people should not support and be integrated in a system that oppresses and victimizes our community. Otherwise they are participating in their own oppression! How does that make sense?

As you can tell, my politics are a bit more radical. I am a revolutionary feminist and prison abolitionist. I don't want to "reform" a broken system of colonialism, genocide, and slavery, I want to overthrow it!!

Fascists will not give up their power structures and stolen land/wealth, they will use the police and military to protect the capitalist ruling class. The U.S. is not a "democracy," it's a fascist police state and unpopular government ran by thugs and criminals. They beat, torture, and murder people like Rodney King, Oscar Grant, and the California Prison Hunger Strikers in solitary confinement.

March 6, 2014

Dear Kris,

Thank you for the postcard February 2014. I
haven't received a support letter. Did you send it
to my attorney? Or to me? Either way, thank you.

As you can see from my address change, I was
transferred from KVSP [Kern Valley State Prison]
to CIM [California Institution For Men in Chino,
California] I've been held in Reception Center
Central for over a month, deprived of all of
my personal property and regular privileges,
purportedly for temporary "out-to-court" status.

The living conditions here are horrendous! We
are locked down 24/7 in dirty and deteriorating
housing units which are infested with mice and
cockroaches. We only come out for yard once a
week, though we recently went from February 20th
to March 4th (12 days!) between yards, in spite of
the bare minimum requirements of 3 days a week
for not less than 10 hours for segregation
housing inmates.

The first time I was in Chino Prison was in June
or July 1989, nearly 25 years ago. I was a young
vulnerable "white" kid from Orange County serving
a 16-month prison term for attempted robbery.

However, easily influenced and manipulated by the
older convicts, I was coerced into sex in 1990 at
the California Rehabilitation Center (CRC), and in
1991 I was sexually assaulted and raped by a cell
mate here in Chino while serving a second prison
term of 7 years for robbery.

I should have done my time and gone home, but instead I was forced into racially motivated violence by the Aryan Brotherhood prison gang. It was "mandatory" for my own survival to assault other prisoners and correctional officers in Folsom Prison. Though I committed these prison offenses under duress, I was charged and convicted in Sacramento County, receiving additional prison terms under the "Three Strikes" law for a total aggregate term of 104 years to life in California State prison.

Since then, I have dropped out of gang association, denounced racism, and disassociated myself from my past criminal behavior.

After suicide attempts and many years of psychotherapy, I "came out" in 2006 as a transgender, underwent a full gender transition and have also been on a regimen of estrogen hormone therapy for nearly 8 years.

I have problems with discrimination and sexual harassment by inmates and staff, which sometimes gets me into fights with homophobic inmates. I was forced to double cell with known sexual predators and raped in Tehachapi SHU (which is documented by Just Detention International and rape crisis counselor Karin Stone of Women's Center — High Desert).

In spite of these facts, prison officials continue to ignore these repeated sexual assaults and even blame me for it! In June 26, 2013, I was given a disciplinary report for "illegal sexual acts" for being sexually coerced in exchange for "protection and safety," even though I did nothing wrong and have even asked to be moved to a women's facility where I belong!

Well, that's all for now, my sister. Enclosed is another visiting form. Have fun in Bangkok! Be safe and good luck! Goddess bless you!

Much love and respect, Jennifer Gann

May 21, 2014

Dear Kristin

Hello! How are you? I hope that all is well and that you received my letter from Chino Prison a couple of months ago. I'm doing ok.

I transferred back to KVSP [Kern Valley State Prison] on 3/24/14, but I was placed in the hole for a fight that happened in CIM [California Institution For Men, Chino]. A child molester was beaten up in the chow hall. I was there with my friend, and the c/o implicated me (actually, he didn't even see it!) and another inmate as "suspects."

So they charged us both with "battery on an inmate with serious injury." I was not involved and my medical report shows "no injuries." Hopefully, I can be cleared by the other inmates, however, the disciplinary hearing process is a "kangaroo court." So I'll probably be on my way to Corcoran SHU for a couple of years.

I'm kinda sad and depressed about my situation. I was doing well, but prison circumstances are beyond my control.

On a more positive note, on 5/2/14 I was evaluated by the psychiatrist, Dr. Dahar, for eligibility and readiness for sex-reassignment surgery (SRS). I meet all criteria and was referred to a "medical team" for "medical and surgical management." This determination was also signed by the Chief Psychiatrist, Dr. Syed. I'm excited!

Also, enclosed is another visiting form.

Goddess bless you! Love, Jennifer XOXO

Enclosures-2

P.S. I started an initiative, the Advocacy Campaign for Trans-Women (ACT!). You can read about and download it from our website: www.blackandpink.org.

September 2, 2014

Dear Kris

Hey lovely lady!

Well, my sister, it seems I'm stuck here at Kern Valley for the time being. I continue my activism with Black & Pink and the Advocacy Campaign for Trans-women (ACT!). Jazzie and Stefany are still here, but they are on other yards and I haven't seen either of them lately…. They also are part of B&P.

Currently, I'm in the Enhanced Outpatient Program — psych unit — for therapy. I'm diagnosed with post-traumatic stress disorder (PTSD) and severe anxiety, resulting from long-term solitary confinement (SHU torture) and past sexual abuse/prison violence, etc.

My short-term goals are to have a Prop. 36 Three Strikes re-sentencing hearing in Sacramento. Would you or TGI Justice members be able to attend my hearing? Or do you still intend to come visit me?

Hopefully, I will be able to get a sentence reduction and a definite parole date in the foreseeable future before I die in this hateful place!!

Additionally, I am pushing to be moved to a women's facility! The men's prisons are not safe for us girls! I'm sad to report that one of our sisters, Carmen, was killed by her cell mate here last Nov. 1, 2013, and this is the latest transphobia murder in California prisons, among a couple of others that I've heard of. Yet, these ignorant prison officials continue to force us into these life-threatening situations based on the mandatory double-cell policy! We are constantly sexually harassed and humiliated by homophobic guards, strip searches, etc. We suffer very inhumane conditions!

The correctional officer had specific forewarning of the threat to Carmen's life and simply disregarded her safety! He is just as guilty as the inmate, but faces no consequences! While the inmate faces the death penalty!

Long live the Amazons! Girl Power! In sisterhood, always, Jennifer XOXO

Ps. Enclosed is my most recent photo. The tat by my eye is a small stem rose (which is a cover-up of a small swastika from my past "Skinhead" involvement).

December 2, 2014

Dear Kris,

Thanks for your letter of Nov 7th. I hope that all is well with you and Schreier. Now to answer your questions: What made you decide to transition finally? What happened to you in that process? Where did you find your strength and courage?

It happened like this: In Sept/Oct 2006, after dropping out of gang involvement, I became sexually involved with another queen. I confided in her my desire to come out as a transgender woman. Since I was very young I've had this strong identification with the female gender, including the same type of feminine (passive) sexual preferences.

Well, we had a fight and broke [up], after which she "outed" me to all the other inmates. Once my "secret" was out, I decided I had nothing more to hide. I was so tired of trying to be this fake person of a "man" that I had attempted suicide more than once. I saw this opportunity to "come out" and be the real me — a woman!

I changed my name to Jennifer and took the
nickname "BabyGirl." I began identifying openly
as a "girl" to other inmates, and I started on
estrogen hormone therapy in early 2007. It took
me a couple of years to fully transition into
my femme gender identity, to adapt and change
some of my behavior and mannerisms. The hardest
thing for me has been dealing with discriminatory
attitudes and policies of prison officials, sexual
harassment and homophobic violence by inmates.

As for the strength and courage to go through
this struggle, I found that long ago when I first
engaged in the prison struggle. I just didn't
realize it! Now I am such a better and happier
person, more loving and caring, more politically
progressive, more spiritual and devoted to the
Goddess. I have a lot of PRIDE in who I am — as a
woman. I despise who I used to be as a "man," and
I regret all the mistakes I've made in my life.
I'm very glad that we can continue to be pen pals
after the book is done! This whole project has
been very encouraging. You are such an inspiration
and incredible woman!!

Much love, Jennifer xoxoxo

January 15, 2015

Dear Kris

Hello there, lovely lady!

What do I usually do during the X-mas and New-
Year? Absolutely nothing! We are usually locked

down on these days. There are no "celebrations" of the holidays in Kern Valley. We get a pecan pie slice for dinner, that's about it!

When I first came to prison in 1989, the state used to hand out bags of X-mas hard candy and mixed nuts to all the inmates, or have a big X-mas dinner…. Those days of courtesy are over. Now it's just a lock down and cell search (to look around for pruno [prison wine])….

We try to have our own small things, such as a special- made meal in our cell from our own canteen and package food items. Maybe have some kind of "spirits" and watch sports events or movies on TV.

I also write and send cards out to family, etc. I put a few cards or X-mas decorations on my wall or cell window. I have a X-mas tree picture I took out of the TGI Justice Project "Stiletto" newsletter. It's snow-covered and colorful pink-and-purple lighted. So beautiful! I taped it to a cardboard and post it in my cell window each year, just to maybe give some good cheer! :)

I will be sure to give your regards to my mom and sister, ok? Xoxo Much love and respect,

Jennifer

①   1/31/2015

Dear Kris ♡

    Hello! ☺ Good news! You have
been approved to visit! Enclosed
is the Notice of Visitor Approval
i just received!
    So, hopefully, i'll see you soon?
Have you visited a California prison
yet? The only problem or issue i've
seen is the dress code, which
they selectively enforce. There's
a visitors center that can help
with that if necessary.
    Also, you can bring about $40
or so in dollar bills & quarters
for the vending machines & photo
tokens. We can have lunch together
girl! ☺ Yay!!! And we'll take
a photo or 2 together!
    Well, i recently sent you
some correspondence via SFINX,
will you receive it?
    How's your man doing? How's
it going with you?
    I'm excited to meet you,
sister! You will be the only
other visitor i've received in

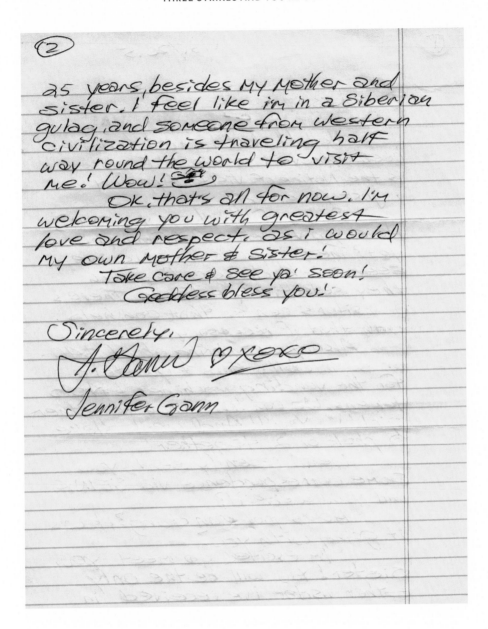

(2)

25 years, besides My Mother and sister. I feel like im in a Siberian gulag, and someone from western civilization is traveling half way round the world to visit me! Wow!

Ok, that's all for now. I'm welcoming you with greatest love and respect, as i would My own Mother & Sister!

Take care & see ya' soon!

Goddess bless you!

Sincerely,

Jennifer Gann

8

HOPEFULLY YOU
TAKE ME SERIOUSLY

More African American adults are under correctional control today—in prison or jail, on probation or parole—than were enslaved in 1850, a decade before the Civil War began. The mass incarceration of people of color is a big part of the reason that a black child born today is less likely to be raised by both parents than a black child born during slavery.

—Michelle Alexander, *The New Jim Crow*[48]

The sky was again appropriately gray on Sunday morning when I left my husband and dog at the hotel in Delano and drove back to Kern Valley State Prison. Having succeeded at getting in to meet Jennifer the day before, I hoped today to meet Jazzie Ferrari (I had approval letters to see both). I drove west along a mostly deserted two-lane road from Delano to the prison, a 14-minute drive that took me past dry fields, occasional rundown mailboxes, and fruit trees galore.

At Kern Valley, as at most prisons, a person cannot see more than one inmate per day, and visits are restricted to Saturdays and Sundays. This meant that Herb and I had time after my visit with Jennifer to get to know Delano. This unfashionably photogenic little town straddles Highway 99 with factories, packing businesses. and ubiquitous billboards advertising bail-out bond services lining the highway. A closed-down cinema, a few sports stores, several banks, and at one end a trailer park suggest a once-developing town now in decline. The hotel where we stayed is incongruously named "Liberty Inn" with a replica of the Statue of Liberty out front welcoming "your tired, your poor, your huddled masses yearning to breathe free." Except there was no sign of the revolutionary Cesar Chavez, nothing that reminded us of the era when Delano was all over the national and international news as a center of struggle for human rights. The hotel is surrounded by three fast-food restaurants and drive-throughs and one old-style local diner, a welcome throwback to the days before nationwide chain eateries.

Jazzie had been the first to write to me from prison in 2013. "Dear Kris," she wrote, "I am a beautiful African American transgender woman…. Hopefully you take me seriously." She said she had been incarcerated for 18 years for a crime she did not commit and had spent a lot of time in solitary confinement. Her descriptions of solitary were painful to read. "Being in the SHU is like being underground," she wrote. "Everywhere you go you are in handcuffs, most of the time you are in your cell 24 hours a day.... You can't have no bowl in the SHU, so we use a potato chip bag to eat out of, and use milk [cartons] to drink out of. Now, to wash your clothes, you use the toilet, very degrading. Now for a woman such as myself, how do you think that makes me feel?"

Her family has not been in touch with her since she told them who she was. In her letters describing her years of imprisonment, she seemed lonely, depressed, and without much hope. A few things made her feel better: she loved to read and was writing a novel. She sent me drawings and beautifully handcrafted cards that she had made with whatever materials were available, usually blue or red pencil on paper. She earned a little cash from selling them to other inmates. In a letter Jazzie sent to me in January 2015, she asked if I could send her a Christmas package—and if I would consider doing this annually. All the people she knew in prison received Christmas presents except her, she said. I unfolded the list of wishes she had included. It read: "Dark and Lovely Perm Relaxer, Blue Magic Organics Conditioner, chili shrimp, mini chocolate donuts, and Mother's Taffy Sandwich Cookies."

I drove into the prison parking lot, parked my car, and made my way back to the "no appointment area," where about 40 people were waiting patiently in line. Like the day before, they were mostly nonwhite people, most of them women and children—*a tragic reality*, I thought.[49] This time I knew how to dress and what to do: fill out forms in the middle of the parking lot, walk to the processing center, wait to be called up, take off my jacket and shoes to go through the scanner, walk through the yards to find the facility, and wait for another 45 minutes for Jazzie to come to the visiting room. Based on my limited experience with prisons, I figured this would take two hours—leaving two hours or so for our visit.

While waiting to get in to see Jazzie, I had time to revisit Kern Valley's website. The newly built prison, with its identical white, box-shaped buildings standing on concrete on what was previously farmland, looks like a movie set for a film about North Korea. Constructed in 2005 to accommodate 2,448 inmates, the prison's population in February 2015 was 3,707.[50] The fact that the prison's capacity is exceeded by 1,200 people could be one of the reasons why Jazzie spends so much time in "the hole." There is simply not enough room. Kern Valley State Prison has an annual operating budget of $155 million. (California spends $8 billion per year on its prisons.[51])

On the webpage, I saw a photograph of the warden standing in front of the American flag. I had written to the Kern Valley warden right at the beginning of this project, asking innocently if I could interview both him and a couple of people I was writing about who were imprisoned there—a really dumb approach, I soon discovered. His secretary wrote back months later to inform me that all journalist requests had to go through the California Department of Corrections and Rehabilitation's media department. I sent the media department a copy of my Norwegian passport and my international press card, as well as my US address. They contacted me once by phone but thereafter never responded to my phone calls or emails. My visitor applications were turned down for the next year and a half—until the week before this visit. The odds of a writer or journalist who is not from a major media organization or backed by a prominent publisher are next to nil. The only way I could get in to see the women, I learned, was to be approved as their friend and visit during general visitation hours. But even this took a very long time.

I had recently read about a prison epidemic of Coccidioidomycosis, or "valley fever," a microscopic fungus that thrives in the Central Valley's fertile soil and and can cause serious lung problems.[52] Around 4,000 California inmates have developed valley fever since 2005, and 53 have died from it.[53] Eighty-three percent of the state's valley fever cases occurred at Pleasant Valley and Avenal state prisons, and a federal judge ordered a transfer of some 2,600 prisoners out of the valley in 2011.[54] Treatment of this disorder alone in the California prison system costs $23 million a year.[55]

But the articles I found about the amount of arsenic in the prisoners' drinking water at Kern Valley State Prison worried me more. *Prison Legal News*, a project of the Human Rights Defense Center, wrote in 2011: "Prisoners at California's Kern Valley State Prison in Delano are being slowly poisoned through their drinking water." The arsenic, they reported, had been discovered only weeks after the opening of the prison in 2005, a prison that cost $379 million to build. Nothing had been done to remedy this. A January 2011 memo to the inmates from Warden Martin Biter read: "This is not an emergency." Prisoners "do not need to use an alternative water supply (e.g., bottled water)."[56] In October 2014, Valley State Prison in Chowchilla was fined for not complying with the requirements of the California Safe Drinking Water Act, after failing to meet standard arsenic levels.[57]

In March 2015, a lawsuit filed in California brought up the question of too much arsenic in some California wines. Naturally, the press is covering it and the public wants answers.[58] However, incarcerated people have no choice about too much arsenic in their water.

Seated with the other visitors in the cold and somber processing center that Sunday morning, I talked with several women who confirmed my own frustration with the impossibility of making appointments online or by phone. A woman who was there to visit her brother told me, "If you want to make an appointment, you have to do it online on Sundays at 8 p.m. If you call the appointment phone number, it will be busy the entire time that you call them on redial."

Suddenly, I heard an officer booming out my name. Oh no! My first thought was that Jazzie was on lockdown. I was wrong, yet close enough. "This is an appointment-only, ma'am," he said, "a noncontact visit only." He handed me a sheet of paper with the same phone number on it that I, like so many others, had been dialing to try to get through all week.

"What does that mean?" I asked. "It means you can only speak with each other through a glass. But you need to make an appointment first."

Even though I had prepared myself for this possibility, I was rattled. How was I going to tell Jazzie that after our two years of corresponding, I had driven all the way down here and stood in line, only to be told that I could not see her? I felt powerless. I felt humiliated for Jazzie's sake. As with visiting Ashley in Georgia, I was so so close, and now it seemed possible that we might never meet.

I said to the officer, "It is absolutely impossible to make an appointment. Why are you making this so difficult for us?" I showed him my yellow visitation approval letter and knew I was about to be childish: "I'm really looking forward to going home to write about this experience!"

I got in my car and drove toward the exit, wanting to get back to the hotel room to a comforting hug from my husband—fulfilling a simple human need, something I knew Jazzie did not have access to. As the guard checked my ID again at the checkpoint and looked in the car trunk (for a possible escapee?), I flashed on the faces of others I had seen turned away: looks of hurt yet resignation and calm. We had waited in line, been herded back and forth from line to line, passing by intimidating buildings that showed no sign of any human presence. A woman who had come from Los Angeles and some elderly people were among those turned away. They were used to it, I could see that. They said little, just turned and walked back to their cars.

Later that week, I thought of Jazzie as I was rereading a paragraph in Michelle Alexander's *The New Jim Crow*: "Once you're labeled a felon, the old forms of discrimination— employment discrimination, housing discrimination, denial of the right to vote, denial of educational opportunity, denial of food stamps and other public benefits, and exclusion from jury service—are suddenly legal. As a criminal, you have scarcely more rights, and arguably less respect, than a black man living in Alabama at the height of Jim Crow. We have not ended racial caste in America; we have merely redesigned it." On another page she compares the United States with the rest of the world: "No other country in the world disfranchises people who are released from prison in a manner even remotely resembling this country. The United Nations Human Rights Committee has stated that America's policies are discriminatory and violate international law."[59]

I do not know how long Jazzie has left to serve. She never told me. There are many things I never got to learn about her. What will she do when she eventually gets out of prison, with no family support, no friends to come home to? It is hard enough for a white person to get a job when re-entering society after imprisonment. But for transgender women of color, the odds are overwhelmingly poor. An article in the *New York Times* published just after my trip to Kern Valley reported that "the share of American men with criminal records—particularly black men—grew rapidly in recent decades as the government pursued aggressive law enforcement strategies, especially against drug crimes. In the aftermath of the Great Recession, those men are having particular trouble finding work." Men with criminal records account for about 34 percent of all nonworking men ages 25 to 54.[60] The "Rehabilitation" part of the California Department of Corrections and Rehabilitation's name is nothing more than an empty promise.

What we do know is that the way we treat people in prisons strongly affects what they do when they come out. This has been demonstrated by the teenagers we lock up, many of whom become "lifers" without the possibility of parole. Our failure to reform and educate is evident. We have still not learned what the poet W. H. Auden warned of in a very different context:[61]

I and the public know
What all schoolchildren learn,
Those to whom evil is done
Do evil in return.

California Correctional Institution, Tehachapi, California. Photo courtesy CDCR

Excerpts from Jazzie's Letters 2013–2015

California Correctional Institution
Tehachapi, California
March 27, 2013

Hello Kris.

I do hope and pray that by the time this meaningful and heartfelt letter reaches its destination, I truly hope that it finds you in the best of health, and in the best of God's care.

Now I would like to introduce myself. First and foremost, my name is Ms. Jazzie Ferrari. I'm a beautiful transgender. I'm a real sweet person and easy to get along with. I was born in South Central Los Angeles, Calif. My birthday is June 15, 1971, sign Gemini. I have been incarcerated for $17\frac{1}{2}$ years, with a few more to go. So the reason for this letter is because a friend of mine gave me your address and asked me if would I be interested in this new project. Once I read and seen what it was about, I would love to be part of the project. Due to the fact that I love to write, I'm looking forward to hearing from you. I'm also writing a book which I've almost finished. I'm into urban fiction. I would love to share some of my prison experiences with you, and boy, do I have some.

I wish that I could have been more professional and that this letter was typed; but due to the fact that I'm in the SHU, I'm unable to do that. So hopefully you take me serious, because I am. And I hope that we can take this much needed journey together, so I truly hope to hear from you. Thank you for your time. So until next, God bless you.

PS: I will sign a release form, Truly, Miss Jazzie

California Correctional Institution
Tehachapi, California
April 7, 2013

Dear Kris,

My birth name is Deshone Bruce, born and I was raised in South Los Angeles, birthday June 15, 1971. I'm a Gemini, 41 years old, brown eyes, weight about 169. Mother's name is Bertha, father's name is John. My father died when I was about 14 years old. He got stabbed in the heart. My mother died when I was about 20. I've always been skinny, I was born premature. The doctor told my mother that I wouldn't make it, but I did. So, when I was about 4 or 5, I got taken away from them and put in a foster home. I was able to go home on Saturday and Sunday. While they went to court and kept fighting to get me back, it was hard on me, by me being young. I didn't know what was going on. So I stayed there (foster home) until I was 9 years old.

Once I came home, I was very happy, but then my mom moved to a neighborhood that had a lot of gangbangers, and my mother's brothers were all in a gang. I knew that I couldn't come out at the

time. I started to gang bang, trying to fit in.
I started smoking weed when I was about 11 years
old, getting into trouble at elementary school,
having fights and stuff. My first time going to
juvenile detention was when I broke into a house.
But about a few weeks later I was back on the
street. So, that's how I got started. I knew that
I was gay at a young age. I told my mother and
she didn't mind. I lived a double life. The older
I got, the harder it was for me to hide who I
was, but I knew they would kill me if I came out.
I kept hiding the fact that I was a transgender.
When I told my mother that I wanted a sex change,
she said "I want some grandkids," so I had a boy
and a girl for her and she got to meet them before
she died. But since I've been down, it's been kind
of lonely, but I'm strong and it would be okay.

Kris, this is just the beginning. So, I hope that
we are on the right track. So far, once my people
found out about me they haven't written to me, but
it's okay.

I truly believe that we came together for a
reason. Like I said, I love to write, and I only
have $2\frac{1}{2}$ months left in the SHU so hopefully one
day we will be able to see each other. Well, here
is a old picture of me. I hope you like it. You
can make a few copies, because this is my last
one. Once I get out of the SHU I'm going to take
some new ones.

Truly, Ms Jazzie

PS: Once I finish my book I would love for you to be part of it. And I hope that you can be a true friend as we go on this journey together.

California Correctional Institution
Tehachapi, California
April 28, 2013

Dear Kris,

Being in the SHU, you really have to be strong to survive. Now, the reason why I'm in the SHU is because my boyfriend had a fight on the yard. That's the regular yard where you can program with everybody. I didn't do nothing, and my boyfriend and his friend told the police that Jazzie didn't have nothing to do with it, but yet they still got me here. Now, once you come to the SHU, you got to send all your shit home, like your CD, CD player, your pictures, clothes, shoes, you really can't have shit in the SHU. You're always in your cell 24 hours a day, you get to go to the store once a month, and if you ain't got nobody on the outside sending you money, it can get bad. When it's like that, you are forced to eat stuff you normally won't eat. The food is horrible, you go outside every 2 or 3 days, it depends on how they feel. Before you go out they put you in a cage and you must strip all your clothes, then bend over and part your ass cheeks. Once you're outside you're in a cage — "what type of shit is that?" People are always stressed out. You can have a TV back here, but you're alone. I'm always thinking.

I try to stay strong and not get into trouble,
but yet my rights get fucked over because I'm a
transgender. So, it's only right that you learn
your rights because it's the right thing to do.
In here you learn how to hide your feelings. Like
I said before, it's hard to trust or show your
true feelings. In here it's all about surviving.
Sometimes girls in here get with a dude, just so
he can protect her or take care of her. If she
ain't got nobody on the outside doing nothing
for her, then she has got to do something. It's
a different world in here. I try to get all the
girls to stay together because sometimes all we
have is each other. I never want to be in the SHU,
and I'm going to try my best not to come back.

So as you can see, it's very hard on me here.
That's why I truly appreciated you letting me
be part of this much needed project. How do you
think it feels to be locked away or in a cell
24 hours a day? Who really are the barbaric
ones? Transgenders face specific and unique
difficulties in prison and jail due to ignorance,
discrimination, and violence from guards and other
prisoners. It is the prison officials' job to
keep transgenders safe from substantial risk of
serious harm, whether they are in a male or female
facility. That's why it's very important to learn
how to protect yourself. Kris, I will always tell
you the real deal, this is just the tip of the
iceberg. Like I said, I've been in prison for $17\frac{1}{2}$
years, and I've seen and been through a lot. I've
been in 5 different prisons. A lot of people won't
understand me. I grew up poor. I know how it feels
to be hungry and have no lights or gas in the
house. I had to grow up fast, learn how to steal

just to feed my little nephews and nieces. So with
that being said, I learned how to adjust to my
surroundings. Yes, I'm in pain every day in here.
I'm not supposed to be in prison at all. We'll
talk about that at another time. In here you've
got to have something to look forward to that
keeps you going. I seen people take their own life
in here because they feel that they have nothing
to live for. That's why I started to write my book.
I wanted to do something good. That's what keeps
me going, and to meet people like you, who really
care. And my LGBTQ family out there makes me feel
that I'm wanted, makes me want to keep fighting
and to stay strong.

Ms Jazzie

PS: I like the pink envelope.

California Correctional Institution
Tehachapi, California
May 21, 2013

Dear Kris,

Now what I want you to do is to lock yourself
in the bathroom, make your bathtub your bed.
Now above the tub put a 13" TV there, also put
a locker by your bed — that's where you put your
food and cosmetics. When you want to write, use
your locker as a desk. You have a window that
you can't open. Sometimes as I sit in my cell
I look around and wonder how can anyone think
about building a place where hopes and dreams are
crushed, a place where a person can be locked up

for so long that his/her loved ones forget that they even exist. And when that happens, where does a person find the strength to keep living? Being in the SHU is like being underground; everywhere you go you are in handcuffs, most of the time you are in your cell 24 hours a day.

Now while you're in that bathroom, imagine someone slamming the door all day long, people hollering, someone taking a shoe or a cup and banging on the bed all day. You can't have no bowl in the SHU, so we use a potato chip bag to eat out of, and use milk [cartons] to drink out of. Now to wash your cloths you use the toilet, very degrading. Now for a woman such as myself, how do you think that makes me feel? The food is so so, you've been away for so long you forgot how real food tastes, or how a real bed feels. Birthday, Christmas, Easter, Halloween, and New Year's just become another day, nothing special, just another day. As a transgender, it's hard to be in a relationship because sometime the dudes just want you for sexual favors and then treat you like shit once they're done. Not all men are bad, but you got to be careful. Some girls sell their body just to survive. (PS: I hope you can feel what I feel). They don't have nobody on the outside doing nothing for them. Some girls put up with their boyfriend beating on them because that's who is taking care of them. Some of the guards are nice and some bad. Being a transgender in prison is hard, due to the fact that some time you might want to dress sexy, you might have one of the girls to make you a nice tank top and some shorts. So you go put it on just to have the guards tell you that you can't wear that. Or you got some lipstick/lip gloss. They even give you a hard time about that. We are trying to get panties/bras. I think they are letting us have the bras, I'm not sure. I will get back to you on that.

Now back to the matter at hand. You ask: how does it feel to be a woman in a male prison? Well for me it can be good because if you find the right man it can be wonderful. You can have great sex and get treated like a queen. Now in a women's prison you can have nice clothes and makeup, all the things that makes you feel good about yourself, but no man. I rather be in a man's prison. Prison is no good for no one, but you got to stay strong if you want to survive. I refuse to give up. I think about the girls that will come in behind me. I got to stay strong for them. Sometimes in here girls have relationships with other girls. To be real with you, I had a relationship with another girl and it was wonderful, and she was beautiful, and I have no regrets. Yes, they have lesbian relationships in here too. Everybody needs somebody, and that's life. Now, prison can be a lonely and depressing place. Sometimes you have to deal with ignorance, discrimination, violence from guards and other prisoners. Many transgender people are placed in male facilities against their will even if a female facility would be more consistent with their gender identity, expose them to less danger and violence, or make more sense to them for other reasons. Some transgenders are placed in female facilities against their will even if a male facility would be better. Some transgenders have brought lawsuits against prison officials for categorizing them as men and placing them in

a male facilities rather than treating them as
women and placing them in female facilities. We
are strip searched by male guards. This is what we
have to face every day. This hurts because I don't
like to see the girls go through that. Your family
just leaves you for dead, and that's what happened
to me. As I sit and write this letter I'm crying.
I'm only human, Kris. Why can't people see that? I
don't have much, but the little I do have I don't
mind sharing, and that's why your writing me means
so much to me. I cherish every letter you write
me. It gives me hope and lets me know that someone
does care and lets me want to do more. I hope that
you can feel what I'm feeling.

I let some of the girls read my book and they
love it. It's because of them that I can't give up.
I work hard, Kris, just to see them smile. They
don't have no one out there. All we have is each
other. Failure is not an option for me. I want
to be successful just to help other people, and
that's what makes me happy. It's a challenge every
day to keep a smile on your face when there's
really nothing to smile about.

With love, Jazzie

California Correctional Institution
Tehachapi, California
Postmark July 17, 2013

Dear Kris,

I was just sitting here thinking about how busy
you must be and yet to find time to write a lonely

woman as myself. My family don't even find time to do that, but yet here is a stranger goes out of her way to write me. And that's why I cherish your letters. Going on 18 years and I never had a visit (wow) just because I want to be myself. It's crazy because I'm proud about who I am and I will never hide that again. I refuse to do that, no matter what the cost. Yes I'm by myself right and because I don't have time for nothing else. I read a lot, and the LGBTQ community is doing a lot. I must join the struggle, so as you see. This is what I promised myself. I've got to get my G.E.D. and finish writing my … book.

Much love, Ms Jazzie Ferrari

Ps: Tell Ms. Janetta I said to keep up the good work xoxoxoxo

---

California Correctional Institution
Tehachapi, California
August 19, 2013

Dear Kris,

Now let me say I'm out of the SHU but in the hole, which is worse than the SHU. The reason I haven't written is because I've been stressed out. Kris, at least in the SHU you got your TV and can take a shower every other day, plus you get to go outside every other day. Now in here you're in your cell 24 hours a day! You go outside maybe once a week and shower like every 3 days. It's bad and you ain't got no TV now. This is crazy. This is CRUEL AND UNUSUAL PUNISHMENT. The [department] of

corrections has an unfair disciplinary system that
is reactionary, and it has become desensitized to
the serious repercussions of prolonged solitary
confinement. The practice of handing out massive
amounts of solitary confinement has a direct
effect on the deterioration of inmates' mental
health as well as recidivism. When I first arrived
over here in the hole it was supposed to be
better, but I was introduced to the most horrible
conditions in my life. The only way I can describe
it is as a physical manifestation of hell. I
became very antisocial because I don't want to get
in no trouble. Then the depression hit me hard
along with other mental [issues]. My SHU time,
now this. Man, Kris, you got to be real strong as
a transgender. It's hard on me. I sit up and cry
every night. I need some help. What these people
are doing to inmates is wrong. The 8th Amendment
speaks out against cruel and unusual punishment.
Kris, I'm tired right now, but please write back
A.S.A.P. and let me know you got this letter and
card. So until next time, you keep your head up
and stay safe.

Much love, Ms Jazzie

Kern Valley State Prison, California
February 24, 2014

Dear Kris,

So you want to have your own stuff, because you
can be killed for touching someone's stuff, and it
gets hard in here if you ain't got nobody on the
outside. I have been without since I been here. I

don't have a TV or radio. And I pay restitution, so when someone sends me money they take 55% so you get little for yourself.

So this is what you have to worry about when you come to prison. I've been here for 18-1/2 years and you eat the same shit each week. You miss out on a lot when you come to prison. It's like you lose all your rights. It's crazy in here. A lot of people took their own life in here. Some people can't take it and take their own life because it's hard in here, Kris. If only you knew how we get treated in here. You got to have someone on the street that cares about you, and I truly mean that. It's very important for these people to know that someone out there has your back, and right now, Kris, you're the only one that's helping me right now. See, Kris, once you go to the SHU they make you send everything home or donate it. Then when you get out of the SHU you have to start all over again. Now you don't have no one out there.

Right now, Kris, you're the only friend I have. Kris, it's a lot that I can't say on paper. No, this is not a transgender friendly prison. I cry every time I write. Sometimes it's hard to stay strong in this lonely place and being a transgender of color (WOW)!! Yes in here they bring your food to your cell and then you have about 10 minutes to eat. Also the food be cold and halfway cooked. You get to go to the store once a month, and if you don't have no food in the cell then you are forced to eat the bullshit they give you.

Much love. Your friend, Ms. Jazzie. XOXO

Kern Valley State Prison, California
April 15, 2014

Dear Kris

The girls here told me that I should start a
website and put my drawings on it. You can be my
manager. I got to do something so I can feel a
part of something.

This can be my way of giving back. I'm a hard
worker. There's no doubt in my mind that it will
work, with your help. I know that we can do this.
PLEASE HELP ME! Just tell me what needs to be
done. See, Kris, in here we are so far behind that
they don't teach you how to write up a business
proposal. Kris, I have to have something to look
forward to once I get out.

You know how important this is. I know you're
a very busy woman. Kris, even the officers in
here are amazed at my work. Everybody in here
buys cards from me. But I give them to the girls
for free. I can easily make a portfolio and make
a beautiful design for the website or whatever
(Facebook, Twitter). And I also send the visiting
form back to you. It's getting late so I'm going
to bed. Until next time. I'm glad the project is
coming along.

Much love your friend, Ms. Jazzie XOXO

Kern Valley State Prison, California
June 15, 2014

Dear Kris,

I got some good news — my boyfriend asked me to marry him, and I said yes. We've been together for about 4 years now so I don't know how this is going to turn out, but I think it's going to happen.

Today is my birthday. I'm just taking it easy. Thinking about my future. Hoping it will be a good one. Kris, I'm working on my G. E. D. and hopefully I graduate next year, and if I do I will love for you to come and you be able to bring some friends. I truly hope to hear from you soon.

Your friend, Ms. Jazzie

Kern Valley State Prison, California
October 5, 2014

Dear Kris

What's going on with you? It's been a while since I heard from you. Now as for myself, I'm still working hard to make sure I make something of myself; my boyfriend is here, right now we are in the process of getting married. We would be the first to get married behind the wall.

I also started a foundation. A lot of girls in here don't have nothing or no one on the outside, so with my art I've been able to help a lot of the girls It's called Help/A/Trans/Out. I don't know why you stop writing to me, but I promise that I haven't done anything wrong, and if I said anything that offended you, I truly apologize from the bottom of my heart. Kris, you know that I finish my first book and am working on my second. It is something to be proud of. I just want you to know I'm still your friend and hope that you're doing fine. Until next time, stay safe, your friend,

Mrs Jazzie

Kern Valley State Prison, California
December 30, 2014

Hello Kris,

I am working hard trying to stay alive in here. I know you've been real busy. And I try to wait to hear from you. But it's very hard in here. I don't got nobody. I didn't hear or get nothing for Christmas. I just sat here and cried. It's really sad. I'm so lonely. I'm trying my best to stay strong. But when I have nobody it makes you want to give up. It's a cold place. Everybody got TV and radios. But I have nothing. So, Kris, I am asking: can you please get me a package once a year? I like to have my own stuff. Because people don't like transgenders here. I hope I'm not being a burden. Right now I'm writing a story called "Trans behind the Wall." I believe you going to like it. So I will keep you updated. I know that it's going to be a juicy story.

Much love, your friend

PS. Sorry so sloppy. I'm kind of stressed out right now. Thank you from the bottom of my heart,

Ms Jazzie

Kern Valley State Prison, California. Undated.
Greeting card from Jazzie:

Well, Kris, I just wanted to show you how much I appreciate your friendship. I sit down and cry because it's been a long time since I had a true friend. In here it's hard to let your guard down and call someone a true friend. Words really don't express the true meaning of your friendship.

You are my inspiration, and I stay strong and keep going 'cause it gets hard in here. The food is bad. I mean real bad. I don't look forward to eating the food here. Kris, you take care of yourself and I hope to hear from you soon. Your friend, Ms. Jazzie XOXO

Initials _Jazzie_ Date _3-1-15_ Writing Project _____ Draft _____ Page _1_

HELLO KRIS

WELL I HOPE THAT THIS LETTER FINDS YOU IN THE BEST OF HEALTH AND PUT A SMILE ON YOUR FACE. WELL I JUST WANTED YOU TO KNOW THAT I GOT YOUR POST CARD AND IT WAS VERY NICE THANK YOU VERY MUCH. SO IM SO BLESS TO HAVE FOUND A TRU FRIEND AS YOURSELF. AND IM SO PROUD OF YOU. WELL IM GETTING MY VISITING CLOTHS READY CAUSE YOUR NOT THE TYPE TO GIVE UP BUT ANYWAY YOUR A BUSY WOMAN, AND SO AM I. SO I GOT TO STAY BUSY, OH THEY GOT A PICTURE PROJECT COMEIN UP THIS MONTH SO I WILL SEND YOU SOME UP TO DATE, SO ITS GOOD

SO KRIS THIS IS NOT GOING TO BE A LONG LETTER IM WORKING HARD ON MY (BIO) THATS KEEPIN ME UP ALL NIGHT BUT ITS FUN HARD WORK BUT FUN. I CANT WAIT FOR US TO WORK TOGATHER CAUSE I GOT SO MUCH TO SAY. AND IF I CAN HELP YOU IN ANY WAY JUST LET ME KNOW CAUSE I TRUST YOU. AND THATS SAYING ALOT DO TO THE FACT THAT ITS HARD TO TRUST ANYBODY BUT TOGATHER WE CAN MAKE IT WORK. NOTHIN BEATS HARD WORK AND DETERMINATION.

WELL I HOPE TO SEE YOU SOON, SO UNTIL THAN YOU TAKE CARE OF YOURSELF AND BE SAFE AND STAY STRONG. MUCH LOVE YOUR FRIEND

MISS JAZZIE
XOXO.

P.S. IS THEY STILL PROTESTING OUT THERE WHERE YOUR AT?

Appendix 8

Sometimes as I sit in my cell I look around and wonder how can anyone think about building a place where hopes and dreams are crushed, a place where a person can be locked up for so long that his/her loved ones forget that they even exist. And when that happens, where does a person find the strength to keep living? Being in the SHU is like being underground; everywhere you go you are in handcuffs, most of the time you are in your cell 24 hours a day.... You can't have no bowl in the SHU, so we use a potato chip bag to eat out of, and use milk [cartons] to drink out of. Now to wash your cloths you use the toilet, very degrading. Now for a woman such as myself, how do you think that makes me feel?

Jazzie in a letter from California Correctional Institution in Tehachapi, 2013

I WATCH THE BRUCE JENNER INTER
VIEW AND I KNOW HOW HE FEEL BE
CAUSE IM going THOugh THE SAME
THing, MY Kids dont KNOW IM TRANS
gENDER I HAD TO HiDE. BECAUSE I
HAD FAMILY THAT I KNOW THAT would
NOT ACCEPT ME. SO MY dAUGHTER NAME
IS KRYSTAL   AND MY
SON NAME IS JERRY

Thank You So Much

THEY STAY IN LOS ANGELES CALIF
SOUTH CENTRAL, AND THEIR MOTHER
NAME IS R   SHE
AbouT 45 YEARS. I HAD MY dAUGHTER
WHEN I WAS 16. AND I HAD MY SON A
YEAR LATER. KRIS I REALLY NEED SOME
HELP FiNdiNG THEM, SO IM SENDING YOU
THESE PiCTURE OF THEM AND WHEN YOU
HAUE TIME CAN YOU PLEASE LOOK THEM
UP FOR ME, ITS UERY IMPORTANT NOW. BE
CAUSE THEY ARE OLDER NOW. I BELIEUE
THAT I CAN GET THEM TO UNDERSTANd.
WELL I HOPE   YOU CAN HELP
I REALLY   NEED TO TALK
WITH MY   dAUGHTER.
SO PLEASE dont   TELL THEM
YET, I WILL   iN TIME
WELL THATS ALL FOR   NOW TALK
TO YOU LATER   MUCH LOUE
YOUR FRIEND no   Jazzie
XOXOXOXOXO.....

I will *bless* you...
and you will be a
blessing. GENESIS 12:2 NIV

I LIKE TO TRULY THANK YOU
FOR BEING THERE FOR ME. IT
MEAN SO MUCH TO HAUE SOMEONE
SO SPECIAL iN YOUR LiFE I GUESS
N THESE CASE YOUR A ANGEL.
YOU MIGHT NOT KNOW iT, BUT IM
HERE TO LET YOU KNOW THAT YOUR
THE REAL dEAL :-) NELL I dont
KNOW iF I TOLD YOU AbouT MY
Kids THAT I LOST CONTACT WiTH

In the card I received from Jazzie in May 2015, she included photographs of her children for the first time. She mentioned the Caitlyn Jenner interview with Diane Sawyer and that she has not told her children about being transgender. She has not had any contact with them for the past several years.

9

THE ONLY PLACE

"I can't lie to you and say that my experience in prison has been that bad," Daniella explained in one of her letters. Daniella Tavake first wrote to me from California State Prison in Corcoran in 2013, then from Kern Valley State Prison, and later from Salinas Valley State Prison in Soledad. She had been in and out of prison since she was 19. Now 38 years old, she was serving a six-year sentence and had two more years to go.

Her story stood out not just because her prison experience had not been traumatic. In her early letters to me, she described something I had never heard before. She kept coming back to prison because she felt more comfortable about who she was behind the prison walls—she felt she was treated like a real woman among some of the incarcerated men.

As a teenager, Daniella had joined gangs and hung out with hoodlums in and around San Mateo, California, and she used drugs to ease the pain of having been abused as a child and being in a body that did not conform to her self-identification as a female. On methamphetamine she could finally feel nothing. In prison, she could share her pain with others and feel less misplaced as a transgender person, since she came from a community that knew little about gender identity issues.

Before I was able to visit her in prison, in December 2014, she got an early release for good behavior. We were out of contact until I found her on Facebook and added her as a friend in January 2015. She quickly accepted and we exchanged phone numbers.

She had found a job at San Mateo County's Vocational Rehabilitation Services (VRS) Workcenter and Catering Connection, which provides paid training and transitional work experience to people with barriers to employment, as soon as she "re-entered" society. Within a month, she was warmly ensconced in her sister's house (with five dogs and two children) and had a full-time job. I was impressed by all that I learned about Daniella in the months that followed.

On the morning of January 8, 2015, I drove from Berkeley across the Bay and down the Peninsula to San Carlos, where Daniella worked. I parked my car outside the VRS Workcenter on Quarry Road, an industrial area of warehouses and factories. A few people, probably trainees, were gathered outside the large, industrial-style building, smoking and talking.

Then Daniella appeared—tall, bald-headed, with big, round eyes, a kind smile, and a little gap between her front teeth. Her eyes twinkled. "Here, this is for you!" she said and gave me a bottle of water.

Bright-pink-and-yellow ethnic dresses decorated the walls at the Afghan restaurant I had found on Yelp where we went for lunch. The waiters were dressed in tuxedos with bow ties. Daniella and I obviously shared a passion for food and ordered a variety of dishes. She told me about her new job at VRS. She said she felt taken care of. For the first time in her life she was being encouraged to plan a future. Her employer and case managers seemed to love the challenge of having their first transgender employee.

"The security guy made a complaint about me using the ladies' bathroom, and my case workers took it seriously and called everyone in for a meeting, where they basically said, 'Daniella is allowed to use any bathroom she likes.'"

Daniella was now getting up at 3:40 every morning and taking a couple of buses to be at work at 6:00 a.m. Sometimes she prepared food and sometimes she drove the food delivery van around the Bay Area. "My boss, Robert, has been in prison himself, so he understands me. We are getting on extremely well. My case workers have been so good to me. I don't even see my probation officer much. My workplace sends him reports, and since I show up every day for work, things are going smoothly."

We talked about her experience in prison. Her time at Salinas Valley State Prison just before she was released had been the most difficult. When I asked Daniella about the differences among the prisons where she had been, she quickly responded:

"San Quentin is more open to us women, and they know how we deserve to be treated. In San Quentin we don't have to fight for our rights. In Kern Valley you have to learn not to demand your rights. You have to find an ally in an officer, and I got what I wanted that way. I was not afraid to use my ability to manipulate a situation to get what I wanted. Salinas Valley is crooked, period! The women there just get denied everything, even though it's supposed to be a hub for us girls. The COs [correctional officers] are just dirty."

A month and half later, Daniella and I met again in San Mateo near where she lived. She said she was exhausted. She had worked 92 hours in two weeks and wanted some time off. We went to a spa for a pedicure and manicure in big, comfortable chairs that massaged us lightly while our feet soaked in hot water. I asked about the nursing degree she had mentioned in one of her letters. "I spoke to a nurse, and she thinks it will be impossible because of my criminal record." "How is Chris doing?" I asked next. Chris was a man still in prison that she had written about extensively in her letters.

"Chris and I will move in together when he gets out in two years' time," Daniella said. "I am never going back to prison. I know I can do it. This time I'm staying out here to build a life for myself." It was Daniella's first time being "out" in the world as a woman, and she found this as liberating as being out of prison. "I don't even like to drink anymore. I may have one beer, but then I stop.

"Chris is my best friend, and we are in love. We figured so many things out while we were incarcerated. His marriage ended. Now he has two years left, and he has already told his parents that he wants to build a life with me."

They planned to settle in Nevada City. "I am the first woman who has said yes to Chris about moving with him to Nevada City," Daniella continued. "I told him: 'what am I supposed to do there?' But my boss believes in me and says that he thinks I will start my own restaurant within the next five years. So perhaps that is what I will be doing," she said, focusing intensely on her long, freshly painted nails.

I began imagining Daniella in Nevada City, a California Gold Rush town set in the foothills of the Sierra Nevada. Curious to learn about its history, I later looked it up and found that the indigenous Maidu people call Nevada City "Ground-Zero" because it was a place where their people were killed by miners and settlers.[62] A Maidu artist wrote in the Nevada City *Union*: "Within a period of two years, the several thousand Maidu people who had lived here for centuries were killed, driven off or died of disease. Seldom in the numerous of local celebrations of the Gold Rush is this particular segment of local history viewed in respect to the Maidu people."[63]

Daniella's father was born in Tonga, a Polynesian nation that was never colonized but was formerly a British protectorate. As a young boy, her father moved in with his mother's sister, Aunt Anna, because they lived near a good school. Eventually, Anna's husband got a US visa, settled in San Mateo, California, and called for Anna and their children to relocate. Anna refused to leave Tonga without her nephew. "Somehow they managed to get my dad over to the States too. I am not sure how they did that," Daniella said.

"My father was 21 years old and my mother was 15 when they first met. A year later they started dating. My mother kicked him out when I was 5 years old. He was an alcoholic. He beat her and was unfaithful. I have always been close to my mother, and I remember how bad I felt when he was mean to her. I used to tell him I hated him. He actually lives just a few houses down from us now, but I have only seen him a couple of times since I got out. I won't give him my phone number, I don't want to have a relationship with him. He always tells me that I am too much like my mother. My mother is a rare woman. Even though he treated her so badly and was not a real father to me, she has never said a bad word about him."

By now, we had been in the nail salon for an hour. My feet were nicely massaged and my toenails were painted dark turquoise, Daniella had new acrylic nails in silver gray. I had recently read several news articles about prison officers and deputy sheriffs betting on fights between inmates, cockfight style, in a San Francisco jail. I asked if she had experienced anything like that.

"Oh yes, they did that to me in '95. When I was in the SHU at Corcoran and still gang banging, they would unlock the cell doors and bet on who would come out and fight with one another. It was entertainment to them. And I did that a couple of times—ran out and fought. And then a guard would come up to me later and say, 'Thanks, mate, you just made me a lot of money!'" As soon as

Daniella along the Bay, San Mateo County, 2015. Photo courtesy Daniella Tavake

Daniella dropped out of the gang, the "cockfighting" ended.

"What about contraband items?" I asked next. The California Department of Corrections and Rehabilitation's website stated that the department was cracking down on the use of cellphones in prison. Officers smuggling a cellphone into prison would be fined up to $5,000 or spend up to six months in county jail. The inmates could lose up to 90 days of good time credit.

Daniella said that as long as you were on good terms with the guards, no punishment was given. "You can easily buy a cell phone for 600 to 800 dollars. Drugs are flowing. It is not the inmates who smuggle the stuff in, it's the correctional officers. They may have debts to pay or want to live a more lavish lifestyle. In Kern Valley I had to use a different approach, though, when communicating with staff there. I knew that if I treated the guards as human beings instead of pigs, I would get what I wanted. They would have my back and I, theirs. When I wanted to use [drugs], they knew about it and didn't interfere."

We went next door to a Chinese restaurant and ordered Mongolian beef and roast duck for lunch. It seemed like a good time to ask her about the crimes that had gotten her into prison. In her letters she had said that this was particularly hard for her to write about.

"I was 19. My friend stole a purse from an old lady, but the lady didn't want to let go and she got injured. I was there, so I was part of it. We got caught. The judge said he could believe that we didn't mean to hurt the lady, but he gave me a six-year sentence. I was incarcerated in San Quentin. At that time I was extremely angry. I did some theft on other occasions, was sent back to prison, and this last time I was in for six years for identity theft." I asked her what had made her change this time to be so determined never to go back to prison again. Daniella responded: "Because I found me."

When I spoke with Daniella on the phone in the end of March 2015, she said her three months with Vocational Rehabilitation Services were up. She was already in a new job at Specialty's Café and Bakery, which provides catering for corporations. "It is a family-owned restaurant," she said. "They are always closed on Saturdays and Sundays and on all holidays. I prepare cookie dough and croissants, and drive the delivery truck. Last Friday I went for an interview to work with adults with special needs. I hope I get that job. Caring for elderly people with dementia or for people who are in different stages of Alzheimer would be a good job."

Daniella's story shows that it is possible for people transitioning out of prison to do it successfully. Several factors appear to be at work in her case: a supportive person in prison who helped her through the difficult process of transitioning and believing in herself; a home with caring family members and friends; a boss who understands what prison can do to a person and the challenges of landing on your feet upon leaving; and case workers making sure things are on track, caring for her and wanting to learn from her gender transition, showing her respect and giving her encouragement. If most inmates had these opportunities going for them, I feel confident we could halve the prison population.

Excerpts from Daniella's Letters 2013–2014

California State Prison, Corcoran, California
March 27, 2013

Dear Kristin,

Hello, my name is Daniella Tavake. I am very interested in your project. I also would like to know more about your project. I am a transgender woman. I would like my story written. Please let me know what I must do to be involved. Thank you for caring about us in prison. It means a lot to me.

I am a 37, half Tongan, half white, and I have been sober since 2008. There is more but I am not sure what you want to know.

Well, take care. Hope to hear from you soon.
Sincerely, Daniella Tavake

April 26, 2013

Dear Kris,

Hello. I received your letter and the story about Damond a few hours ago. I just finished watching a movie. I am enclosing the release form. I am not sure about what you want to know about me.

Who I am? That isn't an easy question to answer. There are so many layers to me. I am gentle, kind, caring, and loyal. Then there is the lady in me, but there is a side of me that will not accept anyone's crap if I don't want to and I will fight if I have to. There was a time where I prided myself on being that gangsteria chica! I was down for my man and my homies and would fight for them. Now I do everything in my power to avoid violence at all costs.

I have been coming in and out of prison since 1994. I used to gang bang. I was born and raised in Redwood City, CA (Bay Area). I used to bang hard. I was angry during my first prison term. I felt like everyone in my life abandoned me. I felt like everyone who said they loved me gave up on me. I don't blame them now; back then I did though. I pushed everyone away from me that was good in my life. I chose banging over the people who loved me. I was abusing alcohol and crack while in prison. By the way I have been sober since 2008. I was 19 when I came to prison the first time. I did 5 years on a 5-year prison term even though I had half time. I was in prison from 1994 to 1999. I became institutionalized. I dropped out of being a Norteno in 1997. I came out of the closet in prison in 1998.

I will not lie to you and say it has been such a horrible experience, that I was preyed on or treated badly. That hasn't been my experience. I am not saying that this experience is everyone's experience. The men here treat me the way I represent myself. I am a lady and they, for the most part, treat me as a lady. Don't get me wrong. There are those who think we all are depositors for their dick and sperm. Those find out pretty quick

When I look in the mirror, I want to cry. I am forced to wear a beard. We are supposed to shave with the clippers on the yard three times a week but the clippers are broken. Apparently there will not be new ones for another three weeks. I appealed this.... I don't understand this. I don't even belong in the hole. I was attacked and I was the one who has all the injuries! It was written up in my favor, but I still shouldn't even be in this place. They are not even investigating the fact that the two men who attacked Naomi and I called us faggots! I can't wait to get out so I can put all this behind me! So moving to this horrible prison has not been good thus far.

— Daniella in a letter in 2013 on being transferred from California State Prison to Salinas Valley State Prison

I am not the one. It isn't easy, Kris, but it is something I have learned to deal with. I just want to cry or be by myself but I get through this. I can't tell you why I haven't experienced what most gay men or transgender go through. Maybe it was divine intervention or just wasn't meant to be.

My childhood was a joke! Haha haha! I will not talk about that until I have had the chance to talk to my mother. I love my mommy with my whole being. She did her best to raise me.

I would get out and dream about going back to prison. I was afraid to function in the real world. I never believed I deserve better. I wanted more of course but I believe I couldn't have anything more than a life in prison. Pretty crazy, huh? Well, that was my reality. I would do well at first but always went back to meth and drinking so I could end up in prison. I don't know why the creator has spared me from getting life in prison but I was spared that fate. I go home in Feb 07 2015. I will be going home to my sister's house in San Mateo.

I don't know what else to say. I am open to meeting you in person. Would you like me to send you a visiting form? I think you asking me questions would help me a lot to know what you need. I just want people to know there is hope and there is more to life than dope, alcohol, gangs, prison, etc. I want to give someone who is willing to learn what was given to me.

I really look forward in working with you and sharing my experience with you. Please don't think

any questions are off limits. If I don't feel
comfortable answering and question(s), I don't have
a problem with saying so.

Please be careful, Kris, there are people in
prison that will try to take advantage of you and
use your cause to somehow advance financially. I
will always keep it real and honest with you. I
come in the name of help, nothing more.

Always, Daniella

California State Prison
April 28, 2013

Dear Kris,

Hello, I wanted to put down a few things about
me in prison. Most of these men have never been
taught the basics in life. Like it is okay to
love, it is okay to hurt, it is okay to be sad, it
is okay to feel different. I am friends with the
most unlikely guys in prison. What I mean by this
is the guys who normally don't talk to us girls or
gays. I am friends with them. I am not sure why,
but I believe it is because I am always up front
that I am not out to pursue them sexually. My
best friend, Kris, is in Kern Valley State Prison
and he told me that I am really a woman and am
naturally feminine and naturally nurturing and
that's what puts most guys' defense down with me.
I am not a threat to them. Kris and I have had a
lot of deep conversations about why I am who I am.
I wish you could read some of his writing. He is
a master with words. I miss him so much. I felt

completely safe with him, the first time I ever
felt that way with anyone.

I dream of being a registered nurse. I want to
work with kids. I want to meet a man that can
love me for me and accept me. I want to feel safe
again. I want to settle down, own my own house,
have a beautiful garden, with tomatoes, herbs,
corn, potatoes, an apple tree, an orange tree,
a lemon tree, lime tree, avocado tree. I love
plants. I would love to have a flower garden too.
I want to learn how to sew so I can make my own
drapes, placemats, bed spread. Please take care.
Thank you for helping us get our voices out there.
We all have a story. I am open to you taking
pictures of me when I go home February 07, 2015.
Less than two years. Yeah, I am excited! Hope to
hear from you soon.

Always, Daniella, XXXXX

PS: You're awesome.

Salinas Valley State Prison, California
July 14, 2013

Dear Kris,

Hello sweetie, how is life. I hope all is well. I
have transferred to Salinas Valley State Prison.
This move from the beginning was horrible. I had
to leave my man Johnny in Corcoran. I cried and
cried the night before I left. It sucked, Kris. I
met Johnny at work. I didn't expect to ever fall
in love with him or even move in with him. It all

came unexpectedly. He goes home 8 or 9 months
before me. He lives in Lindsay, CA. We plan on
seeing each other. He gave me faith in love again.

I was transferred to this prison because Corcoran
wasn't an approved prison for transgenders. Well,
I was attacked by this guy 3 days after I got out
of orientation. I wasn't even in Salinas Valley
for 3 weeks before I was sent to the hole. My
girlfriend Naomi got into an argument with some
guy and he started calling her a faggot. I asked
the guy to stop and then he started calling me
a faggot. Anyways, words were exchanged and then
this asshole and his friends attacked Naomi and
I while we were waiting to be released from the
dining hall. We all were sent to the hole for
participating to a riot. Naomi and I are supposed
to be sent back to the yard after our 115's are
heard.[64] I pray they hurry and get this over. I
have not shaved my face in two weeks. When I
look in the mirror, I want to cry. I am forced to
wear a beard. We are supposed to shave with the
clippers on the yard three times a week but the
clippers are broken. Apparently there will not
be new ones for another three weeks. I appealed
this. The horrible thing is none of these inmates
are even appealing this. I don't understand this.
I don't even belong in the hole. I was attacked
and I was the one who has all the injuries! It was
written up in my favor, but I still shouldn't even
be in this place. They are not even investigating
the fact that the two men who attacked Naomi and
I called us faggots! I can't wait to get out so
I can put all this behind me! So moving to this
horrible prison has not been good thus far.

The biggest thing I miss [about] Corcoran is
Johnny, and how he protected me from all the crap.
I was treated like a lady there and not like I was
the new meat on the yard or the new girl in town.
Had to tell so many guys I wasn't interested. There
were some straight, tacky-ass pigs on the yard.
This one older guy came up to me and said, "Hey
baby, where did you come from with them nice tits!"
I was appalled! Not only was this man at least
half a century but he didn't know how to talk to a
lady! Sick! I told him to have some respect and he
was way too damn old to talk like that!

I was sent to this prison because supposedly
this prison has more programs for transgenders!
That is a lie! They don't offer nothing more than
Corcoran! Also I am supposed to have my blood
drawn every three weeks and see the transgender
specialist every 60 days. It has been more than 60
days since my last visit with Dr. Kumar. I'd seen
the Dr. on Thursday and he said he will make sure
I'd be seen by the gender specialist. This place
is horrible. I am going to appeal it as well.

I am sorry to hear about the problems you are
having with CDCR to get approved to visit. It
doesn't surprise me though [that] CDCR would make
it difficult! You mentioned Kern Valley disapproved
you? You wouldn't happen to be trying to see Jenny
again? She is my girlfriend. I was in Kern Valley
on C facility with her. We were in 1 bunk together
and neighbors for a while. I miss her.

When I was young, I liked playing with dolls,
Barbies and when we played house I always wanted
to be the mom. I would wear my mom's shoes and

clothes, even in high school. I absolutely knew that I was different in 9th grade. When I was younger (in elementary school) I never gave it any thought that I liked what little girls liked. No one around me, except my brother and uncle, said it was wrong! My Auntie Barbra (my grandma's sister) told me I was okay and never mind what they said and just be me. I thought it was okay until high school. That is when I knew how coming out would make people hate you — I even hated this guy named Dillan for coming out. I beat him up, fortunately not because he was gay. He challenged me. We became civil afterwards. I respected him 'cause he was not afraid of me even though I beat his ass. Ironically I knew he would fight me again. He was nice. I got into a lot of fights as a kid. I felt I had to prove I was a gangster or a man, more than my friends. I had a lot of feminine ways. Ironically, when I told my friend Eric I was gay at 26, he said he used to know when I was in 7th grade. A lot of friends from high school knew. There were the ones who couldn't accept it and refused to be my friend. It hurts a lot but I just got drunk or high to get over it. I never got over it until I got sober. I am still not good with rejection, but it doesn't make me want to give up and get high or drunk like it used to. I have done a lot of meth in my life.

I have decided to share with you what happen to me as a child. My mom's brother (not the one who got mad at me for acting like a girl) started molesting me when I was four and a half years old. I knew it was wrong, but he convinced me it was okay. My body betrayed me, I hated what he was doing but it still felt good. He tried to

penetrate me but it hurt too much so he would
have sex with me by putting Vaseline between my
legs and have sex with me and kiss me. It was
gross. He would perform oral copulation on me or
masturbate me and make me masturbate him. When I
got older he would make me perform anal copulation
on him. I hated it but it still felt good. Then
while my uncle was abusing me when I was 6 or 7,
my baseball coach had me have orgies with little
boys and masturbate him while he did the same to
me. This only happened for like 6 months with my
coach. He went to jail. I was molested by my uncle
until I was 14 and living with my dad. I got so
drunk I couldn't move and my cousin made me let
him fuck my mouth. I cried and begged him to stop
and he kept smacking me telling me open my mouth.
I told myself from that point on I would never be
a victim. I have been drinking heavily and daily.
The alcohol dulled the pain and made me forget all
the sexual abuse.

I was kicked out at $16\frac{1}{2}$ of my grandparents' house.
I bounced from friends' houses a few times. I
slept with men for money or a warm place to sleep.
I couldn't [get] over the dirtiness, so that
stopped. That is my worst thus far. Then at 17 I
got introduced to meth. I hated it at first and
then I realized I felt nothing on meth. I thought
meth was the answer to everything. It's what
destroyed my life and almost all the good in me.
Well, here is where I will stop for now. As you
can see, I didn't have a great childhood.

Kris, there is more but I will share more the next
time I hear from you. Maybe my story will help
someone. I have fought so many demons and most of

them I have won. I am constantly learning
and changing.

Thank you for your work and kindness. Love,
blessing, and happiness, honey.

Always, Daniella

July 24, 2013

Dearest Kris,

Hello. How are you? I hope and pray all is well.
I am good. I didn't sleep very well last night. I
don't know why. My anxiety has been so, so. I know
how to deal with it so there are times I don't
even realize I am so wound up. I don't realize
until my shoulders and neck are sore.

There is something I believe that needs to be
told about me. All my life I would always be this
tough ass, hard-core gangster chick. But deep down
I am soft, tender, and all woman. I went through
emotions as a woman and every guy I was with
always treated me as a woman. All my life I just
wanted to be loved and most of all be "safe and be
protected" and know with my whole heart and soul
I was safe and protected. I never ever felt that
until I met Kris and Johnny. With them I could be
me, "Daniella," and totally be safe. I could cry
and know they would make sure I was okay. I never
had anyone in my life do that to me. Even if Johnny
and Kris are not in my life, they gave me something
no one else could or would give me. They made me
believe in love and showed me what real love is.

With every man before them I always settled because they were gorgeous but they didn't treat me good. I always gave more of me than they gave me. I was always sacrificing for them but they didn't do it back. Kris and Johnny are drop-dead gorgeous but they love me for me and they both let me know why they chose me, and love me. They ensured me that everything about me was all woman.

I can be Daniella and still be loved for me. Love is something I have always felt. Everyone in my life (not my mom and sister and older sister) has always given up on me or left. Most of the time I would push anyone that got too close away or purposely sabotage our relationship or friendship. I might as well push them away before they leave and I am broken and hurt again. Oh god I know, Kris, this sounds so so sad, but it is how I lived my life for so long. I am still insecure, but I know who I am now and I know how strong I am and even someone hurts me I won't help it or prevent it. All I can do is not invite scally wags into my life and just live life.

I used to believe I had to fight and hurt someone that did me wrong. I can't be that cruel. That is a prison mentality and I refuse to allow myself to be institutionalized again. Don't get me wrong, it isn't easy not to think like I used to. I mean it makes life so much easier in here. However it is cut-throat and I can't live like that. Not caring who I hurt or who I wrong to get what I want isn't the way I want to live my life anymore.

Here is some wisdom Kris gave me. We were (Kris and I) talking about how mainstream Christians say

I live in sin, but I know that Jesus is my savior and God is my father and God made me because he wanted me to be exactly who I am. Kris looked me in my eyes and said, "It would be a sin for anyone to be anything than who they are." That touched me so deeply. I live my life by this. So I quote Kris and say, "It is a sin to be anything but me." Kris knows me, the real me, he says to me when I am being selfish and stubborn, "My queen, where is my Daniella? Because this isn't my Daniella."

Well, I figured I would share this with you. Thank you for listening and being someone who cares to have our stories be told. Love life in love and the rest will follow. Take care.

Always, Daniella

Salinas Valley State Prison October 22, 2013

Dear Kris,

I just got a letter you wrote me in July and you sent it to Corcoran State Prison. I have been in Salinas Valley since June. It is great to hear from you. Your letter made me cry.

I am still not sure I can parole to my sister's house. I have not heard from them since last year. Also they don't know that I am on hormones and I have made this decision because it is how I have always wanted to live my life. I am petrified they will not accept me. They know I like men but not that I always identified myself as a woman. I never really shared this with anyone until I met

Kris. I started hormones in May of this year. Kris still doesn't know yet. He knows I was thinking about it. He told me he would love me no matter what and I would always be his eternal queen. I never had a man kiss my hands and tell me he loved me. It was more than physical with him. Life and circumstances and my choices have always stole everyone I loved from me. So when you tell me you can help me find my king Kris, it makes me cry and makes me believe life can be good.

One thing I do know, I will make it in this life. I will parole and never spend another day inside a cell. I hate this life. As the days go by, I am reassured that this isn't the life for me.

You asked me if I have people who will take care of me. No one has taken care of me and I don't have anyone helping me. I doubt anyone will be there when I get out. This will not stop me from making it, Kris. I promise you I will make it. All I want out of life is to love and be loved. Everything else will just be what I make of life.

I really am not accustomed to a bunch of guys being dirty. It seems like every week it is a new guy doing some creepy, nasty shit! This guy was showering Sunday during dayroom and he called and walked out of the shower naked and asked me if it made me happy to see him naked. I was shocked and appalled. I have never flirted with this guy, never given him the notion that is appropriate, never acted like I would find something like that funny. Kris, I had to go to my friend Christopher a few weeks ago and ask him if I am doing something to make these weird creepy guys think I like things like that. I cried when I asked him. He was pissed and said hell no, it isn't me and I don't do anything to attract that behavior. I am serious — I haven't been around so many guys who are just nasty. It truly wears me thin. You asked me about gangs. I was a Norteno and I am a Norteno dropout. That life was attractive to me because I wanted to be loved and I wanted to belong. Even though I didn't truly belong, I felt like it was the only place I could feel safe because of the sexual abuse. I felt like I could escape from feeling less than a human. I never really liked the violence, but in a way I just wanted someone to hurt like I was hurting. I wanted my dad to love me. My mom cried but she could only do so much. She had her demons she was fighting. My mom wasn't perfect but my dad wasn't a father at all. If I was good, I was his son. He used to call me the white boy of the family. I just wanted my daddy to love me like he loved my sisters and brothers. I found that in my friends and homies. Although I truly wanted to be a girl, being a troublemaker and gang banger was better than just being lost and feeling violated. Drugs and alcohol. Alcohol at first was everything to me. It made me feel complete and drowned all the distress, shame, and pain. Shame for being molested and shame for knowing I should have been a girl. Then I found meth. Oh my goodness, with meth I could forget everything. I was 18 and I had my first willing encounter with a man. I believe meth was the reason I was able to be so open and free. Then I knew I really wasn't attracted to a girl. I was just doing what was accepted.

Now I am so done with drugs. I don't really take Motrin for a headache. I have good friends in here that are lifers that get high and drink and it doesn't bother me. The other day I dreamt I was getting high again. I don't think I will ever not want to get high. I just know I can't. It takes over my life and I turn into a monster. I don't like the person I am on drugs. I am cut-throat and self-serving and selfish. That really isn't me and I just can't go back to that life. I just know that isn't the life for me. I understand why lifers want to escape. I would love to escape this place mentally but I just can't do it because I am using drugs or getting drunk. I believe I might eventually have a drink every now and then when I am free but not to get drunk.

You asked if I was feminine when I was arrested. Yes, I was. I dressed like a boy but ever since I came out I've always shook my hips and butt like a woman. The guys tease me about my walk in here. They always tell me I am the only girl on the yard that is naturally feminine and my walk isn't rehearsed or practiced. My friend Christopher tells me how much he loves my walk and no one can walk like me. I just laugh at him. Kris, he is so sweet to me. I met him 3 years ago in San Quentin and when I came here we started hanging out again. Every meal we eat in the dining hall we sit together. I love being around him. He makes sure I am safe and that I know I am safe. Sometimes he gets upset when I try to fix things he feels it is his place to fix. I just smile and let him be the manly man he is. He is like my Kris when it comes to his belief that it is the man's job to make the woman feel safe and to fix the problems that arise around them. Oh, Kris, it is very difficult at times because I am a very stubborn, strong-willed woman.

Christopher is a skinhead dropout. Yeah, surprising huh! Skinheads are not gay friendly or empathetic to transgenders. Christopher is the opposite.

Kris is a Blood dropout and Mexican and Christopher is a Skin Head dropout. I'm sure you will meet both of them. Kris goes home in 2018 and Christopher has 7 more years. I am a better person because they are a part of me.

When I get out I can't wait to get my nails done. I want to put acrylic on my nails. My nails used to grow so pretty and long, and were strong until I started my hormones therapy. I miss having long nails. My Kris would always grab my hands and ask me to scratch his chest or back. Now they are so damn weak and brittle. I hate it. I really never liked makeup. I will wear mascara, eye liner, and of course wear makeup to conceal the 5 o'clock shadow until I can afford electrolysis on my face and neck. Then I will only wear mascara, eye liner, and lip gloss. My nails will be long and stay manicured.

Thank you so much for sending me this picture. You are so pretty. So are Grace and Janetta. I can't wait to do things like that. I want to support my sisters in prison. There isn't really unity with us in prison. Most girls in here compete with each other. I make it very clear to all the women everywhere I go, I will not do the catty, back-biting, two-faced, bitchy competition that normally goes on with the girls in prison. I do not participate in any of the talking behind each other's back. If I haven't said it to a person's face then I just don't say it. A few of my so-called sisters have tried to pull me into the drama, but I short stopped it real fast. They now know. I just don't hang around most of them.

I just don't understand it, Kris. Why it has to be so hateful. We are the minority, but so many of the girls create problems because they are insecure. I don't understand. I mean I am not perfect, I have my insecurities but I won't just start problems with a girl because I am insecure. Christopher told me I am so different than most women in prison. I just want my sisters to learn to love themselves. Some sell their body and use men to get things but that life isn't for any of us. Christopher tells me they won't get it until someone hurts them. I see so many girls play with these guys' emotions and use them. There should be some kind of self-building classes for us women in here. There are men groups but not one woman's group. I want to appeal this. I need to talk to my friend who is real good at appealing issues and knows the law very well.

Well, Kris, I should close now. I can't wait to go hiking and go to the ocean. I really hope to hear from you. Stay sweet.

Love always, Daniella

Salinas Valley State Prison, Soledad, CA
October 24, 2013

Dear Kris,

Hey you.

THE ONLY PLACE

I was able to talk to my little brother Victor
this morning. He made me cry, he is so good to me.
I met Victor in 2005 and we got close. I used to
treat him like a little brother and he would tell
everyone I was his sister. I met Victor through
my ex, Joseph. I don't dislike Joseph, but I will
never trust him or be his friend. Joseph was the
only man I loved that hit me and choked me. If I
wasn't strong, he probably would have hurt me. I
watched my mom hurt and good girlfriends get hit.
I would be damned if I ever let a man hit me ever
again. Kris, I hate women beaters. They make me
sick to my stomach. I won't fight a man anymore,
but I will fight a man if he ever hits me.

You know it is pretty crazy how you would have
told me I would grow so much in this prison term,
I wouldn't have believed you in 2008 when I got
arrested. When I got sentenced and sent to San
Quentin in 2010, I was so angry until I got to
Kern Valley. I just couldn't believe I had failed.
It wasn't society's fault or my friends, it was my
fault. I failed and I came back. I had to accept
it and I had to get over it on my own. I did. I
am not delusional, there will be failures in the
future but I will learn from them just like I did
this time. I won't repeat the same failures again.

My mommy let me be me. Around 5 or 6, I would
dress up in my mommy's clothes and wear her heels.
I loved everything feminine. I would wear my
mommy's rings. Ironically, I don't like jewelry
much, even though growing up I loved wearing my
mommy's. I am listening to New Edition, I grew
up on all these songs. I can't wait to get out. I
want to go shake my ass! Haha Haha Haha Haha! I

miss dancing. I think a lot of jewelry is tacky. I like simple jewelry.

My thoughts are scattered right now. Take real good care of yourself. Love and blessings.

Love always, Daniella

November 21, 2013

Dear Kris,

Hello. I got your cute postcard of Stinson Beach. Thank you. You asked me four questions and I am going to answer them.

You asked if I don't get a hold of my sister where will I parole. I don't know, Kris. I don't have an answer to that. I will be homeless.

I started my hormones March of this year. How did it change me psychologically? I don't think it changed me too much. I hate being called him, sir, he, Mr., or Daniel or Danny. Before hormones I didn't mind Danny but now I don't like it. I am truly intense with my emotions. I cry more when I get my feelings hurt, instead of getting angry. When I am hurting it seems like it hurts more now than before. At first I really was moody and an emotional wreck for the first five months. I was bitchy. Smile. Ha ha! Ha ha! I have always thought I was a woman since I was five. I never shared it with anyone. It invoked a lot of feelings when I came out in prison and the nun called me mija, mamas, baby girl, girl, she, etc. I believe that is why I became so comfortable in prison because I was treated as a woman and it never was questioned. I was a woman. So when I went home I felt out of place. I felt like I didn't belong out of prison. I used to dream of being sent back to prison and in my dreams I was always happy and felt like I belonged. I wasn't being treated like a woman when I went home and it truly bothered me. I have experienced that a lot in my life.

Norteno is a Mexican faction in prison and on the street that is called Nuestra Familia (N.F.) that started the Nortenos. You can look up the N.F. on the Internet. I was a soldier for them. I wasn't that important but I became a Norteno when I was 19 and I came to prison.

Before I go on, I would like you to please make sure you include that I in no way agree with gangs and would never promote gang life. I loathe anything to do with gangs and that life. It is all lies and none of it is worth someone losing their life or getting in prison. So please know what I say: by no means am I proud of what I did when I was a gang member.

I have gang tattoos I will be getting removed. I have XIV on my neck. X4 on my right arm, Puro Norte on my chest. The 14th letter is "N," which stands for Nortenos/Norte. Nortenos are from Northern California. General population is where all the NFs and Nortenos are (I am SNY/Sensitive Needs Yard). I made weapons and I was in a few positions of leadership.

I am going to come back to this subject. I really

hate talking about this part of my life. It takes so much out of me.

One of my biggest fears is I will not ever find true real love outside of prison. I will not ever find a man to just love me for me. I am scared I will die alone. What is important to me is going to work, coming home, and making dinner for my man. Making his lunch so he can take it with him to work. Wake up early and make him and I breakfast every morning. I want a real home. This is home to me, Kris. This is love. This is what I dream of. I don't want anything but a real home with a good man. The fancy cars, big bank account don't really matter to me.

There is no program today because all of the correctional officers called in sick because of the Super Bowl.

The transgender doctor changed my hormones from Premarin to Estradiol pills. Well, I broke out in a rash, my ankles swelled up, I was an emotional wreck and I was flashing and angry and arguing with everyone. He lied to me and said CDCR is stopping Premarin prescriptions. Well, he lied. I told him Estradiol had a bad reaction in my body and Premarin never did. Well, he is stopping the Estradiol and continuing my Premarin. I am so happy.

Well, I should close. Love, Daniella XOXO

Salinas Valley State Prison
February 25, 2014

Dearest Kris

Hello. How is life? I hope all is well. I am
well. I received your beautiful postcard. Your
kindness made me cry and I am crying as I
am writing you. Mere words can't describe my
gratitude for your kindness.

I found out there is a guy that is related to my
dad's side of my family. He is very sweet and I
really like him. He is from San Mateo. He knows a
lot of Tongan, but he is white. He is Caribbean and
has a Caribbean accent and Tonga, fresh-off-the-
boat accent all in one. He really treats me like
family. When he sees me he hugs me and holds me
and asks in Tongan if I am okay and how I am doing.

Thank you for saying I am brave. Kristin, for so
long I drowned my feelings and emptiness in meth.
16 years to be precise. I wanted to be at home,
but I couldn't be brave enough to say, "Hey, I am
not a man. I really am a WOMAN!"

I used to wake up crying because I missed prison.
While I was in prison, I would sabotage myself
and fight to get more time, just so I could stay.
Eventually my old man would make me behave. The
longest I stayed out was almost 2 years from 2000
to 2002. Of course I went back to meth and came
back. Then in 2003 I got out for 3 months and 2007
I stayed out for 11 months. The first time I got
out in 1999 I stayed out for 5 months and went
back 10 months for a DUI.

I can't wait to learn how to do my makeup.

This guy I was in Kern Valley State Prison with saw me recently and he was shocked. He said my body has changed and I am starting to have curves like a woman. I left Kern Valley 2 years ago. I have been working out a lot again. I feel so much better about my body now that I am working out.

I talked to Shiloh for 20 minutes this afternoon during day room. She is cute. Her and I were talking about the battle we go through with not fighting someone when they disrespect us. This pig grabbed my ass today and I checked him. He tried to justify his actions with some lame excuse that I hug more than one guy on this yard. I told him to stay away from me. 2 years ago I would have punched him and fought him. The new Daniella just walked away. I am really proud of the woman I am growing to be.

I should close for now. Smile please. Love,
Daniella XOXOXO

March 19, 2014

Dear Kristin

Hello. It's Daniella again. I am well. I hope all is well with you.

So I have not heard from my family still. I really don't know what is going on. Oh well. That is life.

So how was your trip? I hope good.

I kicked it with my girl, Mercedes, yesterday.
She is so terrible sometimes. I love her so much.
I always have fun hanging out with her. We will
hang out tomorrow morning on yard again. I miss
my girl. It's funny because her and I are together
the whole time on yard and there are some girls
I don't talk to that talk to Mercedes and they
walk up to us and talk to Mercedes and they really
think they bother me. Mercedes and me laugh when
they leave, because Mercedes and I know none
of them bother me at all. A few of these girls
attempt to get to me every day and I just move
on and smile. I refuse to allow anyone to get the
best of me.

Love, Daniella XOXOXO

Salinas Valley State Prison
April 25, 2014

Dear Kris,

Hello honey. How are you? I hope everything is
well. I am okay. I am so damn worried about Chris.
I will go into that later.

I apologize for not writing sooner. I have been
focusing all my energy on helping Chris and it has
taken a lot out of me.

I just want to be able to know I can count on
someone and I can depend on a man when I need
it. My only experience with this has been with my
best friend, Chris. So my friendship with him will
be forever, but I want more than a friend when I

go home. Right now I need just a friend with no sex or strings attached. I have never gone home single. I have always left my old man in prison and I felt like I was betraying him by leaving him. I don't want that feeling ever again. I am happy to leave prison for the first time in my life ever.

Well I should close for now. I hope to hear from you soon. The mail stamped the envelope say[ing] they sent your visiting questionnaire to the visiting sergeant. I will write you when I get your approval back.

Take care of yourself, honey. Love always, Daniella XOXOXO

May 10, 2014

Dear Kristin,

Hello! How are you?

I have never really been a girl that slept around and I don't do casual sex. I don't agree with friends with benefits. One person always falls in love. I tried the friends with benefits twice. One time I fell in love and got hurt. The second time he fell in love and got hurt. That comes to being courted. I love being courted. I believe that is how I have become friends with every man I was with before I fell in love, and he fell in love. I would love to be taken out to dinner and walk on the beach with a guy. One of my favorite things to do is go camping. My Ne-Ne and Papa (Grandma and

Grandpa) used to take all of us kids camping. I would love to go with my sister, mom, two nieces, and the guy I am with. I love the ocean. I have never shared my love for the ocean with any man outside of prison. When I was a kid my mom used to take us to the beach and we would BBQ or she would bring stuff to make deli sandwiches. It was so much fun.

I can cook and bake really well. There are some things I cook I don't think anyone can make better. I love my meat sauce that my Ne-Ne taught me how to make. I, Mom and sister know how to make it but I just like mine better. I like my lasagna better too. I love my chocolate chip cookies. Oh Kris, my Mom makes the best peanut butter cookies. I have tried to make them and I never like them. Oh my Mom's are so good — can't wait to go home and ask my Mom to make me some peanut butter cookies.

Well, I should close for now. I hope to hear from you soon. Take care, sweetie. Love always, Daniella XOXOXOXO

June 17, 2014

Dear Kristin,

Hey honey! How are you? I have not heard from you in a while. I hope all is well. I am well. We are on lockdown. The Mexicans (ex-Northerners), blacks, and two black gay boys got into a riot. The one who started all the drama was a big-mouthed gay boy named Naomi.

I just found out a girlfriend of mine is in Chowchilla. She tried to get Salinas Valley to approve us to correspond. Of course, this sorry prison denied it, even though Chowchilla approved it. Oh well, I go home the end of January and I will write her then. Last I heard she was living in San Mateo and working. She didn't have a criminal record as an adult. So I was surprised to hear she was in prison. Lindsey will be surprised. I am now on hormones. She knew I was gay but not that I would ever live my life as a woman. Oh well, I know she will love me no matter what. She was one of the rare friends I met that was loyal to me.

My Christopher is going through it with his wife right now. It hurt me a lot that he is hurting and I can't help him. I wish I could help but I can't. He is my friend and it sucks not being able to help. He thinks his marriage is over.

Well I should close for now. I am 7 months to the house. Ya hoo! I am stoked. Smile, honey. Love, Daniella XOXOX

June 28, 2014

Dear Kristin,

Hey! How is life? Hope good. We are on lockdown again. Some kind of security breach happened on C-facility so they locked down the institution. They are parking officers off our yard to search the facility. We are protective custody inmates on a facility and there is no way we could even come in contact with them or even communicate. Sucks.

I received a notice that you have been approved to visit me. Here is the visiting office's number and extension (831) 678-5500 Ext. 5708. You are allowed to bring $50.00.

Kristen, I truly despise prison! I am so over lockdowns and not being able to run every other day, consistently. Always, Daniella XOXO

July 8, 2014

Dear Kris,

Hello. I received your card today. It is good to hear from you. I am waiting to hear from Records to find out my exact date. Yeah, I did write TGI twice but I still have not heard from them. I received a letter from them concerning a letter I wrote them in 2013. I have not ever heard from Janetta.

We are on lockdown. The white institution is on lockdown. Something was found in a facility. I only hang out with myself when I am on the yard. I talk to a few people, but I am not trying to get caught up in anything.

I am really scared, Kris. I may be paroling to no family. I have not heard from them in quite some time. I sent a letter to my mom and sister and told them both I feel abandoned by both of them. I don't know if I will ever hear from them.

I am down right now. Take care. Love, Daniella

July 10, 2014

Dear Kris,

Hello. I am not doing so well. I am so depressed.
I just want to wither away and just disappear.
I have never felt this way. it is not healthy.
Really it isn't. I am constantly sad and unsure
of myself. My normal confidence is slipping away.
It isn't working, honey, and I don't know why. I
have felt like this the last month and a half.
Sometimes I just cry myself to sleep. Last night
I prayed and begged to be okay. I am not okay. I
have never thought I should ever take depression
pills but I am thinking about it. Really I am. I
keep telling myself I will be okay but I don't
believe that myself. I just want to go home and
leave this awful place. I can't believe I ever
thought this is where I belonged. Sometimes
I doubt myself. I have never felt unpretty or
insecure of my beauty. I have always felt like I
am the baddest bitch, no matter who is around.
I don't feel like that. This is very new to me.
I have never been with an ugly guy. Girls have
always wondered how I have always got the guy
none of the girls with pretty long hair, huge
asses, and huge tits couldn't get. I am pretty
but I am bald. So I have always had to believe
in myself more than most girls. My weight has
always gone up and down. I am getting thinner now
because I am getting too old to carry any extra
weight. I lost 7 pounds. I was 225, now I am 218.
I am just a big-bones girl but I should be more
[like] 200 or 205. 13 more pounds.

Well, I need to work out. I am going to close now.
I hope to hear from you soon.

Always, Daniella XOXOXOXO

July 14, 2014

Dearest Kristin,

Great news! My release date is December 7, 2014.
Yes, 2014! I just found out. I am writing Janetta
when I am done writing you. Will you please write
her and let her know. Thank you. I will be home
for Christmas. I am so excited. In the 20 years
I have been in and out of prison, I have never
gotten a 90-day early kick!

My friend who was adopted by my Grandma's sister's
family gave me a UB-40 CD and my Christopher just
put it on. I love this CD. I grew up on this CD.
I was 14 when this album came out. 1990. I know
every song. It's Labor of Love II. It reminds me
of my brother, Peter. He loves Reggae. I started
listening to Reggae because of him. My big brother
is in his addiction bad. His mind is gone from all
the meth he has done.

Pretty soon I will be home wearing heels, skirts,
dresses, real makeup, and I can't wait to get my
nails done! I want long nails so bad, Kris. You
don't understand how bad I want to slip into some
heels and a cute dress and go job hunting with a
cute-ass handbag and briefcase.

Oh yeah! I have a plant! Yes I do. It's a Japanese red chili pepper plant. My Chris germinated some seeds and now I have my plant. He is germinating green bell pepper seeds right now. Kris, I am so excited. I love plants and I miss having plants. Now I will have two plants! I can't wait to go hiking. I love hiking.

Well, I should close for now. I hope to hear from you soon. Smile for me, please.

Love, Daniella XOXOXO

November 14, 2014

Hey you! How is everything? I got a letter from Janetta and I wrote back two months ago, but have not heard from her. She offered to pick me up on my parole date. I let her know I will be going home December 07, 2014. I would like her or one of her co-workers to come pick me up and [drive] me to my sister's house. I am extremely excited that I am finally going home. Me and my best friend Chris are together. He and his wife are no longer together. I love him like I have never loved anyone before him. We are so good together. It will kill me to leave him here, but he will be home soon. You will meet him when he comes home. He just wants me to do good.

Kris, I would love to meet you. It will be awesome to participate in the project. I am so stoked to go home and start my life over. I am not delusional, I know I have a lot of hard work ahead of me. I am stoked to wear female undergarments, female clothes, and shoes. I can't wait to have a purse! I can't wait to get my nails done. I want long nails so bad, Kris, I want a French manicure. Oh and to wear heels!

Love, Daniella xoxoxo

Daniella getting her nails done with Kevin in San Mateo, California, April 2015

EPILOGUE

At the end of March 2015, I received a Facebook message from Ashley Diamond's sister Diana, letting me know that a reporter from the *New York Times* was coming to interview Ashley's family in two weeks' time—and that Ashley had been transferred from Baldwin State Prison to Georgia State Prison in Reidsville, a maximum security prison. Her family and her lawyers at Southern Poverty Law Center felt that Ashley's transfer from a close security to a maximum security prison was most likely retaliation by the Georgia Department of Corrections because of the lawsuit she had filed against them on February 19, 2015, and because she was receiving considerable and often favorable attention from the media. Ashley wrote to me and said, "The electric chair here is a tourist attraction." Where would they send her next?

My initial reaction when her sister told me about the reporter was that a *New York Times* article would help Ashley's case—the story would cross oceans and move people. But I quickly felt concern for her safety: would an article in such a big media outlet increase the risk of her being abused in prison? Then I reminded myself that Ashley understood this risk better than anyone. From what she had shared with me, I imagined she would feel it was a risk worth taking, she wouldn't want it any other way.

At the time I chatted with Ashley's sister on Facebook, her family had not heard from her in over a week. Diana said she could not stop crying. She had not seen her sister in more than three years, and she was scared knowing that her sister, a nonviolent woman who had already been gang raped, threatened, and tortured in prison, was housed with convicted males who were killers and rapists. Then Diana wrote me something that disturbed me even more, a proof of downright evilness: "My mom sent Ashley a picture you sent her, and they tried to make her throw it away, but she refused so they made her cut it up small and that really hurt her!!"

One Saturday morning in early April, I picked up the paper edition of the *New York Times* on the doorstep and saw the headline: "U.S. Supports Transgender Inmate in Lawsuit—Prisons Cannot Deny Hormone Therapy, Justice Dept. Says."[65] Ashley was right there on the front page, and I felt proud and excited. The article said: "It is believed to be the first time that the Justice Department has weighed in on the question of whether hormone therapy for transgender inmates is necessary medical care that states are required to provide."

Two days later, on April 6, there she was again—on the front page of the paper edition, the second article in the *New York Times* focused on Ashley's family and her criminal case, with the headline: "Every Day I Struggle—Transgender Inmate Cites Attacks in Men's Prison."[66] All the while I was in touch with Diana, who said that she and Ashley's mother were excited about the attention Ashley's case had received. A day or two later, Elton John and Michael Stipes (lead singer of the band R.E.M.) released a joint statement condemning the abuse of Ashley and calling for equal rights for transgender inmates. Newspapers later reported that Ashley was now receiving hormones, although still too low a dose, at Georgia State Prison. As for her other complaints and her sentence, she is still being treated as a dangerous person and a freak, and the abuse against her continues. Her appeal to be moved to a less brutal, less dangerous prison was denied later in April.

Shortly afterward, Ashley's family made the nearly five-hour drive from Rome to Reidsville to visit her. When I asked Diana how it went, she answered, "They [Georgia Department of Corrections] denied us [visitation] and said she is fine, no need for an emergency visit. Rude, rude, rude."

Reporting abuse, writing to the press, participating in lawsuits against correctional institutions, ending up in physical fights (even if not voluntarily) had dire consequences for most of the women in this book. Time after time, many people who are incarcerated who were trying to defend themselves or speaking up, ended up in solitary confinement, or in some cases even have received a second and third strike to their list, leading them to live in prison until their death.

As this book goes to press, I still haven't been able to visit Ashley, Jazzie, or Donna in prison. When I asked Donna to send me a visitation form, she contacted the state corrections institution's media department, who told her that I needed to apply. But I knew from experience that applying to interview Donna as a journalist was not likely to bear fruit. I may be able to visit her one day, if I can get on her visitation list. I'm keeping in touch with the other women too, by mail and by phone.

A few weeks after I visited Jennifer at Kern Valley State Prison in February 2015, she sent me a letter: "Dear Kris. My dear friend and sister! I'm sooo happy to have had the honor to meet you face to face in person! I really enjoyed the lunch and our conversation. I especially enjoyed taking the photos with you!" Before that visit, Jennifer had asked if she could keep writing to me after the book project was done, and I had said yes. After the visit, I was certain we would keep in touch. Jennifer, who will be imprisoned for the rest of her life, sent me an article from the Canadian *National Post* with the headline: "Ontario will now assess transgender inmates based on identity, not anatomy."[67] The new policy will make sure that inmates are referred to by their chosen names and pronouns such as "he," "she," or "ze," are allowed to retain prostheses, and can choose the gender of the staff person performing searches. This is at least a sign of progress, but of course this is in Canada, not the US, although online news reports announced in 2014 that a New York jail was going to open a separate wing for transgender people only.

I think of the women in this book as activists. They are making history, teaching us about the abuse that has been and continues to be done to them.

Grace from Liberia, who generously shared her story, is only one example of the inhumane treatment LGBTQI asylum seekers receive in "detention camps." Many have been locked up and treated as criminals without having committed a single crime. A friend, himself a gay man from Guatemala who was finally granted asylum after many years, sent me a news article from Fusion. A six-month investigation by three Fusion reporters found that the treatment of immigrants in this country is sometimes so torturous that many ask to be sent home again to their even more dangerous homelands in Central and South America. The conditions for transgender women locked up by Immigration and Customs Enforcement (ICE) "are humiliating, dangerous and even deadly. On any given night, some 75 transgender prisoners are detained by ICE. A significant portion are women who have requested asylum."[68]

Shortly before this book was finished, I spoke by phone with Janetta. Since I finished her chapter, she made several trips to Florida to renew ties with her family. She was doing therapy twice a week and felt stronger. Janetta and her colleagues at various organizations had organized demonstrations in San Francisco during the #blacklivesmatters campaigns that were occurring nationwide. Several transgender identified women of color had recently been killed—at least one every week in the US since the beginning of 2015. I had attended a demonstration in San Francisco after Taja Gabrielle DeJesus, a 36-year-old transgender woman of color and a friend of Janetta's, was found fatally stabbed multiple times in a stairwell early on the morning of February 1.[69] The TGI Justice Project, together with their friends, allies, and colleagues, had set up a new coalition, the Trans*[70] Activists for Justice and Accountability (TAJA)[71] and spread their message on Facebook: "We are united in anger and outrage over the murder of Taja de Jesus." They demanded more support from white allies to help stop violence against transgender women of color and for putting aside plans for a new jail in San Francisco—instead building affordable and accessible shelters and housing for people with gender identity issues.

On Thursday August 9, 2015 Shiloh's lawyer Herman Hoying called me with the news; Shiloh had won! A historic settlement was reached with the California prison system that would give her gender-reassignment surgery and move her to a female prison. He asked if he could use a photograph of Shiloh from the book for the press release. The next day her story spread across the country like a tornado. The day Shiloh heard the news it was her birthday.

Daniella is educating her community in San Mateo and her employers about the needs of transgender people.

Tanesh and her husband are currently participating in workshops for men who are in relationships with transgender women. The sessions are held at St. James Infirmary, a health and safety clinic for sex workers and their families in San Francisco.

Almost daily, I ask myself the question: How can any sane, democratic society justify keeping transgender women in maximum security prisons for men? Why are we locking up a nonviolent woman in a male prison, allowing her to be gang raped and beaten? Why is that itself not considered a criminal act? In Ashley Diamond's case, who decided that the alleged thefts and nonviolent burglaries she is accused of are worse than allowing her to be raped by six men in prison and doing nothing about it?

The New York Times Magazine had a cover story in March 2015 called "Prison Planet: How do we treat the world's most dangerous criminals? And what does it say about us?" The same issue included an article titled: "The Radical Humanness of Norway's Halden Prison—The goal of the Norwegian penal system is to get inmates out of it."[73]

Billions of dollars are spent every year to lock away people in US prisons, yet it has not made US society any safer. Quite the opposite is true. The decline in criminal activity in the US owes little or nothing to our massive expansion of the numbers of people we lock away. American prisons are notoriously expensive, punitive, and crowded, yet have a very high recidivism rate. Few resources are spent preparing inmates to leave prison and, when they do, become positive members of society. While researching and writing this book I repeatedly heard stories both from participants in my project and from the news about the fostering of aggression in prison—even to the point of prison guards forcing inmates to fight with each other so they could bet on the results for their own entertainment.[74] San Francisco's Sheriff Deputy Scott Neu was accused of forcing three women (two of them transgender) to perform sexual acts on him in 2006, yet was still allowed to work inside in the city's jail where he continued to abuse and bully inmates, buying them cheeseburgers to silence them, forcing them to fight for entertainment.[75,76] Coming from Norway, which treats even convicted mass-murderers less harshly than some of our nonviolent inmates, the overarching lesson I take away from my research is that prisons are breeding grounds for criminality. They grow mental illness, irreversible in many cases. Even one of the current justices of the US Supreme Court, Anthony Kennedy,[77] has recognized that the criminal justice system "is not human." He stated, "we have no interest in corrections."

Some may argue: What do we owe a "criminal"? To which I would answer that all of us suffer when someone's humanity is denied in the way experienced by so many of our people who end up in US prisons.

We judge people's guilt or innocence, not by what they have actually, provably done but by their life stories. We judge them for the way they were born, for the way they look, and for the way their grandparents lived.

We betrayed these women long before they became adults by not believing what they told us about who they are, by not giving them the opportunity as children to dress and act as who they were. And then when we lock some of them up, we torture them, watch them being raped, and forget that they exist. We take our own freedom for granted. We assume our own sins are easily forgotten—but we do not forget theirs.

We have a responsibility to do better, to make up for the cruel and unusual punishment they have suffered. Call this our shared walk to reconciliation—a walk to find the good in ourselves, beginning by helping people who only ask us to recognize them for who they are. It is never too late to take their hands and lead them across the bridge they thought was burned.

ABOUT THE AUTHOR

Norwegian-born Kristin Schreier Lyseggen, author of The Boy Who Was Not a Lesbian, has studied and worked as a journalist and photographer in Oslo, Birmingham (UK), Bangkok and San Francisco. Now based in Berkeley, California, she is working on long-term independent projects, often with her husband, child psychiatrist Herb Schreier, including a film-project on sexual abuse and human trafficking, and a book about transgender youth in rural areas and townships of South Africa's Eastern Cape. Kristin exhibits and presents her work internationally.

kristinl.com

ACKNOWLEDGMENTS

Thanks to all the strong women in this book and the many other terrific people I met on the way who shared their stories with me. Thanks to Naomi Schneider at University of California Press who connected me with the editor and publicist. Thanks go to my editor, Carolyn Bond, whose give-and-take with me over the creation of the book has made it something we both can be proud of. It was clear that she shared a genuine interest for these women and their strivings. Little did I know how much my publicist, Kathlene Carney, could give to this project, even before she was "officially" involved. A big thanks to my neighbor, design professor Mary Scott, who brought me together with the book designers Kathrin Blatter and Andrew Johnson at un-studio in San Francisco, sensitive artists who wanted the book's appearance to match the intensity of the stories told within. To Jorunn Solli who always brings me back to my center, who is available always to discuss, share and to give. To my transcriber, Jo Ann Wall, and collaborator, Laurie Gibson, whose enthusiasm for the subject has given me heart.

Thanks to Jamison Green, WPATH president, colleague, and friend who connected me with Miss Major and Janetta, with whom I have had several fine discussions on such a variety of topics in so many places on the planet.

To my sister Beate Rostin, a font of support, for her love and friendship. To Fresh! White, a knowledgeable friend and companion always willing to share a much-needed "pint" and a laugh and who constantly reminded me of my strength when I felt a little under the weather. To my family in Norway for their unconditional love. To Marcus Holje and Bo Høilund Martinsen whom I met writing my first book, *The Boy Who Was Not a Lesbian*, lifelong friends and always there for me sharing their humor and interests as their own lives have taken wonder-filled turns. To all the people who took me in during my life and work in Birmingham, UK, "Brum" as they call it. There are too many wonderful Brummies from India, Poland, Pakistan, Germany, Hungary, and Hawaii to mention. Oh what a place to learn! Richard Sealy, my dear friend (who didn't know there was such a word for a human until he was five or six years old when someone told him he was black) who started my quest to really try and understand racism. Thanks to the Bedouins of the Negev desert for taking a woman photographer into their homes, and especially the women who were in a struggle on more than one front; to Birgit Möller in Germany, a close friend who invites Herb and me to present our work there. To my friends Salvador and Kevin and their mother, Milagro, whose perilous escape from persecution across the border always stands out as a reminder for me of the importance of work like this that must be done.

To new friends from Texas, Amanda Blackhear and Felishia Porter, whom we met at the airport in Bangkok and who reluctantly jumped into our cab because there was a man there with me; they became a source of support and inspiration. Thanks to my other neighbors Jack Litewka and Jane W. Ellis, who were always there with a news story on the goings-on in the transgender community and ideas on how to promote the book, get reviews and are always "selling" it.

To my fellow artists and friends Cecilie Berggaard, Ole Marius Pettersen, Bjørg Thorhallsdottir, Dale Sparage, Tomm Wilgaard Christiansen, Ryan Cassata, Robert Powell, Alex Sander Fossoy, A Lise Woldsund Melhus, Jonathan Day, Leigh Ann van der Merwe, Hope Frye, Anni Friis Røyem, Thabisa Moyikwa, Stevie Stallmeyer, Nancy Hollander, Stephen Portugese, Katrine Storebø, Milo Manopoulos Beitman, Dania Sacks March, Deborah Lichtman, Aiden Key, Jackie Beck, Even Rognlien, Ariel Adams, Mikael Scott Bjerkeli, Tone Maria Hansen, Kathrine Sjuls Nygard, Harmil Pardesi, Anna Romanczuk, Sofie Brune, Kine Michelle Bruinera, Bal Rayat, Arsha Arshad, Michelle Lord, and the good people at Symmetry Health Center.

Thank you Edition One Books, Ben Zlotkin and Ken Coburn for your generosity and invaluable help. Thank you, team terrific Photolab in Berkeley, Ginger Fierstein, Mark Weaner, Melissa K. Smith, Joe Glass, Andrea McLaghlin, Drea Gomez, and the rest of the crew, whom our Siberian Suki loves as well. Thank you Looking Glass, especially my very own Rolleiflex expert Carol. To publishing task force Sharon Goldinger and Amy Collins, last-minute saviors. To MJ Bogatin, a lawyer whose advice was extremely useful and comforting.

And last, but not least, to my husband, Herb, for his unflagging support and belief in me and the projects (this my second foray into the crazy world of publishing), constantly reading whatever I thrust in front of him, constantly urging me on. He knows dearly how much our love means to me.

NOTES

[1] Bryan Stevenson, *Just Mercy: A Story of Justice and Redemption* (New York: Spiegel & Grau, 2014).

[2] The term "gender identity issues," or "gender identity differences," covers all translated identities such as transgender, trans*, gender variant, gender nonconforming, intersex, gender queer, and so on.

[3] Jamison Green, PhD, lawyer, sociologist, president of the World Professional Association for Transgender Health (WPATH) and author of *Becoming a Visible Man*.

[4] "Gender dysphoria" is the preferred term over "gender identity disorder," as most professionals no longer see this as an illness.

[5] Valerie Jenness and Sarah Fenstermaker, "Agnes Goes to Prison: Gender Authenticity, Transgender Inmates in Prisons for Men, and Pursuit of 'The Real Deal,'" *Gender & Society* (February 2014), 28:1, 5–31, http://gas.sagepub.com/content/28/1/5.

[6] Lambda Legal; http://www.lambdalegal.org/sites/default/files/publications/downloads/transgender_prisoners_in_crisis.pdf.

[7] One in six black men had been incarcerated as of 2001. If current trends continue, one in three black males born today can expect to spend time in prison during his lifetime; http://www.naacp.org/pages/criminal-justice-fact-sheet.

[8] Valerie Jenness, Cheryl L. Maxson, Kristy N. Matsuda, and Jennifer Macy Sumner, "Violence in California Correctional Facilities: An Empirical Examination of Sexual Assault," Center for Evidence-Based Corrections, Department of Criminology, Law and Society, University of California Irvine, California, 2007.

[9] Nicholas Ray, "Lesbian, Gay, Bisexual and Transgender Youth: An Epidemic of Homelessness," National Gay and Lesbian Task Force Policy Institute; www.taskforce.org.

[10] Jaime Grant, Lisa Mottet, and Justin Tanis, "Injustice at Every Turn: A Report of the National Transgender Discrimination Survey," National Center for Transgender Equality, National Gay and Lesbian Task Force, 2012.

[11] Leonard Shengold, *Soul Murder: The Effects of Childhood Abuse and Deprivation*. (New Haven: Yale University Press, 1989)

[12] Daniel Paul Screber, http://www.nybooks.com/articles/archives/1990/nov/08/another-soul-murder/.

[13] "Memoirs of a Chain Gang Sissy," which she had a friend upload onto YouTube for her.

[14] Keith J. Conron, ScD, MPH, Gunner Scott, BA, Grace Sterling Stowell, MA, and Stewart J. Landers, JD, MCP, "Transgender Health in Massachusetts: Results from a Household Probability Sample of Adults, *Am J Public Health*, January 2012.

[15] http://www.huffingtonpost.com/2013/04/02/kayla-moore-death_n_3000575.html.

[16] The Trans Murder Monitoring (TMM) project was initiated in April 2009 in order to systematically monitor, collect, and analyze reports of homicides of transgender

people worldwide. http://www.transrespect-transphobia.org/uploads/downloads/2013/ TDOR2013english/ TvT-TDOR2013PR-en.pdf.

[17] Huffington Post, Mara Keisling, Dec. 30, 2013 http://www.huffingtonpost.com/mara-keisling/ 10-transgender-wins-of-20_1_b_4505453.html; Arizona Senate Bill 1045, dubbed "no loo for you" by local residents, would permit business owners to restrict access to gender-specific facilities based on a person's gender identity or gender expression. Introduced by Arizona Representative John Kavanagh. Transgender Law Center, San Francisco 2013.

[18] The Netflix series is based on Piper Kerman's memoir, *Orange Is the New Black: My Year in a Women's Prison.* Laverne Cox is making a film, *Free CeCe,* with producer and director Jacqueline Gares, about the arrest and imprisonment of transgender woman CeCe McDonald, to be released in 2016.

[19] The Crips and the Bloods are rival violent, often murderous gangs. Founded in Los Angeles in the '60s, they spread across the US and now are a dominating presence in the US prison system.

[20] Levels of security at a prison system's various facilities are usually classified on a range that includes minimum, medium, and maximum security. County jails and detention centers, intended for nonfelony offenses or short-term stays, are where people arrested are first held, or where they are awaiting trial or transfer to "mainline" institutions.

[21] Embarrassing someone by sharing information about that person without his or her consent.

[22] The incident was captured on many cell phone and digital video cameras and later turned into a major motion picture called *Fruitvale Station.*

[23] http://kalw.org/post/transgender-immigrant-detainees-face-isolation-detention.

[24] http://sfist.com/2014/06/27/the_gay_rights_fight_started_in_cal.php.

[25] ILGA (International Lesbian, Gay, Bisexual, Trans and Intersex Association); http://old.ilga.org Statehomophobia/ILGA_map_2013_A4.pdf.

[26] http://www.theguardian.com/world/2012/mar/19/nobel-peace-prize-law-homosexuality.

[27] Laurel Anderson, "Punishing the Innocent: How the Classification of Male-to-Female Transgender Individuals in Immigration Detention Constitutes Illegal Punishment under the Fifth Amendment, *Berkeley Journey of Gender, Law, and Justice,* May 21, 2010, p. 6.

[28] Seth Hemmelgarn, "Transwoman Sentenced to Prison after Stabbing," *The Bay Area Reporter,* April 17, 2008.

[29] Close security is a level between medium and maximum security.

[30] "Pro se" means advocating on one's own behalf before a court, rather than being represented by a lawyer. Courts are seeing an increase in the numbers of litigants who represent themselves.

31 Equal Justice Initiative: http://www.eji.org/files/Slavery%20in%20America%20short%20 version.pdf.

32 The Southern Poverty Law Center (SPLC) was founded by Alabama lawyer and businessman Morris Dees and another young Montgomery lawyer, Joe Levin. They took pro bono cases few others were willing to pursue at the time, some of which resulted in desegregation of recreational facilities, the reapportionment of the Alabama Legislature, the integration of the Alabama State Troopers, and reforms in the state prison system. Southern Poverty Law Center was formally incorporated in 1971, and civil rights activist Julian Bond was named the first president. They have received numerous death threats from groups like the Ku Klux Klan.

33 Mark S. Hamm, *In Bad Company: America's Terrorist Underground* (Boston: Northeastern University Press, 2002), p. 12. Hitler's paramilitary storm troopers had a significant gay element, initially approved by Hitler (see *Gay Berlin* by Robert Beachy) until SS head Heinrich Himmler announced that all gays would be sent to concentration camps "and shot if they tried to escape." Small groups of gay Neo-Nazis dotted the European landscape after the war, while in America homosexuality continues to be a "secret of postwar American National Socialism," according to Jeffrey Kaplan, a well-known scholar of extremism. http://www.splcenter.org/get-informed/intelligence-report/browse-all-issues/2000/fall/the-fringe-of-the-fringe.

34 Trần Lệ Xuân, or Madam Nhu, died in Italy in 2011. Monique Brinson Demery, *Finding the Dragon Lady: The Mystery of Vietnam's Madame Nhu* (New York: PublicAffairs, 2013).

35 The Phoenix Program (1965–72) was, according to the CIA, "a set of programs that sought to attack and destroy the political infrastructure of the Viet Cong" but is said to have led to the most horrific forms of torture and killings such as gang rapes by American soldiers.

36 California Department of Corrections and Rehabilitation: http://www.cdcr.ca.gov.

37 "Jailhouse Snitch Testimony: A Policy Review," The Justice Project, Washington, D.C., 2007.

38 As of early 2015, people with gender identity issues still could not serve in the military. Things are changing, however. An article in the March 6, 2015, edition of *Time* magazine reported that "the U.S. Army just got one step closer to allowing transgender soldiers to serve openly." The army had just announced "that it will elevate the authority to discharge transgender soldiers from local unit commanders to the Assistant Secretary of the Army"; http://time.com/3736103/trangender-troops-army-military/.

39 "In 2001, San Francisco became the first city in the country to cover the cost of sex-change surgeries for transgender city employees. In 2007, it became the first city in the country to provide health care for all uninsured residents through its Healthy San Francisco program. Now, San Francisco is combining those firsts into yet another pioneering move by becoming the first city in the country to cover the cost of gender reassignment surgeries for its uninsured transgender residents. The Department of Public Health has long been on the cutting edge of providing medical care for transgender patients. It established a special clinic for them in 1994 and offers hormone therapy, counseling and primary care services." *San Francisco Chronicle*, November 17, 2012.

[40] Nicolas Krystof, "When Whites Just Don't Get It," *New York Times*, August 30, 2014; http://www.nytimes.com/2014/08/31/opinion/sunday/nicholas-kristof-after-ferguson-race-deserves-more-attention-not-less.html.

[41] The Sentencing Project and Bureau of Justice Statistics.

[42] Bryan Stevenson, *Just Mercy: A Story of Justice and Redemption* (New York: Spiegel & Grau, 2014).

[43] Speech by Cesar Chavez, President United Farm Workers of America, AFL-CIO, The Commonwealth Club of California, San Francisco, November 9, 1984; http://www.ufw.org/_page.php?menu=research&inc=history/12.html.

[44] https://www.law.stanford.edu/organizations/programs-and-centers/stanford-three-strikes-project/three-strikes-basics.

[45] Center for Constitutional Rights, "Solitary Confinement at the Pelican Bay Security Housing Unit Fact Sheet"; http://ccrjustice.org/solitary-factsheet.

[46] http://www.legalmatch.com/law-library/article/three-strikes-laws-in-different-states.html.

[47] Stanford Law School Three Strikes Project, "Prop. 36 Progress Report"; https://www.law. stanford.edu/organizations/programs-and-centers/stanford-three-strikes-project/proposition- 36-progress-report.

[48] Michelle Alexander, *The New Jim Crow: Mass Incarceration in the Age of Colorblindness* (New York: The New Press, 2012).

[49] Latinos make up 41% of the population in California's 33 adult prisons; African Americans, who represent only 5.8% of the state's population, 29%, and other races make up 6%. Public Policy Institute of California, June 2013; http://www.ppic.org/main/publication_show. asp?i=702.

[50] http://www.cdcr.ca.gov/Facilities_Locator/KVSP-Institution_Stats.html.

[51] http://www.vera.org/files/price-of-prisons-california-fact-sheet.pdf.

[52] www.kerncountyvalleyfever.com.

[53] http://www.motherjones.com/environment/2015/01/valley-fever-california-central-valley-prison.

[54] http://www.sacbee.com/news/politics-government/article2605061.html.

[55] Patricia Leigh Brown, "A Disease without a Cure Spreads Quietly in the West," *New York Times*, July 4, 2013.

[56] https://www.prisonlegalnews.org/news/2011/aug/15/california-prisoners-still-forced-to-drink-arsenic-laced-water/.

[57] http://www.waterboards.ca.gov/drinking_water/programs/documents/ddwem/dwp%20 enforcement%20actions/Madera/2014/03_11_13R_01A_2010801_02.pdf.

[58] http://www.npr.org/blogs/thesalt/2015/03/25/395091550/arsenic-in-california-wines-should-drinkers-be-concerned.

[59] Michelle Alexander, *The New Jim Crow*, pp. 2, 158.

[60] New York Times/CBS News/Kaiser Family Foundation poll; http://www.nytimes.com/ 2015/03/01/business/out-of-trouble-but-criminal-records-keep-men-out-of-work.html?_r=0.

[61] W. H. Auden, "September 1, 1939," in *Another Time* (New York: Random House, 1940); http://www.poets.org/poetsorg/poem/september-1-1939.

[62] Elisabeth Rose Middleton, "We Were Here, We Are Here, We Will Always be Here: A Political Ecology of Healing in Mountain Maidu Country." PhD thesis, University of California Berkeley, 2007, p. 387.

[63] Judith Lowry-Croul, "Other Voices: My Grandmother Liked to Eat Grasshoppers," *The Union*, Oct. 12, 2007.

[64] 115: A rules violation report (CDC Form 115) can lead to disciplinary action. It may be classified as either "administrative" or "serious." http://aren.org/prison/documents/ dictionary/words.htm.

[65] Matt Apuzzo, "U.S. Supports Transgender Inmate in Lawsuit—Prisons Cannot Deny Hormone Therapy, Justice Dept. Says," *New York Times*, April 4, 2015; http://nyti. ms/1ClDmkU.

[66] Deborah Sontag, "Every Day I Struggle—Transgender Inmate Cites Attacks in Men's Prison," *New York Times*, April 6, 2015.

[67] Laura Strapagiel, "Ontario will now assess transgender inmates based on identity, not anatomy," *National Post*, January 26, 2015; http://news.nationalpost.com/news/canada/ ontario-will-now-assess-transgender-inmates-based-on-identity-not-anatomy.

[68] Cristina Costantini, Jorge Rivas, and Kristofer Rìos, "Why did the US lock up these women with men?" Fusion, November 17, 2014; interactive.fusion.net/trans/.

[69] Mitch Kellaway, "Suspect found dead as family, friends mourn death of San Francisco Trans Woman," *The Advocate*, February 9, 2015.

[70] The * at the end of the term trans* is an attempt to be more inclusive and include all gender identities, not just trans women and trans men.

[71] TAJA's Coalition includes leadership from TGI Justice Project, El/La Para Translatinas, Trans March, Community United Against Violence, Transgender Law Center, St. James Infirmary, The SF LGBT Center, Trans Employment Program (TEEI), TRANS:THRIVE, Dimensions Clinic, Center of Excellence for Transgender Health and Trans Life at the SF AIDS Foundation.

72 Bob Egelko, "Prison must allow sex-change surgery." *San Francisco Chronicle*, April 4, 2015; www.sfgate.com/news/article/State-prison-officials-ordered-to-allow-6178228. php?cmpid= email-desktop.

73 Jessica Benko, "The Radical Humaneness of Norway's Halden Prison—The goal of the Norwegian penal system is to get inmates out of it." *New York Times Magazine*, March 26, 2015.

74 Adam Gopnik, "The caging of America: Why do we lock up so many people?" *New Yorker Magazine*, January 30, 2012.

75 Vivian Ho, "San Francisco jail inmates forced to fight, public defender says." *San Francisco Chronicle*, March 26, 2015.

76 Vivian Ho, "Deputy in inmate fights faced 2006 complaints." *San Francisco Chronicle*, March 28, 2015.

77 The Editorial Board, "Justice Kennedy's Plea to Congress" *New York Times*, April 4, 2015.